ETYMOLOGICAL DICTIONARY

OF

FAMILY AND CHRISTIAN NAMES.

WITH AN ESSAY,

ON THEIR DERIVATION AND IMPORT.

BY

WILLIAM ARTHUR, M.A.

NEW YORK:
SHELDON, BLAKEMAN & CO.
No. 115 NASSAU STREET.
1857.

PREFACE.

The Author has been induced to publish this volume, from the opinions expressed by a number of literary friends, that a work on the origin and import of Family Names would be a valuable addition to the current literature of this country. He is not aware that a Dictionary of this kind has ever before been published, embracing surnames derived from the English, Saxon, Dutch, Danish, German, Welsh, Gaelic (Celtic), Cornish-British, and other languages.

From this consideration he is inclined to indulge the hope that the book will be acceptable not only to the Philologist, but to readers in general who may have the curiosity to know the origin and signification of their own names.

Much labor has been spent upon the Dictionary. It has been prepared by long and careful research and study of the several languages from which the names are derived.

In the outlines of the Introductory Essay the author is indebted for much valuable information to the "learned Camden,"—" Camden's Remaines concerning Britaine," London, 1614.

iv PREFACE.

He has read with pleasure an interesting and amusing "Essay on English Surnames," by Mark Antony Lower, M.A., London, 1849, from which he has taken many curious observations and humorous anecdotes on several names given in that work.

Available aid has also been obtained from a series of articles on Irish Surnames, by Mr. John O'Donovan, published in the "Irish Penny Journal," Dublin, 1841; from "Bailey's English Dictionary," 20th edition, 1764; "Playfair's British Family Antiquity," London, 1811; and from "Burke's Genealogical and Heraldic Dictionary of the Landed Gentry of Great Britain and Ireland," London, 1848.

In a volume of this size it is not to be expected that the origin and meaning of every surname can be found, nevertheless, from an attentive perusal of the Introductory Essay, and the several derivations of the names given, a majority of Family and Christian names may be ascertained with a good degree of accuracy.

From the nature and difficulty of the work, arising in many instances from the mutation and corruption of the original names, the change of customs and language, and the frequent similarity of the roots from which many of the words are derived, it can not be otherwise than in many respects imperfect.

NEWTONVILLE, ALBANY CO., N.Y.,
November, 1856.

AN ESSAY

ON

THE ORIGIN AND IMPORT

OF

FAMILY NAMES.

NAMES commenced in Eden. The Creator bestowed on the first man the name of *Adam*, denoting his origin from the earth. Eve gave to her first born the name of *Cain*, implying acquisition, a standing testimony of her faith in the first promise made to man in Eden.

The signification of the Hebrew names recorded in the 5th chapter of Genesis, when arranged in order, present an epitome of the ruin and recovery of man through a Redeemer:

ADAM,	*i. e.,*	"Man in the image of God;"
SETH,		"Substituted by ;"
ENOS,		"Frail Man ;"
CANAAN,		"Lamenting ;"
MAHALALEEL,		"The blessed God ;"
JARED,		"Shall come down ;"
ENOCH,		"Teaching ;"

6   ESSAY ON THE ORIGIN AND

METHUSELAH,   " His death shall send;"

LAMECH,   "To the humble;"

NOAH,   " Rest or consolation."*

These names in the order in which they are recorded, read thus: "To man, once made in the image of God, now substituted by man frail and full of sorrow, the blessed God himself shall come down to the earth teaching, and his death shall send to the humble, consolation."

The son of Abraham and Sarah, by divine direction was to bear the name of *Isaac*, signifying laughter, in allusion to the circumstances recorded of the father of the faithful in the 17th chapter of Genesis. In like manner Jacob received the name *Yaakob*, that is, he shall "hold by the heel" or supplant, a prediction which was fulfilled when he supplanted his brother Esau, in the matter of his birthright.

The ancient Hebrews retained the greatest simplicity in the use of names, and generally a single name distinguished the individual. Where it was necessary the name of the father was added, and sometimes that of the mother, if she happened to be more celebrated.

Names were first given for the distinction of persons, and each individual had, at the beginning, but

* Dr. Cummings.

SIGNIFICATION OF NAMES. 7

one proper or given name, as *Joseph* among the Jews, *Amasis* among the Egyptians, *Arbaces* among the Medians, among the Greeks *Ulysses*, among the Romans *Romulus*, the Germans *Ariovistus*, the British *Caradoc*, the Saxons *Edric*, etc.

The Jews named their children the eighth day after the nativity, when the rite of circumcision was performed. The Greeks gave the name on the tenth day, and an entertainment was given by the parents to their friends, and sacrifices offered to the gods.

The Romans gave names to their female children on the eighth day, and to the males on the ninth, which they called *Dies lustricus*, the day of purification, on which day they solemnized a feast called *Nominalia*.

The name given was generally indicative of some particular circumstance attending the birth or infancy, some quality of body or mind, or was expressive of the good wishes or fond hopes of the parent. Objects in nature, the most admired and beautiful, were selected by them to designate their offspring. The sun, the moon and stars, the clouds, the beasts of the field, the trees and the flowers that adorn the face of nature, were all made subservient to this end.

Pythagoras taught that the minds, actions, and

8 ESSAY ON THE ORIGIN AND

success of men would be according to their fate, genius and *name*, and Plato advises men to be careful in giving fair and happy names.

Such hopeful names as *Victor*, conqueror, *Felix*, happy, and *Fortunatus*, lucky, were called by Cicero, "bona nomina," good names, and by Tacitus, "fausta nomina," prosperous names.

" Such names among the Romans were considered so happy and fortunate, that in the time of Galienus, Regilianus who commanded in the ancient Illyricum, obtained the empire in consequence of the derivation of his name. When it was demanded during a banquet, what was the origin of Regilianus, one answered, '*a Regno*,' to reign, to be a king; another began to decline '*Rex* (a king), *Regis*, *Regilianus*,' when the soldiers began to exclaim, 'Ergo potest Rex esse, ergo potest regere, Deus tibi regis nomen imposuit,' and so invested him with the imperial robes."*

Lewis the Eighth, King of France, sent two of his embassadors to Alphonso, king of Spain, to solicit one of his daughters in marriage. When the young ladies, whose names were Urraca and Blanche, were presented to the embassadors, they made choice of Blanche, though far less beautiful than her sister, assigning as a reason that her name would be

* Camden.

SIGNIFICATION OF NAMES.

9

better received in France, as *Blanche* signified fair and beautiful.

So the proverb, "*Bonum nomen bonum omen*"—A good name is a good omen.

Names, epithets, and soubriquets were often bestowed by others than the parents, at a more advanced age, expressive of character or exploits, of personal beauty, deformity or blemish—such as, among the Greeks Τελεμάχος (Telemachus), able to sustain the war; Φίλλιππος (Philip), a lover of horses ; Ἀλέξανδρος (Alexander), a benefactor of men, and Γρυπὸς, eagle-nose. Among the Romans, *Victor,* a conqueror; *Strabo,* squint-eyed ; *Varus,* bow - legged. Among the Britons, *Cadwallader,* the leader of the war. Among the Gaels or Celts, *Galgach,* or *Galgachus,* the fierce fighter of battles; *Curaidh,* a hero.

Among the Britons and Gaels, names were taken from those animals which excelled in swiftness, fierceness, boldness, strength or courage, as the *Lion,* the *Bear,* the *Wolf,* the *Mastiff.* The following are examples: Llew, Llewelyn, Arthur, Kee, etc.

Others from valor, skill · in war, and various mental qualities, as *Caw, Cadwallon, Cadwallader, Hardd; Donald, Duncan, Fergus, Colom, Coel, Caractacus.* *

* For the signification of these names, see Dictionary.

10   ESSAY ON THE ORIGIN AND

Others from color. Lloyd, Brych, Winne, Goch, Gorm, Gwrmain, Glass, Dhu or Du, Da or Day, Melyn, Bane, Cane, Roe, &c.

The ROMANS introduced such names as Julius, Claudius, Felix, Constans, Constantine, Augustus, Augustine, etc. The SAXONS the names of Charles, Edward, Edmund, Baldwin, Oswald, etc. The Danes, such as Hengist, Horsa, Sweyne, Canute; and the NORMANS chose such as Robert, William, Richard, Henry, etc.

Before the general introduction of surnames, the Britons and Celts, for the sake of distinction, used *explanatory names*, descriptive of personal peculiarities, individual pursuits, mental or bodily qualities, accidental circumstances, or the performance of certain actions. These names have been called Soubriquets, Cognomens, and Nicknames—such as Howel *Da*, or Howel the good; Howel *y Pedolau*, or Howel of the horse-shoes, so called from being able to straighten them or bend them by manual strength; Cadrod *Hardd*, or the beautiful; Ririd *Vlaidd*, or Ririd the Wolf; Cunedda *Wledig*, or the Patriotic; Howel *y Fwyall*, or the Battle-axe; Caswallon *Law hir*, or the long hand; Llywarch *Hen*, or the aged; Donald *Gorm*, or Blue Donald; Malcolm *Canmore*, great head.

The Gaels of Ireland had also the same kind of

SIGNIFICATION OF NAMES. 11

cognomens or descriptive names, as Niall *Roe,* or Niall the Red; Niall *More,* Niall the Great; Con *Bachach,* Con the Lame; Henry *Avrey,* Henry the Contentious; Shane au *Dimais,* John the Proud; Shane *Buidhe,* or John with the yellow hair; Shane *Gearr,* John Short; Seumas *Reagh,* James the Swarthy; O'Connor *Don,* the Brown-haired O'Connor.*

Sir Henry Piers, in the year 1682, in a letter to Anthony, Lord Bishop of Meath, gave the following account of Irish sobriquets and cognomens:

* * * "They take much liberty, and seem to do it with delight, in giving of nicknames; and if a man have any imperfection or evil habit, he shall be sure to hear of it in the nickname. Thus, if he be blind, lame, squint-eyed, gray-eyed, be a stammerer in speech, be left-handed, to be sure he shall have one of these added to his name; so also from his color of hair, as black, red, yellow, brown, etc.; and from his age, as young, old; or from what he addicts himself to, or much delights in, as in draining, building, fencing, or the like; so that no man whatever can escape a nickname who lives among them, or converseth with them; and sometimes, so libidinous are they in this kind of raillery, they will give nicknames *per antiphrasim,* or contrariety of speech.

* Mr. John O'Donovan, Irish Penny Journal, 1841.

12 ESSAY ON THE ORIGIN AND

Thus a man of excellent parts, and beloved of all men, shall be called *Grana*, that is, naughty, or fit to be complained of. If a man have a beautiful countenance or lovely eyes, they will call him *Cueegh*, that is, squint-eyed; if a great housekeeper, he shall be called *Ackerisagh*, that is, greedy."

The same custom prevailed in England, and other countries, in reference to *descriptive* names, many of which in after times became surnames; as William the Lion; Henry the Fowler; Edmund Ironside; Harold Harefoot; William Rufus (the Red); Henry Beauclerk (fine Scholar); Richard Cœur de Lion (the Lion-hearted; John Lackland; Edward Longshanks; David Crookshanks. Some of this class indicate mental qualities, as Good, Goodman, Goodenough, Best, Sage, Wise. Others are derived from personal appearance or bodily peculiarities, as Big, Meikle, Little, Lightbody, Lightfoot, Armstrong, Greathead.

Among these are included names denoting complexion, color of hair and dress, as Black, Blond, Brown, Gray, Grissel, Red, Rufus, Rous, Russel, Rothe (Germ. red), Rothman, Ruddiman, Blacket or Blackhead, Whitelock, and Whitehead.

Among names of costume are found Capet, Curthose (short hose), Robe, Mantle, etc.

The custom of giving nicknames to individuals

SIGNIFICATION OF NAMES. 13

bearing hereditary surnames has not yet been discontinued; and in many localities, the peasantry are better known by soubriquets than by their proper surnames. This is especially the case where several families bear the same sur-names.

Mark Antony Lower, M. A., in his interesting and amusing Essay on Family Nomenclature, relates the following story, as given by a correspondent of Knight's Quarterly Magazine: "I knew an apothecary in the collieries, who, as a matter of decorum, always entered the real name of his patients in his books; that is, when he could ascertain them. But they stood there for ornament; for *use*, he found it necessary to append the soubriquet, which he did with true medical formality, as, for instance, 'Thomas Williams, *vulgo dict.* (vulgarly called) 'Old Puff.' "

A story is told of an attorney's clerk, who was professionally employed to serve a process on one of these oddly-named persons, whose real name was entered in the instrument with legal accuracy. The clerk, after a great deal of inquiry as to the whereabouts of the party, was about to abandon the search as hopeless, when a young woman, who had witnessed his labors, kindly volunteered to assist him.

"Oy say, *Bullyed*," cried she to the first person

14   ESSAY ON THE ORIGIN AND

they met, "does thee know a mon neamed Adam Green?" The bull-head was shaken in token of ignorance.

"*Loy-a-bed*, dost thee?"

Lie-a-bed's opportunities of making acquaintance had been rather limited, and she could not resolve the difficulty.

Stumpy (a man with a wooden leg), *Cowskin*, *Spindleshanks*, *Cockeye*, and *Pigtail* were severally invoked, but in vain; and the querist fell into a brown study, in which she remained for some time. At length, however, her eyes suddenly brightened, and slapping one of her companions on the shoulder, she exclaimed triumphantly, "Dash my wig! whoy he means moy feyther!" and then turning to the gentleman, added, "yo should'n ax'd for *Ode* (old) Blackbird."

It is stated that "few of the miners of Staffordshire bear the names of their fathers; and an instance is given of a certain pig-dealer in that county whose father's name was Johnson, but the people call him *Pigman*, and *Pigman* he calls himself. This name may be now seen over the door of a public-house which this man keeps in Staffordshire."*

In this connection Mr. Lower adds: "There were

* Mark Antony Lower, M. A., on English Surnames,

SIGNIFICATION OF NAMES. 15

lately living in the small town of Folkestone, Co. Kent (Eng.), fifteen persons whose hereditary name was HALL, but who, *gratiâ distinctionis*, bore the elegant designations of

DOGGY HALL,	FEATHERTOE,
BUMPER,	BUBBLES,
PIERCE-EYE,	FAGGOTS,
CULA,	JIGGERY,
PUMBLE-FOOT,	COLDFLIP,
SILVER-EYE,	LUMPY,
SUTTY,	THICK-LIPS.
OLD HARE.	

A SURNAME is an additional name added to the Proper or given name, for the sake of distinction, and so called because originally written *over* the other name, instead of after it, from the French *Surnom*, or the Latin *"Super nomen,"* signifying above the name.

Surnames have originated in various ways. Some are derived from the names of places; others from offices and professions; from personal peculiarities; from the Christian or proper name of the father; from the performance of certain actions; from objects in the animal, mineral, and vegetable world, and from accidental circumstances of every varied character.

16 ESSAY ON THE ORIGIN AND

The introduction of surnames arose from the necessity of the case. Soon after the diffusion of Christianity among the nations of Europe, their Pagan names were generally laid aside, and the people began to take Hebrew names, such as Moses, Aaron, Malachi, David, Matthew, Mark, Luke, John, Peter, James. As the families increased, many persons were found bearing the same name. The Johns, and the Jameses, and the Peters became numerous.

For a long time, soubriquets and nicknames, like those of which we have spoken, and patronymics, were appended to the name to distinguish the individual, which were in some cases retained, and became surnames, but by degrees this means of remedying the confusion became insufficient, and to identify the individual more distinctly, surnames were found necessary.

It is impossible to state at what precise period names became stationary, or began to descend hereditarily. According to Camden, surnames began to be taken up in France about the year 1000, and in England about the time of the Conquest (1066), or a very little before, under King Edward the Confessor.

He says: " And to this time doe the Scottishmen referre the antiquitie of their surnames, although

SIGNIFICATION OF NAMES. 17

Buchanan supposeth that they were not in use in Scotland many yeares after.

"But in England, certaine it is, that as the better sort, euen from the Conquest, by little and little, took surnames, so they were not settled among the common people fully vntil about the time of King Edward the Second, but still varied according to the father's name, as *Richardson*, if his father were Richard; *Hodgson*, if his father were Roger, or in some other respect, and from thenceforth began to be established (some say by statute) in their posteritie.

"This will seem strange to some Englishmen and Scottishmen, which, like the Arcadians, think their surnames as ancient as the moone, or, at the least, to reach many an age beyond the Conquest. But they which thinke it most strange (I speake vnder correction), I doubt they will hardly finde any surname which descended to posteritie before that time; neither have they seene (I fear) any deed or donation before the Conquest, but subsigned with crosses and single names, without surnames, in this manner, in England—✠ *Ego Eadredus confirmaui;* ✠ *Ego Edmundus corroboraui;* ✠ *Ego Sigarius conclusi;* ✠ *Ego Olfstanus consolidaui*, etc.

"Likewise for Scotland, in an old booke of Duresme in the Charter, whereby Edgare, sonne

18 ESSAY ON THE ORIGIN AND

of King Malcolme, gave lands neare Coldingham to that church, in the year 1097, the Scottish noble-men, witnesses thereunto, had no other surnames but the Christian names of their fathers, for thus they signed—*S.* ✠ *Gulfi filii Meniani. S.* ✠ *Culuerti filii Doncani,* etc."

On the authority of Dr. Keating* and his cotem-porary Gratianus Lucius, we learn that surnames first became hereditary in Ireland, in the reign of Brian Boru, who was killed in the battle of Clon-tarf, in the year 1014, in which battle the Danes were defeated. Previous to this time, individuals were identified by Tribe names, after the Patriarchal manner. These tribe names were formed from those of the progenitors by prefixing the following words, signifying race, progeny, descendants, etc.: *Corca, Cineal, Clan, Muintir, Siol, Sliocht, Dal, Tealach, Ua, Ui,* or *O,* which signifies grandson or descendant.

It is asserted on the authority of the ancient Irish Manuscripts, that King Brian ordained that a cer-tain surname should be imposed on every tribe or clan, in order that it might be more easily known from what stock each family was descended; and

---

* See Irish Penny Journal, 1841, p. 365, "Origin and Meanings of Irish Family names, by John O'Donovan."

SIGNIFICATION OF NAMES. 19

that these names should become hereditary and fixed forever. In the formation of these names, care was taken that they should not be arbitrarily assumed. The several families were required to adopt the names of their fathers or grandfathers, and those ancestors were generally selected who were celebrated for their virtues or renowned for their valor.

Many of the surnames now common in Ireland were derived from the chiefs of the several clans who fought against the Danes at the battle of Clontarf, under King Brian, and others were assumed from ancestors who flourished subsequently to the reign of that monarch. Soon after the invasion of Ireland by Henry the Second, in the year 1172, the Anglo-Norman and Welsh families who had obtained large grants of land in that kingdom, in reward for their military services in subduing the inhabitants, from intermarriages and other causes, began by degrees to adopt the language and manners of the people, and in process of time became "*Hibernis ipsis Hiberniores,*" more Irish than the Irish themselves. They not only spoke the Irish language, but conformed to the Irish custom of surnames, by placing "MAC," which signifies "*son,*" before the Christian name of their father. This was particularly the case in regard to those

English and Welsh families who settled in the province of Connaught. Thus, the descendants of William De Burgos were called MacWilliam, that is, the son of William, and the De Exeters assumed the name of MacJordan, from Jordan De Exeter, who derived his name from Exeter, a town in Devonshire, England.

In the year 1465, in the reign of Edward the Fourth, it was enacted by statute, that every Irishman dwelling within the English pale, then comprising the counties of Dublin, Meath, Lowth, and Kildare, in Ireland, should take an English surname.

"At the request of the Commons, it is ordeyned and established by authority of said Parliament, that every Irishman that dwells betwixt or among Englishmen, in the county Dublin, Myeth, Uriell, and Kildare, shall goe like to one Englishman in apparel, and shaveing off his beard above the mouth, and shall be within one year sworn the liege man of the king, in the hands of the lieutenant, or deputy, or such as he will assigne to receive this oath for the multitude that is to be sworne, and shall take to him an English surname of one towne, as Sutton, Chester, Trym, Skyrne, Corke, Kinsale; or colour, as White, Black, Brown; or art or science, as Smith, or Carpenter; or office,

SIGNIFICATION OF NAMES. 21

as Cook, Butler; and that he and his issue shall use this name under payne of forfeyting of his goods yearly till the premises be done, to be levied two times by the yeare to the king's warres, according to the discretion of the lieutenant of the king or his deputy."—5 Edward IV., cap. 3.

In obedience to this law, Harris, in his additions to Ware, remarks that the *Shanachs* took the name of Fox, the *McGabhans* or *McGowans*, that of *Smith*, and the *Geals* the name of White. In consequence of this statute of Edward, many Irish families were induced to translate or change their names into English.

The ancient prefixes of *Mac* and *O* are still retained in Irish names, the former denoting *son*, and the latter *grandson*, or descendant. To distinguish the individual the father's name was used, and sometimes that of the grandfather after the manner of the Scripture. Thus, should *Donnel* have a son, he would be called *Mac*Donnel, that is, the son of Donnel, and his grandson would be termed O'Donnel; O'Neal, the grandson of Neal, or the descendant of Neal; *Mac*Neal, the son of Neal.

The Welsh, in like manner, prefixed *Ap, mab, ab,* or *vap* to the given or first name to denote *son*, as David Ap Howell, David the son of Howell; Evan Ap Rhys, Evan the son of Rees; Richard Ap Evan,

Richard the son of Evan; John Ap Hugh, John the son of Hugh. These names are now abreviated into *Powell, Price, Bevan,* and *Pugh.*

The name of the ancestor was appended in this manner for half-a-dozen generations back, and it is no uncommon occurrence to find in their old records a name like this:

"Evan - ap - Griffith-ap-Jones-ap-William-ap Owen-ap-Jenkin-ap-Morgan-ap-Rheese."

Lower tells of a church at Llangollen, Wales, dedicated to "St. Collen-ap-Gwynnawg-ap-Clyn-dawg-ap-Cowrda-ap-Caradoc- Freichfras - ap - Llyn-Merim-ap-Einion-Yrth-ap-Cunedda-Wledig—a name that casts that of the Dutchman '*Inkvervankodsdor-spankkinkadrachdern*' into the shade."

Surnames were not adopted in Wales until long after they were in England and Scotland. The old manner was retained as far down as the time of Henry the Eighth. It is related in Camden, "That in late yeares, in the time of King Henry the Eight, an ancient worshipful gentleman of Wales beeing called at the pannel of Jurie by the name of '*Thomas ap- William-ap- Thomas-ap- Richard-ap-Hoel-ap-Euen- Vaghan,*' was advised by the judge to leave that old manner; whereupon he after called himself *Moston,* according to the name of his principall house, and left that surname to his posteritie."

SIGNIFICATION OF NAMES. 23

About this time, the heads of the Welsh families either took the names of their immediate ancestors as surnames, or adopted names from their estates, after the English manner.

The old Normans prefixed *Fitz*, a son, the same as *Fils* in French, and *Filius* in Latin, to the name of the father as a patronymic, as *Fitz William*, the son of William, the same as Williamson.

In Ireland, after the invasion of Strongbow, in the time of Henry the Second, names commencing with Fitz frequently occur, as Fitzhugh, Fitzgerald, Fitzgibbon, Fitzsimmons, Fitzpatrick, which are of Anglo-Norman origin. Camden informs us that in the reign of Henry the First, the daughter and heir of Fitzhamon, an English nobleman of wealth, refused the hand of Robert, the natural son of the king, saying,

"It were to me a great shame
To have a lord withouten his twa name."

Whereupon, the king gave him the name of Fitz Roy, "the son of the king." Children born out of lawful wedlock not unfrequently have had Fitz prefixed to the name of their mother or reputed father. The children of his Royal Highness, William, Duke of Clarence, and Mrs. Jordan, took the surname of Fitzclarence.

24   ESSAY ON THE ORIGIN AND

WITZ, a termination common in Russian names, denotes *son*, and is somewhat analogous to the Norman *Fitz*, as Peter Paulowitz, Peter the son of Paul.

SKY is used in a similar manner by the Poles, as James Petrowsky, James the son of Peter.

. ING, Teutonic, denoting progeny—which Wachter derives from the British *engi*, to produce, bring forth—was affixed by the Anglo-Saxons to the father's name as a surname for the son, as *Cuthing* the son of Cuth, *Ælfreding* the son of Alfred, *Whiting* the Fair offspring, *Browning* the Dark offspring. *Gin*, in Gaelic, signifies to beget; *An*, Gaelic, is a termination of nouns implying the *diminutive* of that to which it is annexed, and *an*, in the Welsh, as an affix, conveys also the idea of *littleness*. The termination *son* was also added to the father's name, and instead of saying John the son of William, the name was written John Williamson; Peter Johnson, in place of Peter the son of John. While the English affixed *son* to the baptismal name of the father, the Welsh merely appended "*s*," as John Matthews, that is, John the son of Mathew; David Jones (Johns), David the son of John; John Hughs, John the son of Hugh.

Kin, kind, ling, let, et, ot, cic, cock, are diminutives. From the German *kind*, a child, is formed the

SIGNIFICATION OF NAMES. 25

diminutive termination *kin*, as Watkin the son of Wat or Walter; Wilkin the son of Will or William. *Kin* or *kind* has the same signification as the Greek γένος and the Latin *genus*, race, offspring, children.

LING at the end of a word conveys the idea of something young or little, as *darling* or *dearling*, *firstling*, *gosling*, and denotes also the situation, state, or condition of the subject to which it is applied, as hireling, worldling.

LET, Anglo-Saxon *lyt*, is sometimes used for *little*, as hamlet, ringlet, streamlet, Bartlet; *i. e.*, little Bart or Bartholomew. The terminations *et* and *ot* are used in the same sense, as *Willet, Willmot*, the son of William or little William.

The termination *cic* or *cock* is also a diminutive, and signifies *little* or son, as *Hiccic, Hiccock*, the son of *Hig* or Hugh; Wilcock, the son of William; Babcock, the son of Bob or Robert.

LOCAL NAMES form the largest class of our surnames. First among these are those which are national, expressing the country whence the person first bearing the name came; as ENGLISH, SCOTT, IRISH, FRENCH.

GERMAN or GORMAN, BRETT and BRITAIN.

FLEMING, from Flanders.

2

26 ESSAY ON THE ORIGIN AND

BURGOYNE, from Burgundy.

CORNISH and CORNWALLIS, from Cornwall.

GERMAINE, ALMAN and D'ALMAINE (D'Allemagne), from Germany.

CHAMPAGNE and CHAMPNEYS, from Champagne, France.

GASCOYNE and GASKIN, from Gascony.

ROMAYNE, from Rome.

WESTPHAL, from Westphalia.

HANWAY, from HAINAULT.

JANEWAY, a Genoese—etc., etc.

These names had commonly *Le* (the) prefixed to them in old records.

The practice of taking names from patrimonial estates, or from the place of residence or birth, was prevalent in Normandy and the contiguous parts of France in the latter part of the tenth century, and was generally adopted in England and Scotland after the Conquest.

Names were taken from almost every county, city, town, parish, village, and hamlet, and from manors, farms, and single houses, such as *Cheshire, Kent, Ross, Hastings, Cunningham, Huntingdon, Preston, Hull, Compton, Goring,* etc., so that local names of this class number many thousands.

Where the name was taken from the patrimonial estate, it was assumed by the individual himself;

SIGNIFICATION OF NAMES. 27

when from the place of residence or birth, it was probably bestowed by others. A person who had removed from his native place and settled in another, received from the inhabitants of the town or village in which he took up his abode the name of his native place as a surname, which descended to his children.

These names were first given with the prefix "*of,*" shortened frequently to "*O*" or "*à,*" signifying *from* (or it may be sometimes an abreviation of "*at*"), as *John O'Huntingdon, Adam à Kirby.* These prefixes were after a time dropped, and *Adam à Kirby* became *Adam Kirby,* and *John O'Kent, John Kent.*

Besides these, we have a great number of local surnames which are general and descriptive of the nature or situation of the residence of the persons upon whom they were bestowed, as *Hill, Wood, Dale, Parke,* etc. The prefix *At* or *Atte* was generally used before these names, as *John At Hill,* John at the hill, *James At Well, Will At-Gate, Tom At-Wood,* now Atwell, Adgate, and Atwood. *Atte* was varied to *Atten* when the following name began with a vowel, as *Peter Atten Ash,* now *Nash, Richard Atten Oak,* now *Noakes* or *Nokes.*

Sometimes "*à*" was used instead of *at,* as *Thomas à Becket, Jack à Deane.* *By* and *under* were used as prefixes, as *James By-field, Tom Under-hill.*

ESSAY ON THE ORIGIN AND

In this way men took their names from rivers and trees, from residing at or near them, as *Beck*, *Gill*, *Eden*, *Trent*, *Grant*, and *Shannon*; *Beach*, *Vine*, *Ashe*, *Bush*, and *Thorn*.

Local names prefixed with *De* (from) and terminating in *ville*, originated in Normandy, and were introduced into England at the time of the Conquest. These names were taken from the districts towns, or hamlets of which they were possessed, or in which they resided previously to their following the fortunes of William the Conqueror, such as *De Mandeville*, *De Neville*, *De Montague*, *De Warren*, *De Beaumont*, etc. The prefix *De* was generally dropped about the reign of Henry the Sixth. All these names introduced into England at the time of the Conquest, from Normandy and the contiguous parts of France may easily be distinguished by the prefixes *De*, *Du*, *Des*, *De La*, *St.*, and the suffixes, *Beau*, *Mont*, *Font*, *Fant*, *Ers*, *Age*, *Ard*, *Aux*, *Bois*, *Eux*, *Et*, *Val*, *Court*, *Vaux*, *Lay*, *Fort*, *Ot*, *Champ*, and *Ville*, the component parts of names of places in Normandy, the signification of most of which we give in the derivation of those names into the composition of which they enter.

The greater part of English local surnames are composed of the following words or terminations: *Ford*, *Ham*, *Ley*, *Ey*, *Ney*, *Ton*, *Tun*, *Ing*, *Hurst*,

SIGNIFICATION OF NAMES. 29

Wick, Stow, Sted, Caster, Combe, Cote, Thorpe, Worth. Burg, Beck, and *Gill.* There is an ancient proverb—

"In Ford, in Ham, in Ley and Ton,
The most of English surnames run."

To which *Lower* has added—

"Ing, Hurst, and Wood, Wick, Sted and Field,
Full many English surnames yield,
With Thorpe and Bourne, Cote, Caster, Oke,
Combe, Bury, Don, and Stowe, and Stoke,
With Ey and Port, Shaw, Worth and Wade,
Hill, Gate, Well, Stone, are many made;
Cliff, Marsh, and Mouth, and Down, and Sand,
And Beck, and Sea, with numbers stand."

FORD, Welsh, *Fford,* signifies a way, a road. *Ford,* Saxon, from the verb *Faran,* to go or pass, denotes a shallow place in a river, where it may be passed on foot, whence Bradford, Crawford, Stanford, etc.

HAM, Saxon, a house, a home, a dwelling-place; German, *heim,* a home. It is used in the names of places, as Waltham, Durham, Buckingham, etc. *Ham,* in some localities in England, indicates a rich, level pasture; a plot of land near water; a triangular field.

LEY, LEGH, and LEIGH, a pasture, field, com-

30 ESSAY ON THE ORIGIN AND

mons; uncultivated land. *Lle*, Welsh, a place, Stanley, Burkeley, Raleigh, etc.

EY, NEY, EA are applied to places contiguous to water; a wet or watery place, as Chertsey, Lindsey, Ilsley.

TON and TUNE, Saxon, and TUIN, Dutch, signify an inclosure; DUN and DIN, Gaelic and Welsh, a hill, a fortified place; now a town, *dun, tune, town.* If the residence of the Briton was on a plain, it was called *Llan*, from *lagen* or *logan*, an inclosed plain, or a low-lying place; if on an eminence, it was called *Dun*. *Dun*, in the Gaelic, signifies a heap; a hill, mount; a fortified house or hill, fortress, castle, or tower.

The surnames terminating in *den, din, ton* and *tun*, are numerous, as Houghton, Leighton, Chittendin, Huntington.

ING is a meadow; low flat lands near a river, lake, or wash of the sea, as Lansing, Washington.

HURST, a wood, a grove; a word found in many names of places, as Bathurst, Hayhurst, Crowhurst, Reddenhurst.

WICK, in old Saxon, is a village, castle, or fort; the same as *vicus* in Latin; a bay, a port or harbor, whence Wickware, Wickliff, Warwick, Sedgewick.

STOW, a fixed place or mansion, whence Barstow, Bristow, Raystow.

SIGNIFICATION OF NAMES. 31

STED, in the Danish, signifies a place inclósed, an inclosure; a *fixed* residence; whence Halsted, Olmsted, Husted, Stedham, Grinsted.

CEASTER, Saxon, a camp, a city; Latin, *castrum*, whence Rochester, Winchester, Chichester, Exeter.

COMBE, Anglo-Saxon, a valley; Welsh, *cwm*, a vale, from which we have Balcombe, Bascombe, Slocum.

COT, CETE, Saxon, a cottage; COTE, French, the sea-coast; a hill, hillock; down; the side. Several names are composed of these words, as Cotesworth, Lippencot, Westcot.

THORPE, Anglo-Saxon, a village. Dutch, *Dorp*, from this comes Northrop, Northrup or Northorp, Winthorp or Winthrop.

WORTH, a possession, farm; court, place; a fort, an island. Such names end in *worth*, as Bosworth, Farnsworth, Wordsworth, Woodworth.

BURG, BURY, a hill; Dutch, *Berg*, a mountain, a hill; now, a court, a castle, a town. From these words we have the names Kingsbury, Loundsbury, Waterbury, Salisbury, Rosenburg or Rosenbury.

TRE, TREF, Welsh, a town, Coventry, the town of the Convent; Trelawny, Tremayne.

The Britons of Cornwall derived many of their surnames from local objects, while most of the Welsh names are patronymics. The following

32   ESSAY ON THE ORIGIN AND

couplet expresses the usual character of Cornish names :

"By *Tre*, *Ros*, *Pol*, *Lan*, *Caer*, and *Pen*,
You know the most of Cornish men."

These words signify town, heath, pool, church, castle, and promontory.

BY is a termination of Danish names of places, and denotes a dwelling, a village, or town, as Willoughby, Busby, Ormsby, Selby, Goadby.

OVER. The Anglo-Saxon *over* corresponds to the German *ufer*, and signifies a shore or bank, as *Westover*.

BECK, a brook, Anglo-Saxon, *Becc*, from which we have Beckford, Beckwith, Beckley, etc.

A majority of Dutch surnames are local, derived from places in Holland. VAN, Dutch, VON, German, signify *of* or *from*, and denote locality, as *Van Antwerp*, belonging to or coming from the city of Antwerp; *Van Buren*, from the town of Buren in Holland. Nearly all the Dutch local names have this prefix.

SURNAMES DERIVED FROM CHRISTIAN OR BAPTISMAL NAMES are probably next in number to the local surnames. For a long time, before and even after the introduction of stationary surnames, the name of the father was used by the child as a surname.

SIGNIFICATION OF NAMES.   33

Camden says we have many surnames formed of such forenames as are now obselete, and only occur in Doomsday Book and other ancient records, of which he gives a list.

I have already shown how the Normans prefixed *Fitz* to their father's name for a surname, to denote son; the Welsh *Ap*, and the ancient Irish, *Mac*.

The surnames formed from Christian or baptismal names are very numerous; as many as ten or fifteen are frequently formed from a single Christian name. Lower forms no less than twenty-nine from the name of William.

First we have the names terminating in *son*, which was added to the name of the father, as *Williamson, Johnson, Thompson, Wilson*, etc.

The Welsh merely appended "*s*" instead of *son*, as *Edwards, Davis, Jones* (Johns), *Hughs*.

Then we have those formed from nicknames, nursenames, and abbreviated names, as *Watson*, the son of Wat or Walter; *Watts*, the same; *Simpson, Simms; Dobson*, the son of Dob or Robert; *Dobbs, Hobson, Hobbs*, etc., etc.

A great many are formed of these abreviated or nursenames, with the addition of the diminutive terminations *ette, kin*, and *cock* or *cox*, all of which signify "little" or "child." From the termination

2*

34 ESSAY ON THE ORIGIN AND

ette we have such names as *Willett*, little Will, or the son of Will; *Hallett*, little Hal or Henry.

From *kin* or *kins* we have *Wilkins*, *Tompkins*, *Simpkins*, *Atkins*, *Hawkins*, *Higgins*, *Dobbin*, and *Gilkin*. From *cock* or *cox*, *Wilcox*, *Simcox*, *Babcock*, the son of Bab or Bartholomew; *Alcock*, the son of Hal or Henry, and *Hickcox*, the son of Hig or Hugh.

NAMES OF TRADE, OCCUPATIONS, AND PURSUITS, are next in number, as Smith, Carpenter, Joiner, Taylor, Barker, Barber, Baker, Brewer. Sherman (a shearman, one who used to shear cloth), Naylor (nail-maker), Chapman, Mercer, Jenner (Joiner), Tucker (a fuller), Monger (a merchant), etc., etc.

These names originally had the Norman prefix " *Le*" (the), as *Le Spicer*, *Le Dispenser*, *Le Tailleur*.

OFFICIAL NAMES, including civil and ecclesiastical dignities, viz., King, Prince, Duke, Lord, Earl, Knight, Pope, Bishop, Priest, Monk, Marshall, Bailey, Chamberlain, etc., etc.

Many of these titles, as King, Prince, etc., were imposed on individuals from mere caprice, as few of these *kings* or *dukes* ever held the distinguished rank their names indicate.

It is said that nearly nine hundred Kings are born annually in England and Wales.

SIGNIFICATION OF NAMES. 35

We find the following in Lower's Essay, as taken from the "History of Huntingdon."

"TRUE COPY of a jury taken before Judge Doddridge, at the assizes holden at Huntingdon, A.D. 1619. (It is necessary to remark, 'that the judge had, at the preceding circuit, censured the sheriff for empanneling men not qualified by rank for serving on the Grand Jury, and the sheriff being a humorist, resolved to fit the judge with sounds at least.') On calling over the following names, and pausing emphatically at the end of the Christian, instead of the surname, his lordship began to think he had, indeed, a jury of quality:

Maximilian KING of Toseland,
Henry PRINCE of Godmanchester,
George DUKE of Somersham,
William MARQUIS of Stukeley,
Edmund EARL of Hartford,
Richard BARON of Bythorn,
Stephen POPE of Newton,
Stephen CARDINAL of Kimbolton,
Humphrey BISHOP of Buckden,
Robert LORD of Waresley,
Robert KNIGHT of Winwick,
William ABBOTT of Stukeley,
Robert BARON of St. Neots,
William DEAN of Old Weston,

36 ESSAY ON THE ORIGIN AND

John ARCHDEACON of Paxton,
Peter ESQUIRE of Easton,
Edward FRYER of Ellington,
Henry MONK of Stukeley,
George GENTLEMAN of Spaldwick,
George PRIEST of Graffham,
Richard DEACON of Catworth.

"The judge, it is said, was highly pleased with this practical joke, and commended the sheriff for his ingenuity. The descendants of some of these illustrious jurors still reside in the county, and bear the same names; in particular, a Maximilian King, we are informed, still presides over Toseland."

Personal characteristics have given origin to another class of surnames, descriptive of mental or bodily peculiarities. Among these are many names of color and complexion, as Black, Brown, Blond, White, Gray, Grissel (grayish), Rous (red), Dunn (brown); and from the color of the hair, Whitehead, Whitlock, Fairfax (fair-hair), Brunel, Roth (red), Swartz (black), Fairchild, Black, Blackman, etc.

Those which indicate the mental or moral qualities are such as Good, Goodman, Goodfellow, Giddy, Wise, Wiley, Meek, Merry, Moody, Bliss, Joy, Gay, Sage.

SIGNIFICATION OF NAMES. 37

Those derived from bodily peculiarity and from feats of personal strength or courage, Strong, Mickle, Little, Long, Short, Strongfellow or Strengfellow, Hardy, Proudfit, Lightbody, Ironside, Armstrong, Crookshanks, Turnbull, and Camoys.

> "Round was his face, and *camuse* was his nose."
> CHAUCER.

We find such names bestowed among the Greeks and Romans. The Greeks had their Sophocles (wise), Agathios (good), and Strabo (squint-eyed), and Paulus (little). The Romans, their Pius, Prudentius, Longus; their Naso (bottle-nose), Calvus (bald-pate), Flaccus (loll-eared), Varus (bow-legged), Ancus (crooked arm), Crispus (curly-headed), etc. As I have before remarked, the Britons, Gaels, and Celts bestowed many names descriptive of personal peculiarities, and mental and bodily qualities, as Cadrod *Hardd*, Cadrod the beautiful; Con *Bachach*, Con the lame; Shane *Buidhe* (Boyd), John with the yellow hair; Seumas *Reagh*, James the swarthy; *Vaughan*, little; *Gough*, red; *Gwynne*, white, etc.

Some surnames are derived from animals, such especially as were noted for fierceness or courage, as the bear, the wolf, the lion, whence the names *Byron*, or bear; Wolf, French *Loupè*, German *Guelph*, the surname of the existing Royal Family of Great

38   ESSAY ON THE ORIGIN AND

Britain; Wild-boar or Wilbur, Lovel or Luvel, from *Lupellus*, a little wolf; Bull, Brock (a badger), Todd (a fox), Hare, Hart, Leveret, Roe, Stagg, etc., to which some add the name of *Hog* and *Hogden*, a sheltered swine pasture.

A writer in the Edinburg Review, April, 1855, has remarked that *Eber* or *Eafer*, a boar, is the root of the following names: Eber, Ever, Ebers, Everard, Evered, Everett, Everingham, Everington, Everly, and Everton.

Richard the Third was called the *Boar* or the *Hog*, "and so gave occasion to the rhyme that cost the maker his life :

> "The Cat, the Rat, and Lovel the Dog
> Rule all England under the Hog."*

The names of fishes have been taken as family names. From this source we have Pike, Burt, Chubb, Mullet, Bass, Fish, etc.

Birds also come in for a share in our surnames. We have Dove, Raven, Lark, Wren, Peacock, Finch, Sparrow, Swan, Culver, Gosling, Heron, Wild-goose or Wilgus, Jay, and many others.

The mineral and vegetable kingdoms have contributed their full quota of names. In this list we

---

* EDINBURG REVIEW, *April*, 1855.—"The allusion to the names of Ratcliff and Catesby is obvious. Lovel is said to have borne a dog as his arms."

SIGNIFICATION OF NAMES.

39

find Garnet, Jewel, Gold, Silver, Salt, Steel, Iron, Flint, and Stone.

From flowers, plants, shrubs, and trees, we have Lilly, Rose, Ferne, Furze, Heath, Broome, Primrose, Pease, Peach, Oak, Cherry, Beach, Ash, Thorn, Alder, Pine, and Burch.

We find such names among the Romans—Taurus, a bull; Vitulus, a calf; Porcius, like a hog; Caprillus, like a goat; Leo, lion; Lupus, a wolf; and the names of Fabius, Lentulus, Cicero, and Piso, were given respectively for skill in cultivating beans, lentils, peas, and vetches.

Many names were taken from the signs over the doors of inns, or the shops of various tradesmen, where goods were manufactured and sold.

Camden informs us, " that he was told by them who said they spake of knowledge, that many names that seem unfitting for men, as of brutish beasts, etc., come from the very signs of the houses where they inhabited. That some, in late time, dwelling at the sign of the Dolphin, Bull, Whitehorse, Racket, Peacocke, etc., were commonly called *Thomas at the Dolphin, Will at the Bull, George at the Whitehorse, Robin at the Racket,* which names, as many other of the like sort, with omitting *at,* became afterward hereditary to their children."

40 ESSAY ON THE ORIGIN AND

In olden times, in London, might be seen the sign of the Boar's Head, the Crosskeyes, the Gun, the Castle, the Crane, the Cardinal's Hat, the Angell, the Bell, the Swan, the Bowles, the Barrell, the Crosier, the Griffin, the Coney, the Jugg, the Kettle, the Potts, the Pitcher, Sword, Shears, Scales, Tabor, Tub, etc.

In the cities and towns, every kind of beasts, birds, and fishes, objects animate and inanimate, were taken by tradesmen as signs to distinguish their shops from others, and to excite the attention of customers. From many of these, names were bestowed, and we can account in this way for many surnames which would otherwise seem strange and absurd.

Armorial ensigns and heraldic bearings have given surnames to families. Many of the old knights took their names from the figures and devices they bore on their shields.

The royal line of Plantagenet (Broome) took their surname from the broom plant, Fulke, Earl of Anjou, the founder of the house, having worn a sprig of broom, as a symbol of humility, and adopted it as his badge after his pilgrimage to the Holy Land.

Names were borrowed from armor and costume, as Fortescue (strong-shield), Strongbow, Harness,

SIGNIFICATION OF NAMES.   41

Beauharnois, Broadspeare, Shakespeare, Shotbolt, Curthose, that is, short hose, Curtmantle, a name given to Henry the Second from his wearing shorter mantles than were then in fashion; Freemantle, Coates, Capet. "Hugh Capet, the founder of the royal line of France, in the tenth century, is said to have acquired that surname from a freak of which, in his boyhood, he was very fond, that of snatching off the caps of his play-fellows. De La Rocque, however, gives a different origin for this name, deriving it from 'le bon sens et esprit qui residoit à sa teste!'"

We have names taken from the seasons, the months, and the days of the week, holidays and festivals of the church, most of which probably originated from the period of birth, such as Summer, Spring, Winter, Fall, Monday, Friday, May, March, Morrow, Weekes, Day, Christmas, Paschal, Holiday, Noel (Christmas), etc.

Many surnames have originated in soubriquets, epithets of contempt, and ridicule, and nicknames, imposed for personal peculiarities, habits, and qualities, or from incidents or accidents which happened to the original bearers. Such names are very numerous, and can be accounted for in no other way.

42 ESSAY ON THE ORIGIN AND

They are such as Doolittle, Hearsay, Timeslow, Houseless, Tugwell. Steptoe, Goelightly, Bragg, Trollope, that is, slattern; Parnell, a woman of bad character; Lawless, Silliman, Bastard (William the Conqueror was not ashamed of the illegitimacy of his birth, as he often signed his name *William the Bastard*), Crookshanks, Longshanks, Addlehead, and Leatherhead, Gubbins, that is, the refuse parts of a fish; Gallows, and Devil!

We can easily imagine how some ridiculous incident or foolish act or saying would confer a soubriquet or nickname upon a person by which he would be known and called through life, and which would even descend to his children, for we often see this in our day.

The following anecdote from Lower is an illustration: "The parish clerk of Langford, near Wellington, was called Redcock for many years before his death; for having one Sunday slept in church, and dreaming that he was at a cock-fighting, he bawled out 'a shilling upon the red cock!' And behold, the family are called *Redcock* to this day."

We have gone through the principal sources from which the greater part of our surnames are derived; but many names yet remain for the origin of which we are at a loss to account.

But shall we wonder when we consider that

SIGNIFICATION OF NAMES. 43

names have been taken and bestowed from every imaginable incident and occurrence unknown to us, and that many of them have been so corrupted in process of time, that we can not trace their originals. *All names must have been originally significant.*

In the words of our old friend Camden:

"*To drawe to an end*, no name whatsoeuer is to be disliked, in respect either of originall or of signification; for neither the good names doe disgrace the bad, neither doe euil names disgrace the good. If names are to be accounted good or bad, in all countries both good and bad have bin of the same surnames, which, as they participate one with the other in glory, so sometimes in shame. Therefore, for ancestors, parentage, and names, as Seneca said, let every man say, *Vix ea nostra voco.* Time hath intermingled and confused all, and we are come all to this present, by successive variable descents from high and low; or as he saith more plainly, the low are descended from the high, and contrariwise the high from the low."

AN

ETYMOLOGICAL DICTIONARY

OF

FAMILY NAMES.

In the following Dictionary, in giving the languages from which the names are derived, I have used these abbreviations:

Nor. Fr.	Norman French.	Ger.	German.
Sax.	Saxon.	Teut.	Teutonic.
Cor. Br.	Cornish British.	Lat.	Latin.
Fr.	French.	Gr.	Greek.
Du.	Dutch.	Heb.	Hebrew.
A. S.	Anglo-Saxon.	Dan.	Danish.

The term *Gaelic* is often used instead of what is commonly called the *Celtic*. The Celts of Ireland call their language the *Gaelic* or *Gaelen*, and the Welsh writers call the Irish *Guidhel* or *Gael*. The Gaelic is spoken in different dialects, by the descendants of the ancient Celts or Gaels, in a large portion of Ireland, in the Highlands of Scotland, in the Hebrides, and, to some extent, in the Isle of Man.

The names of many of the rivers, headlands, hills, and mountains in Britain are found to be of Gaelic or Celtic origin.

The ancient British or Welsh language, spoken and written by the people of that name, is more nearly allied to the Gaelic than the Teutonic.

The Cornish-British is a dialect of the Celto-Belgic or Cambrian, formerly spoken throughout Cornwall, but now extinct.

46 ETYMOLOGICAL DICTIONARY

The Saxon, so named from the people who spoke it, in its idiom, resembled the modern Low Dutch.

The Anglo-Saxon was a compound of the idioms spoken by the Angli, the Saxons, and the Jutes, who, invited by the British to assist them against the Scots and Picts, finally took possession of the country.

AARON. (Hebrew.) Signifies a *mountaineer*, or mount of strength.

ABBOT. So named from his office in the church; the chief ruler of an abbey—derived from the Syriac *Abba*, signifying *father*.

ABDALLAH. (Turkish.) The servant of God.

ABEL. (Hebrew.) Vanity, breath.

ABENDROTH. (Ger.) From *abend*, evening, and *roth*, red. The name might have been given to a child born at the close of day.

ABERCROMBIE. (Celtic and Gaelic.) Local, The name of a parish in Fife, Scotland, on the northern shore of the Frith of Forth, whence the possessor took his surname; from *Aber*, marshy ground, a place where two or more streams meet; and *cruime* or *crombie*, a bend or crook. *Aber*, in the Celtic and Gaelic, and also in the Cornish British, signifies the confluence of two or more streams, or the mouth of a river, where it flows into the sea; hence it is often applied to marshy ground, generally near the confluence of two rivers. It also signifies, sometimes, a gulf or whirlpool.

ABERDEEN or **ABERDENE.** (Gaelic and Celtic.) Local. The name of a city in Aberdeenshire, whence the surname was taken. It is derived from *Aber*, the mouth, as above, and *Don*, the name of a river, at the mouth of which it is situated.

OF FAMILY NAMES.

ABERNETHY. (Gaelic and Celtic.) Local. From a town in Strathern, Scotland, on the river Tay; derived from *Aber*, as given above, and *nethy*, in the Gaelic, dangerous. *Nith* or *Nithy*, is also the name of a river in the south of Scotland, and the name may have been taken from a town at or near its mouth—*Abernithy*.

ABNEY. (Nor. Fr.) Local. A corruption of Aubigny, a town of France, in the department of Berry, whence the surname is derived; so *D'Aubigny* is corrupted to *Dabney*.

ABRAHAM. (Heb.) The father of a great multitude.

ACHESON. (Cor. Br.) An inscription or memorial.

ACKART. (Saxon.) From *Ack*, oak, and *ard*, nature, disposition; firm-hearted, unyielding.

ACKERMAN. (Saxon.) From *Acker*, oaken, made of oak, and man. The brave, firm, unyielding man.

ACKERS. (Saxon.) Camden derives this surname from the Latin *Ager*, a field. The name, however, is Saxon, and signifies *the place of oaks*, or oak-man; *ac* and *ake* being old terms for oak.

The termination *er*, in many nouns has the same signification as the Latin *vir*, a man—as *Plower*, i. e., Plowman; Baker, Bakerman.

Like oak, the first Acker might have been firm and unyielding in his disposition, or he might have used or sold acorns.

ACKLAND. (Saxon.) Local. The name of a place in North Devonshire, England, whence the surname is derived; so called, because it was situated among groves of oaks—from *ack*, oak, as above, and *land*.

ACTON. (Saxon.) Local. The oak-town or oak-hill—the name of a town in Middlesex, England, whence the name is derived.

ADAIR. (Celtic and Gaelic.) Local. From *Ath*, a ford, and *dare*, from *darach*, the place of oaks, "The ford of the oaks." There is the following tradition of the origin of this surname:

48 ETYMOLOGICAL DICTIONARY

"Thomas, the sixth Earl of Desmond, while on a hunting excursion was benighted, and lost his way, between Tralee and Newcastle, in the county of Limerick, where he was received and hospitably entertained by one William McCormic, whose daughter he subsequently married. At this alliance, the family and clan took umbrage. Resigning his title and estate to his youngest brother, he fled to France in 1418, and died of grief at Rouen, two years afterward. The King of England attended his funeral. He had issue, Maurice and John; Robert, the son of Maurice, returning to Ireland, with the hope of regaining the estates and title of Thomas, his ancestor, slew Gerald, the White Knight, in single combat at *Athdare, the ford of the oaks*, whence he received the name of Adaire. He embarked for Scotland, where he married Arabella, daughter of John Campbell, Lord of Argyle."

ADAMS. (Hebrew.) Man, earthly, or red. The surname of *Adam* is of great antiquity in Scotland. Duncan Adam, son of Alexander Adam, lived in the reign of King Robert Bruce, and had four sons, from whom all the Adams, Adamsons, and Adies in Scotland are descended.

ADCOCK, little Ad or Adam, *cock* being a diminutive termination. (See Alcock, Wilcox, etc.)

ADDISON. The same as Adamson, the son of Adam, *Adie* or *Addie* being, in the Lowland-Scotch, a familiar corruption of Adam, hence *Addie-son*.

ADEE or ADIE. The same as Adam. (See Addison.)

ADKINS. Little Adam, or the son of Adam, from *Ad* and *kins*, a diminutive, signifying *child*, from the German *kind*, so *Wilkins, Tompkins*, etc.

ADLAM. (Saxon.) Local. From *adel*, fine, noble, and *ham*, a village or castle. *Adelham*, contracted to *Adlam*.

ADLAR. (Dutch.) From *Adelaar*, an eagle.

OF FAMILY NAMES.

49

ADRIAN or HADRIAN. (Latin.) Local. From the city *Hadria*, which Gesner derives from the Greek ἀδρὸς, great or wealthy.

AFFLECK. (Gaelic and Celtic.) Local. Said to be a corruption of the name *Auchinleck*, which was assumed by the proprietors of the lands and barony of Auchinleck, near Dundee, in Angusshire, Scotland. The name is pronounced *Affleck* by the natives. (See Auchinleck.)

AGAN or EGAN. (Gaelic.) From *Eigin*, force, violence; hence, strong-handed, active. The name may be local, and named from Agen, a town in Guienne, France; also *Agen*, Welsh, local, a cleft.

AGAR. (Gaelic and Celtic.) *Aighear* signifies gladness, joy, gayety. If from the Latin *ager*, it denotes a field or land.

AGLIONBY. (Nor. Fr.) Local. From *Aglion*, an eaglet, and *by*, a residence or habitation—the eagle's nest.

AGNEW. (Nor. Fr.) Local. From the town of Agneau in Normandy, whence the family originated. They went from England into Ireland with Strongbow. *Agneau*, in Nor. Fr. signifies a *lamb*.

AIKEN. (Saxon.) Oaken; hard or firm.

AIKMAN. (Sax.) From *ack*, oak, and man.

AINSWORTH. (British and Welsh.) Local. From *ains*, a spring, a river, and *gwerth*, a place, possession, or court. In the British and Gaelic, *Aun, Ain, Au, Hain, Aon, and Avon*, signify a river; the place or possession on the river.

AITKIN. Probably the same as *Atkins* (which see).

AITON. (Nor. Fr.) Local. From *ea* or *eau*, water, and *ton*, a town; the town near the water; the same as Eaton.

AKEMAN or ACKMAN. (Saxon.) The same as Oakman, from his strength or disposition. From *ack*, or *ake*, oak, and *man*.

3

ETYMOLOGICAL DICTIONARY

AKERS. (Saxon.) The same as *Ackers* (which see).

AKIN and **AKEN.** The same as *Aiken* (which see).

ALAN or **ALLAN.** Derived, according to Julius Scaliger, from the Sclavonic Aland, a wolf-dog, a hound, and Chaucer uses *Aland* in the same sense. Bailey derives it as the same from the British. Camden thinks it a corruption of *Ælianus*, which signifies sun-bright. From the same we have Allen, Allin, Alleyne. In the Gaelic, *Aluinn* signifies exceedingly fair, handsome, elegant, lovely; Irish, *Alun*, fair, beautiful.

ALANSON. The son of Alan.

ALBERT. (German.) All bright or famous; *beort* or *bert*, signifies famous, fair, and clear, bright; so *Sebert* and *Ethelbert* were sometimes written *Se bright* and *Ethel bright*. *All*, *Eal*, and *Æl*, in old English and Saxon compound names, have the same signification as the English *All*, as Al-dred, Al-win, etc.

ALBRECHT. (Saxon.) The same as Albert—All-bright.

ALCOCK. From *Hal* or *Al*, a nickname for Henry; and *cock*, a termination meaning *little*, a diminutive, the same as *ot* or *kin;* little Hal or Al, so Wilcox, little Will, and Simcox, little Sim, etc.

ALDEN or **ALDAINE.** (Sax.) Local. From *ald*, old, and *den* or *dun*, a hill or town; old-town, or it may be high-town, from *alt*, high, Gaelic, and *dun*, a hill, castle, or town.

ALDERSEY. (Sax.) Local. The isle of alders.

ALDIS. (Saxon.) A contraction of *ald-house*, the old house.

ALDJOY. (Sax.) The same as the English *all-joy*.

ALDRED. (Sax.) All-fear—see Albert.

ALDRIDGE. (Sax.) The same as Aldred, of which it is a corruption.

OF FAMILY NAMES. 51

ALEXANDER. (Greek.) An aider or benefactor of men. From Ἀλέξω, to aid or help, and ἀνὴρ, a man. A powerful auxiliary.

ALFORD or ALVORD. (Saxon.) Local. From Alford, a town in Lincolnshire, England, signifying *the old ford* or *way*, from *ald*, old, and *ford*, a ford, way, or pass.

ALFORT. (Local.) A village in France, two leagues from Paris.

ALFRED. (Saxon.) All-peace, from · *all*, and *fred* or *friede*, peace, like Alwin and Albert.

ALGAR. (Gaelic.) Noble.

ALLEN. The same as *Alan* (which see).

ALLENDORF. Local. A town in Hesse, Germany, signifying the old town; *dorf*, a town or village, the same as Olden-dorf.

ALLGOOD. (Saxon.) The same as the English All-good.

ALSOP. (Local.) From *Alsop*, Co. Derby, England. One might imagine it a corruption of *Ale-shop*, a name given to one who kept an ale-shop. A very appropriate name at the present day; for "*Alsop's ale*" is celebrated all the world over.

ALVERSTON or ALVERTON. (Cor. Br.) Local. A high green hill; from *al*, high, *ver*, green, and *don* or *ton*, a hill.

ALVIN or ALWIN. (Saxon.) All-winning or victorious, the *v* and *w* being interchangeable.

ALVORD. (Saxon.) The same as Alford (which see).

AMAKER. (Local.) Derived from *Amager*, a small Danish island to the east of Copenhagen.

AMBLER. (French.) From *Ambleur*, an officer of the king's stables; anciently "*le Amblour.*"

AMBROSE. (Greek.) From ἀμβρόσιος, divine, immortal.

ETYMOLOGICAL DICTIONARY

AMERY. (German.) Always rich, able, and powerful, from the old German *Emerich* or *Immer-reich*, always rich.

AMES. (French.) From *Amie*, a friend, belóved; or if from the Hebrew *Amos*, a burden. Some think it is a contraction of *Ambrose* (which see). *Amesbury* in England was originally *Ambrosebury*.

AMHERST. (Saxon.) Local. From *ham*, a town or village, and *hurst* or *herst*, a wood, the town in the wood, the "*H*," by custom, being dropped or silent. It may have been derived from *Hamo*, who was sheriff in the county of Kent, in the time of William the Conqueror; a descendant of his was called *Hamo de Herst*, and the Norman *de*, and the aspirate "*h*" being dropped—Amherst. AMHURST, the connected grove, or conjoined woods; "*am*," in the British, as a prefix, has the sense of *Amb, amphi, circum*, i. e., about, surrounding, encompassing; hence, the surrounding grove, or *Amhurst*.

AMMADON. (Gaelic.) From *Amadan*, a numskull, a simpleton; may be so called by way of *antiphrasis*, because he was wise; as Ptolemy received the surname Philadelphus (from the Greek φίλος, a lover or friend, and ἀδελφος, a brother), because he charged two of his brothers with forming designs against his life, and then caused them to be destroyed.

AMPTE. (Dutch.) *Ampt*, an official situation; the house in which an officer transacts his business; a lordship of the Netherlands.

ANDARTON. (Br.) Local. The oak-hill; from *an*, the; *dar*, an oak, and *ton*, a hill.

ANDERSON. The son of Andrew (which see).

ANDREW. (Greek.) From ἀνδρεῖος, manly, courageous.

ANGEVINE. So named because coming originally from *Anjou*, in France. The natives of Anjou were called *Angevines.*

OF FAMILY NAMES. 53

ANGLE or **ANGEL.** (Greek.) From ἄγγελος, a messenger; also the name of a town in France where the family may have originated.

ANGUS. Local. A county of Scotland, sometimes called Forfarshire, and took its name, according to Halloran, from *Aongus Fer*, grandson to Carbre Riada, who, with others, invaded the modern Scotland, A.D. 498. Angus or Aongus is derived from *Aon*, excellent, noble, and *gais*, boldness, valor.

ANNAN. Local. A river and borough of Scotland. From the Gaelic *aon*, *aon*, one, one, or the river that divides the dale in two shares. *Amhan*, Avon, or An-oun, in Gaelic, may signify the slow running water; a gentle river.

ANNESLEY. Local. From a town in Nottinghamshire, England, and named, perhaps, from *Anclo*, a city in Norway, by the free-booters or conquerors of Briton. *Annansley*, the *lea*, lying on the Annon.

ANSELL. Supposed to be an abbreviation of Anselm; also the name of a bird.

ANSELM. (German.) From the Teutonic *Hamstzhelm*, a defender of his companions.

ANSON. The son of Ann, or the same as Hanson, the son of Hans or John—the "H" being dropped in pronunciation.

ANSTRUTHER. (Gaelic.) From *Anstruth*, an ancient order of historians or bards among the Celts, next in rank to the *Allamh*, or chief doctor of the seven degrees in all the sciences. His reward was twenty kine. He was to be attended by twelve students in his own science, to be entertained for fifteen days, and to be protected from all accusations during that time; and he and his attendants supplied with all manner of necessaries. *Anstruth* is derived from *Aon*, that is, good, great; *sruth*, knowing, discerning, and *er* put for *fear*, a man.

ANTHON. A contraction of Anthony, from the Greek ἄνθος, a flower; but, by way of excellency, appropriated to Rosemary flowers.

ANTHONY. (Greek.) From *ανθος*, a flower; flourishing, beautiful, graceful.

APPLEBY. Local. A town in Westmoreland, England, called *Aballaba* by the Romans, from which the name is derived. *By* signifies a town,—the apple-town.

APPLEGARTH. Local. The orchard, apple-garden, or close.

APPLETON. Local. The town abounding in apples.

ARBLASTER. A corruption of *Balistarius,* a cross-bowman, one who directed the great engines of war used before the invention of cannon.

> " In the kernils (battlements) here and there,
> Of *Arblastirs* great plenty were."
>
> ROM. OF THE ROSE.

ARBUTHNOT. Local. First assumed by the proprietors of the land and barony of Arbuthnot in the Mearns, Scotland. The name is said to have been anciently written *Aberbuth-noth,* which signifies the dwelling near the confluence of the river with the sea, from *Aber,* the mouth of a river, *both,* a dwelling, and *neth,* a stream that descends, or is lower than some other relative object.

ARCHIBALD. (German.) The same as *Erchenbald,* a powerful, bold, and speedy learner or observer. In the Gaelic this name is called Gillespie—a favorite name with the Scotch.

ARDAL or **ARDGALL.** (Celtic.) Bravery or prowess. *Ardol,* local, Welsh, from *ar,* upon, and *dol* or *dal,* a vale, on the vale, or a place opposite the dale.

ARGYLE. (Gaelic.) An extensive shire on the western coast of Scotland. The name is derived from the Gaelic *Earra Ghaidheal,* that is, the country of the western Gael, or, according to Grant, the breeding-place of the Gael.

ARLINGTON. Local. From a village in Sussex, England.

ARLON. A local name, and derived from *Arlon,* a town in the Netherlands, thirteen miles east from Luxemburg.

OF FAMILY NAMES.

ARMISTEAD and **ARMSTED**. (Saxon.) The place of arms.

ARMITAGE. Local. The same as *Hermitage*, the cell or habitation of a hermit, formerly a wilderness or solitary place; a convent of hermits or minor friars.

ARMOUR. Defensive arms; all instruments of war. The name is probably contracted from *Armorer*, a maker of armor.

ARMSTRONG. A name given for strength in battle. Historians relate the following tradition:

This family was anciently settled on the Scottish border; their original name was Fairbairn, which was changed to Armstrong on the following occasion:

An ancient king of Scotland having had his horse killed under him in battle, was immediately re-mounted by Fairbairn, his armor-bearer, on his own horse. For this timely assistance he amply rewarded him with lands on the borders, and to perpetuate the memory of so important a service, as well as the manner in which it was performed (for Fairbairn took the king by the thigh, and set him on the saddle), his royal master gave him the appellation of *Armstrong*. The chief seat of Johnnie Armstrong was Gilnockie, in Eskdale, a place of exquisite beauty. Johnnie was executed by order of James·V., in 1529, as a "Border Freebooter." Andrew Armstrong sold his patrimony to one of his kinsmen, and emigrated to the north of Ireland in the commencement of the seventeenth century. The Armstrongs were always noted for their courage and daring. In the "Lay of the Last Minstrel," when the chief was about to assemble his clans, he says to his heralds:

> "Ye need not go to Liddisdale,
> For when they see the blazing bale
> Elliots and *Armstrongs* never fail."

ARNOLD. (German.) The same as *Ernold;* from *are* or *ehre*, honor, and *hold*, faithful or devoted to—faithful to his honor. How unworthy of the name was the notorious Benedict!

ETYMOLOGICAL DICTIONARY

ARTHUR. (British.) A strong man; from *Ar* (Lat. *vir*), a man, and *thor*, strong. In the Gaelic, *Air* is the same as *Fear*, a man; and the ancient Scythians called a man *Aior*. *Thor* was the Jupiter of the Teutonic races, their god of thunder. In Welsh, *Arth* is a bear, an emblem of strength and courage, and *ur* a noun termination, a man. Arthur, a bear-man, a hero, a man of strength; the name of a British prince.

ARTOIS. (Local.) From the province of Artois in the Netherlands.

ARUNDEL. Local. From a town in Sussex, England, on the river Arun; a corruption of *Arundale*—"the dale on the Arun."

ASCALL or **ASGALL.** In the Gaelic, means a sheltered place, a bosom, a covert. *Aisgiodal* or *Aisgall* was one of the Danish commanders at the battle of Clontarf, near Dublin. The name is expressive of courage and strength. From this may be found the name of *Hascall.* If the name is of British origin, it would signify the sedgy moor, from *Hesg*, and *hal* or *hayle*—low grounds, meadows.

ASHBURTON. Local. From a town of the same name in Devonshire, England. *Burton* signifies the town on the hill, and *Ashburton* the town on the hill covered or surrounded with ash trees. *Ash* may be, in some cases, a corruption of the Gaelic or Celtic *uisge*, water.

ASHBY. (Sax.) Local. The house by the "ash," or the village on a place abounding in ash-trees; *by* signifying a villa or habitation.

ASHFORD. (Sax.) Local. A town in Kent, England, on the river Ash or Esh—the ford over the Ash.

ASHLEY. (Sax.) Local. The lea, field, or pasture abounding in ash-trees. *Leegh, ley*, or *lea*, signifying uncultivated grounds or pastures; lands untilled, generally used as commons.

ASHTON. (Sax.) Local. The ash-hill or town.

OF FAMILY NAMES.

ASKEW. (Sax.) Local. *Acksheugh,* hilly lands covered with oaks. Aschau, local, a town on the bend of a river in Sleswick, Denmark. *Askew,* crooked, from the Danish.

ASPINWALL. (Sax.) Local. The aspen-vale.

ASTLEY. (Sax.) Local. A corruption of *Estley* or *Eastley,* the east meadow or field. (See *ley,* under *Ashley.*)

ASTON. (Sax.) Local. A corruption of *Eston* or *Easton,* the east town.

ASTOR. Local. Oster, a town in North Jutland. Ἀστήρ, Greek, a star. *Austeuer,* German, a dowry, a portion. *Ooster,* the east part.

ATHERTON. (Sax.) Local. From Atherstone, a town in Warwickshire, England.

ATHILL. Local. At (the) hill. This family formerly bore the name of "*De la Hou,*" that is, "*of the hill,*" which was anglicized into *Athill.* They came originally from Normandy.

ATHOL. (Celtic and Gaelic.) Local. A district of Perthshire, Scotland; from *ath,* a ford, and *al,* an old word for a rock, a stone,—Rockford, or the ford of the rock.

ATHOW. Local. The same as Athill; *how* or *hoo,* a high place.

ATKINS. Camden derives it from *At,* a familiar abbreviation of Arthur, and *kins,* a diminutive, signifying a child, having the same meaning as the German *kind,* a child, an infant, *i. e.,* the son of Arthur, so Wilkins, Simpkins, etc.

ATTREE. Local. At (the) tree.

ATWATER. Local. At (the) water.

ATWELL. Local. At (the) well.

.ATWOOD. Local. At (the) wood.

3*

AUBREY. A corruption of the German *Alberic*, a name given in hope of power or wealth, *ric* signifying rich or powerful; always rich.

AUCHINLECK. Local. A parish in Ayrshire, Scotland. The etymology of the name may be found in the Gaelic *Ach*, an elevation, a mound, or round hill, generally level at the top; and *leac*, a flat stone, a tombstone. In several parts of Ayrshire may be traced the remains of cairns, encampments, and Druidical circles. *Auchinleck* appears to have been one of those places where the ancient Celts and Druids held conventions, celebrated their festivals, and performed acts of worship.

AUCHMUTY. (Gaelic.) Local. The field or mount of law; an eminence in which law-courts were held, *moot-hills*, as they were called; from *Ach*, an elevation, a mound, and *mod*, a court, an assembly, a meeting.

AUDLEY. (Sax.) Local. From *ald* or *aud*, old, and *ley*, a field or pasture—the old field.

AUSTIN. (Latin.) A contraction of Augustine, from *Augustinus*, imperial, royal, great, renowned.

AVERILL. Local. A corruption of Haverhill, the aspirate being dropped. Haverill is a town in Suffolk, England, so named from the Dutch *Hyver*, Teut., *Haber*, oats, and *hill*—the hill sown with oats.

AVERY. (Gaelic.) From *Aimhrea* (the "mh" having the sound of "v"), denoting contention or disagreement. It may be from *Avery*, a granary, or from *Aviarius*, Latin, a bird-keeper.

AVIS. *Avis*, in French, is a projector, schemer, busy-body. *Avus*, Latin, a grandfather, ancestor. *Avis*, a bird.

AYLMER. This family trace their name and descent from *Ailmer* or *Athelmare*, Earl of Cornwall, in the time of King Ethelred. *Allmor*. in Welsh, signifies a valley or dale.

AYLSWORTH. This name admits of several meanings; *Eal*;

OF FAMILY NAMES.

59

Saxon, finished, completed, and *worth*, a farm-house or village. *Ayles*, Cor. Br., low meadow, flat lands, washed by a river, sea, or lake, and *gwerth*, a worth, farm, house, village.

AYLEWARD. The ale-keeper.

AYRES. Local. Derived from a river, town, and district of the same name in Scotland. *Air*, Gaelic. Derivation uncertain. It may come from *Iar*, west—the course in which the river runs; or *Air*, slaughter, the place of battle. The Celtic *Aer*, and the Welsh *Awyr*, signify, radically, to open, expand or flow clearly; to shoot or radiate. In Thorpe's catalogue of the deeds of Battle Abbey, we find the following legendary account of this name:

" Ayres, formerly Eyre. The first of this family was named Truelove, one of the followers of William the Conqueror. At the battle of Hastings, Duke William was flung from his horse, and his helmet beaten into his face, which Truelove observing, pulled off, and horsed him again. The duke told him ' Thou shalt hereafter from Truelove be called Eyre (or Air), because thou hast given me the air I breathe.' After the battle, the Duke, on inquiry respecting him, found him severely wounded (his leg and thigh having been struck off); he ordered him the utmost care, and on his recovery, gave him lands in Derby, in reward for his services, and the leg and thigh in armor, cut off, for his crest; an honorary badge yet worn by all the *Eyres* in England."

BABA. German, *Bube*, a boy; Greek, Bába, an inarticulate sound, as of an infant crying out; hence, a little child; to say *Baba*, that is, father or Papa. The word is nearly the same in all languages; it signifies a young child of either sex.

BABER. (Gaelic.) *Babair* or *Basbair*, a fencer or swordsman; one who, by his blows, produced death; from *Bas*, death, and *fear*, a man.

BABCOCK. Little Bab, or Bartholomew; from *Bab*, a nickname for Bartholomew, and *cock*, small, little, a son; *cic*, *cock*, *el*, and *et* are diminutives, and include the ideas of kind-

60   ETYMOLOGICAL DICTIONARY

ness and tenderness, associated with smallness of size. It may be from *Bob*, the nickname for Robert; *Bobcock*, the son of *Robert*, *Robertson*.

BACHELOR. From the Dutch *Bock*, a book, and *leeraar*, a doctor of divinity, law, or physic. When applied to persons of a certain military rank, it may be a corruption of *Bas chevalier*, because lower in dignity than the *milites bannereti*. Killian adopts the opinion that as the soldier who has once been engaged in battle, is called *battalarius*, so he who has once been engaged in literary warfare, in public dispute upon any subject. Calepinus thinks that those who took the degree of Bachelor, were so called (*Baccalaurei*), because a chaplet of laurel berries was placed upon them. The word, however, has probably but one origin, which would account for its various applications.

BACKMAN. German, *Bach*, a brook, and *man*. *Boekman* bookman. *Back*, in some places, a ferry; Backman, a ferry-man.

BACKUS. (Germ.) From *Back-haus*, a bake-house.

BACON. Bacon, from the Anglo-Saxon *bacan*, to bake, to dry by heat. Some derive this surname from the Saxon *baccen* or *buccen*, a beech-tree. Upon the monument of Thomas Bacon, in Brome Church in Suffolk (Eng.), there is a beech-tree engraven in brass, with a man resting under it. It appears, also, that the first Lord-keeper, Sir Nicholas Bacon, with his two wives, are represented in a similar manner.

BADEAU. (Fr.) Camden says this was a name given to the Parisians who admired every thing that seems a little extra-ordinary.

BADGER. A licensed dealer in grain; a hawker, a peddler; also, the name of a small animal.

BADGELY. Bagasly, local. From a town in Scotland.

BAGLEY. (Sax.) Local. The rising or swelling ground that lies untilled; from *bælge*, rising or swelling, and *leagh* or *ley*, plain or pasture land.

OF FAMILY NAMES.

61

BAGOT. (Fr.) A stay or walking staff; a gunstick or drumstick, from *Bagnette*. It may be a corruption of *Bigot* (which see). *Bagad*, in the Welsh, signifies a great many.

BAILEY. A name of office; a corruption of *Bailiff*, which is derived from the French *bailler*, to deliver. A municipal officer in Scotland corresponding to an alderman.

BAILLIE. (Fr.) *Baille*, a bailiff; same as Bailey.

BAIN or **BAINE.** (Celtic.) Whiteness, fairness. Bain is also a bath or hot-house. The name may be local, from *Bain*, a town in France.

BAISLEY. *Baisealach*, Gaelic, proud.

BAITS. A word used in several languages, and signifies to feed, to rest for refreshment; one who kept a house of entertainment.

BAKER. (Sax.) A name of trade, a baker; from the Saxon *bacan*, to dry by heat.

BALL. (Cor. Br. and Gaelic.) *Bal*, a mine, the top of a hill, the top.

BALCOMBE. Local. From *Bal*, Gaelic, a round body, any thing thrown up; a building, house, town; and *combe*, a valley; the round valley; tin-works thrown up in a valley, or a dwelling in such a place.

BALDWIN. (Ger.) The speedy conqueror or victor; from *bald*, quick or speedy, and *win*, an old word signifying victor or conqueror, as *Bert-win*, famous victor; *All-win*, all victorious, etc.

BALEN. *Belen*, in the Cor. British, is the same as *Melen*, a mill. *Bellyn*, local, a town in Lower Saxony. *Balaen*, Welsh, steel, denoting strength and durability.

BALFOUR. Local. From the barony and castle of Balfour, near the confluence of the rivers Or and Leven. (Scot.) *Ball* and *Balla*, in Gaelic, signifies a casting up, raising, like the Greek Βάλλω, and denotes a wall, fortress, house, a village. Balfour, *i. e.*, the *Keep*, or castle on the river Or. *Balfoir*, the castle of deliverance or security.

BALLANTINE. Local. A place where *Bal* or *Belus* was worshiped by the Celts; from *Bal* and *teine*, fire.

BALLANTYNE. Local. A place of ancient, pagan worship among the Celts, whose principal deity was *Belen* or *Baal*, the sun. To the honor of this deity, the Celts lighted fires on the 1st of May and Midsummer day. *Baalantine* signifies " the fire of Baal," from *Baalen* and *teine*, Gaelic, fire.

BALLARD. (Celtic and Gaelic.) From *Ball*, a place, a round elevation; and *ard*, high. The Gaelic word *Ballart* signifies noisy, boasting. *Bal* also signifies a lord, and *ard*, high.

BANCHO. (Gaelic.) The white dog; from *ban*, white, and *chu* or *cu*, a dog. *Bankhoo* (Eng.), the high bank.

BANCROFT. Local. From the Cor. Br. *ban*, a mount, hill, or high ground; and *croft*, a small field near a dwelling—a green pasture.

BANGS. This name may be a corruption of Banks, or from the French *bain*, a bath, a hot-house.

BANNATYNE. Local. The name of a place in Scotland, signifying the hill where fires were kindled.

BANNERMAN. A name of office in Scotland borne by the king's standard-bearer.

BANNING. *Baaning*, Danish, a home, a dwelling.

BANNISTER. The keeper of a bath; from the French *bain*, a bath.

BANT. (Welsh.) A high place; *Bant-lle*.

BANTA. (Gaelic.) Local. From *Beaunta*, hills, mountains.

BANVARD. (Cor. Br.) Local. From *ban*, a mount, hill, or high ground; and *vard*, a rampart, that is, a fortified hill or castle.

BAR. Local. A town of France. Barr, a parish in Ayrshire, Scotland.

BARBER. A name of trade, one who shaves and dresses hair.

OF FAMILY NAMES.

BARCLAY. (Sax.) Local. A corruption of Berkeley; a town in Gloucestershire, England, derived from the Saxon *beorce*, a beech-tree, and *leagh* or *ley*, a field, and so called because of the plenty of beech-trees growing there.

BARCULO. (Dutch.) Local. From *Borkulo*, a town in Holland. The name was originally *Van Borkulo*.

BARD. (Celtic.) Local. From *bawr*, a top or summit, the highest; and *eidde* or *oidde*, instructor—the chief preceptor, instructor, or poet.

BARDEL. (Welsh.) Local. A fortification.

BARHYDT. (Dutch.) From *Barheid*, sharpness, roughness, severity.

BARKER. A tanner.

> "What craftsman art thou, said the king,
>   I pray thee tell me trowe?
> I am a *Barker*, sir, by my trade,
>   Now tell me, what art thou?"
>   PERCY'S RELIQUES.

BARNARD. The same as Bernard (which see).

BARNES. A distinguished family of Sotterly, Co. Suffolk, England. *Bearn*, local, a city in France. *Barnyz*, Cor. Br., a judge.

BARNET. Local. A town in Hertfordshire, England.

BARNEY. A familiar abbreviation or corruption of Bernard, or Barnard (which see).

BARNWELL. Local. From the old English *Bearne*, a wood, and *veld*, a field.

BARNUM. Local. A corruption of *Bearnham*, the town in the wood or hill. *Bern*, in the Swiss language, signifies a bear. This family was originally of Southwick, County Hants, England.

ETYMOLOGICAL DICTIONARY

BARR. (Celtic.) Local. The top or summit of any thing; any thing round. *Bar*, Gaelic, an old word for a bard or learned man. *Bar*, local, a bank of sand or earth, a shoal; the shore of the sea. It may be derived from Barre, a town in France, or from Barr, a parish and village in Ayrshire, Scotland.

BARRAS. (Saxon.) Local. From *Baerwas*, Saxon, groves, a place among trees; a town in England.

BARRELL. (Gaelic.) From *Barrail*, excellent, surpassing.

BARRET. (Fr.) Cunning; from the old French *barat*, strife, deceit.

BARRINGER. Local. A corruption of Beranger (Lat. Berengarus); from *Beringer*, a town in France, where a battle was fought between the French and the English.

BARRON or **BARON.** The word *Baron* is of Celtic extraction, and originally synonymous with *man* in general. It has this meaning in the Salic law, and in the laws of the Lombards; in the English law, the phrase *baron and feme* is equivalent to *man and wife*. It was afterward used to denote a man of respectability, a stout or valiant man; and *Barone* was also used by the Italians to signify a beggar.

From denoting a stout or valiant man, it was employed as a name for a distinguished military leader, who having fought and conquered under some great commander, was afterward rewarded by him with a part of the lands which he had acquired.

As a surname, it was originally *Le Baron*, The Baron. Gaelic, *Baran*, a baron.

BARROW. Local. A circular earthen mound, marking the place of interment of some noted person; also a place of defense. The name of a river in Ireland.

BARRY. Local. From the Barry Islands in Glamorganshire, Wales; so called, says Bailey, from *Baruch*, a devout man who was interred there.

OF FAMILY NAMES.

BARSTOW. Local. May have various significations. *Barr*, the top of a hill, and *stow*, a place or depository. *Bar*, in the Gaelic, Welsh, and Cornish-British, means the summit or top of any thing. The Gaelic or Irish *aran* and *barr*, signify bread, a crop of grain; Welsh, *bar*, bread, an ear of corn; Saxon, *bar* and *bere*, corn, barley. *Barstow*, a place where grain is stored.

BARTHOLOMEW. (Heb.) The son of him who maketh the waters to mount, or a son that suspends the waters.

BARTLETT. A diminutive of Bartholomew—little Bart.

BARTON. (Sax.) Local. From a town in Lincolnshire, England; a corn town, or barley village, from *bere*, barley, and *ton*, an inclosure, a house, a village. *Barton*, a curtilage. In Devonshire, it is applied to any freehold estate not possessed of manorial privileges.

BARTUL. (Ger.) An abbreviation of Bartulph, which is from *Beorht*, and *ulph*; that is, *help in counsel*, or famous helper. *Bartel*, an abbreviation of Bartholomew, used in Holland.

BARWICK or BERWICK. Local. A town in Northumberland, Eng., at the mouth of the river Tweed. The name signifies, the town at the mouth of a river, from *aber*, the mouth, and *wick*, a town or harbor. *Berewick*, the corntown, from *bere*, barley, corn.

BASFORD. Local. The shallow ford or way.

BASIL. (Greek.) From Βασιλευς, royal, kingly.

BASSET. (Fr.) A little fat man with short legs and thighs, from the French *Basset*.

BATEMAN. May have two significations, Baitman, a keeper of a house of entertainment, and Bateman, a contentious man, from *bate*, Saxon, strife, to beat, contention.

BATES. *Bate*, Anglo-Saxon, contention.

66   ETYMOLOGICAL DICTIONARY

BATH. (Sax.) Local. A town in the county of Somerset, Eng., famous for its hot baths; so named from the Saxon, *bad*, Teutonic, *bad*, a place to bathe or wash in. It was called by the Saxons *Acmanceaster*, or the "sick folks' town;" and by the Britons, *Caerbaddon*, from *Caer*, a fortified place or city, and *baddon*, a bathing-place, from *badd*, a bath.

BATHURST. (Sax.) Local. From *Bath*, as above, and *hurst*, a place of fruit-trees, a wood or grove. *Boothhurst*, the house or lodge in the grove.

BAUM. (Germ.) A tree. It may be derived from a town in France by that name.

BAXTER. (Anglo-Saxon.) *Bagster*, a baker.

BEACH. Local. The shore of the sea, lake, or river.

BEACHER. A dweller on the beach or bay.

BEAL. Local. *Biel*, a town in Switzerland. The Gaelic word "*Beul*," signifies the mouth, and by *metonymy*, eloquent, musical.

BEADLE. A name of office; a messenger or crier of a court; an officer belonging to a university or parish.

BEATTY. From the Celtic *Biatach*. Anciently, in Ireland, lands were assigned by the government to a certain number of persons who were appointed to keep houses of entertainment, and to exercise hospitality in the different provinces; they were called *Biatachs*. The office was considered honorable, and besides the lands assigned by the king, they were the lords of seven boroughs or villages, feeding seven herds of one hundred and twenty oxen each, besides the grain raised from seven ploughs every year. *Beathaich*, in the Gaelic, signifies to feed, nourish, to welcome, to support. "*Beata mor*," Irish, to have a great estate. *Beatha*, Gaelic, life, food, welcome, salutation.

BEAUCHAMP. (Nor. Fr.) *De Beauchamp*, from the fair or beautiful field; in Latin. *De Bello Campo*.

OF FAMILY NAMES.

BEAUFORT. (Nor. Fr.) *De Beaufort*, from the fine or commodious fort. *De Bello Forti.*

BEAUMONT. (Nor. Fr.) *De Beaumont;* a city in France, on the river Sarte, in the province of Mayne; *the fair mount. De Bello Monte.*

BEAUVAIS. (Fr.) *De Beauvais.* From a town in France of that name, signifying the sightly or beautiful place.

BECK. (Anglo-Saxon.) Local. From *becc*, a brook.

BECKETT. Local. A little brook. (By no means appropriate to the furious St. Thomas of Canterbury!

BECKER. (Ger.) From *becker*, the same as *backer*, a baker. It may be from *becher*, a cup or goblet, from *bechern*, to tipple; *" der Becher"* (Ger.), drinker, a tippler; the same in Dutch.

BECKFORD. (Sax.) Local. The brook-ford.

BECKLEY or **BEAKLEY.** Local. The meadow or pasture by the brook; from *beck*, a brook, and *ley*, field or meadow.

BECKMAN. A dweller by a brook or stream, or on a *bec*, or neck of land.

BECKWITH. Local. The same as *Beckworth*, the farm or place by the brook, from *beck*, a brook. and *worth*, a farm.

BEDALE. Local. From a town in England by that name.

BEDE. He that prayeth, or a devout man. "To say our *Bedes*, is but to say our prayers."

BEDDAU. (Welsh.) Local. Graves. *"Rhos-y Beddau,"* the heath of the graves, referring to Druidical rites.

BEDEAU. (Fr.) From *bedeau*, a beadle, mace-bearer; a petty officer in parishes.

BEDELL. The same as *Beadle*, of which it is a corruption; an officer belonging to a court, university, ward, or parish.

ETYMOLOGICAL DICTIONARY

BEDFORD. Local. A town and shire in England; from the Saxon *bedan*, battle, war, slaughter, and *ford*, a way or shallow place for crossing a river. *Byddin-ffordd*, Welsh, the route or way of the army.

BEECHER. (Fr.) *Beau chère*, fine entertainment; or from the beech-wood.

BEERS. Local. From *Beer*, a town in Dorsetshire, England; so called from *bere*, grain, barley; a fruitful place. In the Dutch, *beer* signifies a bear, a boar.

BEGG. From the Gaelic *Beag*, little, young, small of stature.

BELCHER. (Old French.) *Bel-chère*, good cheer, fine entertainment; a happier name than to be a *Belcher*, and swell with pride or passion.

BELDEN. (Cor. Br.) The beautiful hill; or *Beildin*, the hill of Belus, a place of Druid-worship.

BELL. A name taken from the sign of an inn or shop. The sign of a bell was frequently used. "John at the Bell" became "John Bell." *Bel*, French, beautiful, handsome, fine.

BELLAMONT. (Fr.) *De Bellamont*, from the fair or beautiful mount. *De Bello Monte.*

BELLAMY. Local. From *Bellesme*, a town of France; or it may be *Belami*, French, a dear and excellent friend; from *bel*, fair or beautiful, and *ami*, a friend or companion.

BELLEW. (Nor. Fr.) *De Bellew*, a corruption of *De Belle Eau*, that is, "from the beautiful water." The family originally came from Italy; they went into England with William the Conqueror, and afterward settled in Meath, Ireland.

BELLINGER. Local. From *Bellinger*, a town in South Jutland.

BELMONT. (Fr.) *De Belmont*, from the fair mount; the same as Bellamont—*De Bello Monte.*

BELVIDERE. (Italian.) Pleasant to behold; from *Bello*, pleasant, and *videre*, to see.

OF FAMILY NAMES.

BENEDICT. (Latin.) From *Benedictus*, blessed, well spoken of, or a person wishing all good.

BENJAMIN. (Heb.) The son of the right hand; the youngest of Jacob's twelve sons.

BENNETT or **BENNET.** A contraction or rather a corruption of Benedict, from *Benedictus*, blessed.

BENT. Local. A plain, a moor, covered with the bent-grass.

BENTLEY. Local. From *bent*, as above, and *ley*, uncultivated ground, a pasture.

BENSON. Ben's-son, the son of Benjamin.

BEORN. (Saxon.) A chief.

BERESFORD. The *bears'-ford*, from *beris*, bears, according to Chaucer. *Barrasford*, from *barra*, an old word for a plain, open heath.

BERKELEY. (Sax.) Local. From the town of Berkeley, in Gloucestershire, England, derived from the Saxon *Beorce*, a beech-tree, or the box-tree, and *leagh* or *ley*, a field, and so called because of the plenty of beech-trees there growing.

BERNARD or **BARNARD.** (Sax.) From *Bearn* or *Bairn*, a child, and *ard* (Teut.), nature, disposition; of a child-like disposition; filial affection. Verstegan brings it from *Beorn*, heart—one of a stout heart.

BERRY. (Fr.) Local. From the province of Berri, in France.

BERTRAM or **BERTRAND.** (Sax.) Fair and pure.

BETTS. (Latin.) A contraction of the Latin *Beatus*, happy.

BETHUNE. Local. From the town of Bethune, a fortified town, and capital of a county in Artois, Netherlands.

BEVAN. (Welsh.) A contraction of *Ap Evan*, or *Ivan*, the son of John; from *ap*, son, or literally *from*, and *Ivan*, John. So Brice, from Ap Rice; Pritchard, from Ap Richard, etc.

70   ETYMOLOGICAL DICTIONARY

BEVERIDGE. Local. From a town in the county of Dorset, England. *Bever* is probably a contraction of *Belvoir* (Fr.), that is, fine prospect; and *ridge*, the back or top of a hill. A town located on a hill.

BEVERLY. Local. From the borough of Beverly in Yorkshire, England; from *Belvoir*, a beautiful prospect, and *ley*, a place or field. Some say "the lake of beavers," from *Beverlac*, and so called from the beavers which abounded in the river Hull, near by.

BEWLEY. A corruption of the French *Beaulieu*, that is, a beautiful place.

BICKERSTETH. Supposed to come from the Welsh word *bicra*, to fight, to bicker, and *steth*, a corruption of *staff*, used for tilting or skirmishing. Probably taken from the sign of an inn. *Beker* (Dutch), is a drinking-cup, *Bekeren*, to drink, to tipple, guzzle, with the termination *steth*, for *sted*, a place.

BIDDLE. The same as Bedell and Beadle (which see).

BIDDULPH. Probably the same as *Botolph*, which Camden derives from *Boat*, and *ulph* (Saxon), Help, because, perhaps, he was the mariner's tutelar saint, and for that reason was so much adored at Boston, in England.

BIGALOW. *Bygglu*, in the Welsh, signifies to hector, to bully. In the Cor. Br., *Bygel* is a herdsman, a shepherd, and the name may have been applied to the commander of an army.

BIGGAR. Local. A town in Lanarkshire, Scotland. *Buygar*, in Danish, signifies a builder.

BIGLER. (French.) One who squints. *Bygylor*, Welsh, a hector.

BIGGORE. Local. An ancient province of France.

BIGOT or BIGOD. A name given by the French to the Normans, because, as Camden says, " At every other word they would swear '*By God*,' " from which they were termed *Bigodi*. It became the surname of Roger de Montgomery,

OF FAMILY NAMES.

one of the followers of William the Conqueror, who was called *Roger Bigod*. The English word *bigot* has probably the same origin.

BIGSBY. (Danish.) The place near the town; from *bigs*, near, and *by*, the town.

BILLINGS. Local. From the town of Billing, in Lincolnshire, England. *Beilean*, Gaelic, loquacious; a prattling person.

BING. (Danish.) Local. Any thing that incloses; from the Danish *binge*, a pen, a bin, a corn-bin; a name given to a place where supplies or provisions were kept.

BINGHAM. Local. From the town of Bingham, in Nottinghamshire, so named from the Danish *Bing*, a place where provisions were deposited; and *ham*, a town or village. *Bingham*, a depository for grain; a place tilled, inhabited.

BINNEY. Local. From the Cor. Br. *Bin*, a hill; and *ey*, water; or from *Buinne*, Gaelic, a cataract, a stream. *Binneach*, in the Gaelic, also signifies hilly, pinnacled, mountains.

BIORN. (Danish.) A bear; denoting courage and strength, the same as *Byron*. *Beren*, Saxon, belonging to a bear.

BIRCH. Local. A name probably given from residing at or near a birch-tree. "John at the birch," etc.

BIRNIE and BIRNEY. Local. A parish in the shire of Elgin, Scotland. It was formerly named *Brenuth*, from *brae-nut*, as many hazel-trees grew there. The natives called it *Burn-nigh*, that is, *a village near the Burn or river*, now corrupted to *Birnie*.

BIXBY. (Danish.) Local. The house or village among the box-trees.

BLACKBURN. Local. The black brook or stream.

BLACKWOOD. Local. This family derived their name from the lands of Baron Dufferin and Claneboye, in Scotland, called Blackwood.

ETYMOLOGICAL DICTIONARY

BLAIN. (Fr.) Local. From the town of Blain, in Bretagne, France. *Blaen*, in the Welsh, signifies the summit or top; the same as *pen*, *brig*, and *bar*, the highest part of a mountain; the end or top of an object; the inland extremity of a glen; a leader or chief.

BLAIR. (Celtic.) Local. From *Blair* or *Blar*, which originally signified " a cleared plain," but from the Celts generally choosing such plains for their fields of battle, *blair* came to signify a battle. There is a small village called the *Blair* near Lochord, about two miles from Lochleven, in Fifeshire, Scotland. It signifies a spot where a battle was fought, *" locus pugnæ."* Here, it is supposed, an engagement took place between the Romans and the Caledonians, A.D. 83.

BLAISDALE. Local. From the old English word *Blase*, sprouting forth, luxuriant; and *dale*, a valley.

BLAKE. A corruption of the British *Ap Lake*, from *Ap*, signifying from, or son, and *Lake*,—the son of Lake. The family went into Ireland with Strongbow, where the name became corrupted into Blake. *Ap Lake* was one of the knights of Arthur's Round Table.

BLAKEMAN. A corruption of Blackman, a name probably given from having a dark complexion.

BLAND. Mild, gentle, smooth.

BLANEY. Local. Welsh, *Bluenae*, the inland extremity of a valley.

BLASEDALE. Local. A place in Lancashire, England.

BLAUVELT. (Ger.) Local. The blue field; from *Blau*, blue, and *veld* or *feld*, field.

BLEECKER or **BLEEKER.** (Dutch.) From *Bleeker*, a bleacher or whitener of linen. In Danish, *bleger*.

BLIN. (Welsh.) Local. The same as *Blaen*, a point, the inland extremity of a valley. *Blin* also signifies weary, troublesome.

OF FAMILY NAMES. 73

BLISS. In English, is a very happy name, imposed by others on the individual. *Blys*, in the Welsh, signifies desiring, longing.

BLIVEN. (Danish.) From *Beleven*, affable, genteel, kind.

BLOOD. In the Dutch, signifies timorous, cowardly; a simpleton. Lower informs us that Godkin, Blood (S'blood), and Sacre, may be regarded as clipped oaths, and given as names to the persons in the habit of using them; and that in the neighborhood of a fashionable square in London, are now living surgeons whose names are *Churchyard*, *Death*, *Blood*, and *Slaughter*.

BLOSS. Local. From *Blois*, the chief town of a territory of the same name in Orleans, France.

BLOUNT, BLOUND, or BLOND. (Nor. Fr.) Of fair hair or complexion; from the French *Blond*. This family trace their origin to the *Blondi* or *Brondi* of Italy, so named from their fair complexion. They went into England with William the Conqueror.

BLUNDELL. (Nor. Fr.) From *Blund* or *Blond*, fair-haired, and having the same signification, only in a lesser degree. *Blundell*, a little fair-haired, so *Russell*, from *Rous*—red.

BLUNT. The same as Blount (which see).

BLYTH. Glad, gay, joyful. *Blyth*, local, a town in England.

BOARDMAN. One who keeps a boarding-house.

BOCK. (Dutch.) *Bock*, a book; *bok*, a goat.

BOCOCK. *Beaucock*, a fine fellow; a straggler.

BODINE. (Fr.) Waggish, merry, sportive. *Boodinne*, in the Dutch, signifies a she-messenger.

BODLEY. (Cor. Br.) Local. The house on the lea; from *Bod*, a house, and *ley*.

BOGART. (Dutch.) Local. From *boomgard*, an orchard.

4

BOGUE. Local. From the residence being near a *bog*, or from the Saxon *boga*, a bend, a bow, a corner; a town in France; the name appears on ancient coins in Sussex, England.

BOLINGBROKE. Local. A town in Lincolnshire, England, the birth-place of Henry IV. "The brook or bridge near the round hill."

BOLSTER. (Cor. Br.) Local. A place in St. Agnes, Wales, and signifies an entrenchment; from *Bolla*, a casting or throwing up, and *ter*, the earth. *Bolwestur*, Welsh, a Hanger-on.

BOLTON. Local. A town in England; the round hill; the abrupt, steep, round hill.

BOND. The father of a family, "*Pater familias*," whence husband, that is, *house-bond*. *Bonde*, in Danish, is a peasant, countryman, also a villager.

BONAR. Local. A town in Scotland; a chain of hills; hills for tillage; also, the hill of slaughter. Cornish British, *Bonar*, the house of slaughter.

BONNAL. (Cor. Br.) Local. The house on the cliff.

BONNER. (Fr.) From *Bonheur*, happiness, good-fortune, prosperity.

BONNEY. (Scot.) Genteel, fine, spruce. French, *Bon*, *Bonne*, good, handsome.

BONTECOU. (Fr.) *Bonte*, goodness, strength, fruitfulness, and *cul* (pron. *ku*), the bottom behind; denoting, figuratively, the humor or turn of mind.

BOORMAN. (Sax. and Ger.) A countryman or farmer.

BOOTH. A small cottage.

BORDOEL. Local. A town in Lower Saxony.

OF FAMILY NAMES.

75

BORLAND. (Cor. Br.) Local. The high land; the swelling or rising land; from *bor*, swelling, rising, and *land*. If from the Saxon, it signifies the land belonging to the common people. *Bordlands* were lands which the lords kept in their hands for the maintenance of their board or table.

Borland is the name of a village in Fifeshire, Scotland, whence the family may have originated.

BORRAIL. (Gaelic.) From *Borrail*, swaggering, boastful, haughty, proud. *Borrel*, in old English, signifies a plain, rude fellow, a boor.

BOSCAWEN. (Cor. Br.) Local. From the town of Boscawen, in Cornwall, which signifies the house surrounded by elder trees.

BOSTWICK. (Cor. Br.) Local. The house near the haven or creek; from *Bos*, a house, and *wick*, a haven or creek. It may be from the Dutch *Bosch*, a wood, and *wick*, the town in the wood. *Boswick*, in the Cornish-British, is the dwelling near the harbor or village.

BOSWELL. Local. A corruption of *Bosseville;* from *Bosch*, a wood, and *ville*, a village. *Bothel*, Gaelic, the house of the powerful.

BOTTESFORD. Local. A town in England.

BOUGHTON. Local. From *Boughton*, a place in Northamptonshire, England; the bowing or bending hill. *Bouton*, the steep or abrupt hill.

BOUVIER. (Fr.) A drover.

BOTTOM. Local. Any low grounds; a dale or valley.

BOURNE. Local. From the town of *Bourne*, in Lincolnshire, England, which is so named from the old English *Bourne*, a small river or spring-well.

BOUCHER. (French.) A butcher; a blood-thirsty man.

BOVIE. (Fr.) Local. A corruption of *Beauvais*, a town in France, whence the surname originated, and which signifies

76　　　ETYMOLOGICAL DICTIONARY

the sightly or beautiful place. The family settled in Holland from France.

BOWERS. From *bur*, Saxon, a chamber; a cottage; a shady recess.

BOWEN. (Welsh.) A corruption of *Ap Owen*, the son of Owen, so *Price* from Ap Rice, and *Prichard* from Ap Richard.

BOWES. This surname, according to Grose, originated as follows: about the time of the Conqueror, there was a town (on the site of the Castle of Bowes), which the tradition of the family states, was burned. It then belonged to the Earls of Brittany and Richmond. The castle was built, as Mr. Horseley thinks, out of the ruins of the Roman Fortress, by Alan Niger, the second earl of that title, who, it is said, placed therein William, his relation, with five hundred archers to defend it against some insurgents in Cambridge and Westmorland confederated with the Scots, giving him for the device of his standard the arms of Brittany, with three bows and a bundle of arrows, whence both the castle and the commander derived their names; the former being called *Bowes Castle*, and the latter, *William de Arcubus*, or *William Bowes*.

BOWLES. Probably from the sign of an inn, as "John at the *Bowl*," i. e., at the sign of the bowl. *Boel*, local, a town in South Jutland, Denmark. *Boel*, Dutch, an estate, also one who keeps a mistress.

BOWMAN. A military cognomen; an archer.

BOWNE. (Cor. Br. and Welsh.) Signifies ready, active, nimble.

BOWYER. An archer, one who uses a bow; one who makes bows.

BOYD. (Gaelic.) From *buidhe*, yellow-haired. *Boyd*, a river of England that unites with the *Avon*.

BOYER. A name given to a Grandee among the Muscovites.

OF FAMILY NAMES.

BOYNTON. Local. From Buvington, in the Wolds, in the East Riding of Yorkshire, England, now called Boynton Dugdale, so named from its being higher in place or altitude.

BRACY. (Fr.) Local. From *Bracy*, a town in Normandy.

BRAINE. Local. A small town and abbey on the river Vesle, in France. *Brain*, Gaelic, a chieftain; a naval commander; a captain of a ship.

BRADBURN. Local. The wide or broad brook.

BRADFORD. Local. A town on the *Avon*, in Wiltshire, England, whence the surname is derived, and which signifies *the broad ford*, there being at that place a ford across the Avon.

BRADY. (Gaelic.) *Breada*, handsome.

BRAGG. *Brag*, among the Scandinavians, was the god of eloquence, and the word was anciently used in the sense of eloquent; also, accomplished, brave, daring.

BRAMAN. *Bramin*, a priest among the Hindoos. *Bremen*, local, a city of Germany.

BRAN. (Gaelic.) Poor; black; a raven, a mountain-stream. Welsh, *bran*, a crow; the name of dark rivers.

BRAMHALL. A place where goods are sold; *bram*, Danish, goods on sale.

BRAND. In all the Teutonic dialects *brand* signifies to burn; also a *sword*, either from its brandishing, or from its glittering brightness. *Brant*, a hill; steep, high; Welsh, *Bryn*.

BRANDE. Local. A town in Denmark.

BRANDON. Local. A market-town in Suffolk, England, and means either the *burnt town*, or the *crows' hill*.

BRANDRETH. Bailey defines this name "the curb of a well," but I think the name is local, and may be derived as follows: *Bran*, both Welsh and Gaelic, signifies a swift

78 ETYMOLOGICAL DICTIONARY

river, and *dreth*, the sandy shore or strand. Brandreth may also mean the sandy shore frequented by wild-fowl, from *Bran*, a crow, and *dreth*, as above. *Brwyndreth*, in Welsh, denotes the shore abounding with rushes, from *brwyn*, rushes, and *treth*, the shore. I prefer, however, to use *Bran* in the sense of *dark*, *black*, and then we have the "*dark shore*," or water, or a place on the shore of the river *Bran*.

BRATT. (Danish.) Brave, valiant, courageous.

BRECK. Local. An old word signifying *broken*, a gap; *Brecca*, an old law term which we find in old Latin deeds, was used to denote a breach, decay, or want of repair. *Breck* is also used in some parts of England to denote pasture. *Breck*, Gaelic, is a wolf or wild savage.

BRECKENRIDGE. Local. From *Brecken*, broken, out of repair; and *ridge*, Sax., *ryg*, the top of a hill; a house.

BREED. (Dutch.) From *Breed*, broad, large. *Brede*, local, a town in Sussex, England, and in the Danish, signifies brim, margin; sea-side, shore, river-side.

BREESE. (Welsh.) A contraction of *Ap Reese*, the son of Reese, or Rice (which see); so *Bevan* from *Ap Evan*, *Brice* from *Ap Rice*, etc. *Brys*, Welsh, agility, quickness; Bresse, local, a small territory in Burgundy, France.

BRENDON. (Cor. Br.) Local. The crow's hill; from *Bren*, a crow, and *dun* or *don*, a hill.

BRENIGAN. (Cor. Br.) A limpet.

BRENIN. (Cor. Br.) From *Brenhin*, a tributary prince; a king. *Brenin*, Welsh, a chief.

BRENTWOOD. Local. A town in Essex, England, and signifies burnt-wood; *brent* signifying burnt, from the Anglo-Saxon *brennan*, to burn.

BREWER, BREWISTER, BREWSTER. A brewer of malt liquor.

OF FAMILY NAMES.

BRET and **BRETT.** Probably contracted from *Breton,* a Briton; *brette,* French, a long sword; *brat* and *bretyn,* in the Welsh, signify an urchin.

BRETON. (British.) A native of Britain; Bretton, a town in Flintshire, Wales.

BREUILLY. (Fr.) Local. A coppice.

BRIAN or **BRION.** (Gaelic.) *The nobly descended,* from *Bri,* dignity, honor, and *an,* diminutive of that to which it is annexed, belonging to it; Gaelic, *gin* or *gen,* begotten. *Bri,* Welsh, honor; *briadd,* honorary. Bailey derives Brian from *Bruiant,* French, clamorous. *Brian,* in the Gaelic, also implies one who is fair-spoken, wordy, specious.

BRIANT or **BRYANT.** (Gaelic.) Dignity, honor; from *Bri,* exalted, and *ant,* a termination, implying the *being* or *state* of that to which it is annexed; equivalent to the Greek *av,* and the Latin *ens.*

BRIENNE. Local. A town of France, either so called from its elevation, or being the ancient meeting-place of the *Brians* or nobles.

BRILL. (Dutch.) Local. So called from *Bril,* a neat city in the Netherlands.

BRIARE. Local. From *Briare,* a town in the province of Orleans, France.

BRIERLY. Local. The briar-lee; French, *bruyere,* shrubs growing on commons and heaths.

BRICE. (Welsh.) A contraction of Ap Rice, the son of Rice, which is the same as Rhys or Rhees (see Rhees). *Brys,* Welsh, haste, quick, lively.

BRICK. A corruption of Breck (which see). We cut the following, on this name, from a newspaper:

A certain college-professor, who had assembled his class at the commencement of the term, was reading over the list of names to see that all were present. It chanced that one of

80 ETYMOLOGICAL DICTIONARY

the number was unknown to the professor, having just entered the class.

"What is your name, sir?" asked the professor, looking through his spectacles.

"You are a brick," was the startling reply.

"Sir," said the professor, half starting out of his chair at the supposed impertinence, but not quite sure that he understood him correctly, "sir, I did not exactly understand your answer."

"You are a brick," was again the composed reply.

"This is intolerable," said the professor, his face reddening; "beware, young man, how you attempt to insult me."

"Insult you!" said the student, in turn astonished. "How have I done it?"

"Did you not say I was a brick?" returned the professor, with stifled indignation.

"No, sir; you asked me my name, and I answered your question. My name is U. R. A. Brick—Uriah Reynolds Anderson Brick."

"Ah, indeed," murmured the professor, sinking back into his seat in confusion—"it was a misconception on my part. Will you commence the lesson, Mr. Brick?"

BRIDGE and BRIDGES. Local. Any structure of wood, stone, or other materials, raised over rivers for the passage of men and other animals.

BRIDGMAN. One who attends a bridge; a builder of bridges.

BRIDE. (Gaelic.) From *Brighid*, a hostage, pledge, or security. The son of Bridget. Cormac, Archbishop of Cashel, in his glossary, defines *Brighid* "fiery dart," and that it was the name of the Muse who was believed to preside over poetry, in pagan times, in Ireland. *Breochuidh*, a term given to those virgins who kept the perpetual fire of *Beil* or *Belus* among the Druids and ancient Celts.

BRIGGS. From the Anglo-Saxon *brigg*, a bridge; *brig*, Welsh, height, the top of any thing.

OF FAMILY NAMES. 81

BRIGHTON. Local. A town on the coast of Sussex, England, anciently called *Brightelmstone*, from *Brithelm*, i. e., bright helmet, who was bishop of Bath and Wells, about the year 955. The bright town.

BRIMMER. From the Anglo-Saxon *Bremman*, *Breme*, or *Brim*, to extend, to amplify to the utmost limits; to be violent, furious, to rage; a violent, bold, furious man; "Foughten breme," that is, "He fought furiously." *Bremmer*, a native of *Bremen*, Germany.

BRINKERHOFF. (Dutch.) *Brengerhof*, messenger of the court, or head messenger or carrier; from *Brenger*, a messenger, and *hof*, a court, or *hoofd*, head, chief, a leader.

BRISBAN or **BRISBIN.** This name is local, and may signify the Mount or Hill of Judgment, a place where courts were held and law administered, among the Celts and Britons, from the Cornish-British *brez* or *brys*, a judgment, a trial at law, and *ban*, a hill, a mount. In Gaelic, *Breasban* signifies the royal mount; *Briosgabhain*, the rapid river; *Brisbeinn*, the broken hill or cliff.

BRISTED. (Sax.) Local. From *brihs*, bright, pleasant, and *stead*, a place—a bright, pleasant place.

BRISTOL. (Gaelic and Welsh.) Local. A city in England. The name signifies "The broken chasm;" from *bris*, Gaelic, broken, and *tull*, Welsh, *tol*, a hole, cleft or chasm. This corresponds to the ancient name of Bristol, which was *Caer Oder*, i. e., "the City of the Gap" or chasm, through which the Avon finds a passage to the sea.

BRISTOW. (Sax.) Local. From *brihs*, pleasant, bright, and *stow*, the same as *stead*, a place.

BRITTE. A word used in Dutch poetry for a *Brittainer*.

BRITTON, BRITTEN, and **BRITTAN.** A native of Britain, the ancient name of England. Several derivations have been given to Britain, such as *Brydon* or *Prydyn*, Welsh, the fair tribe, or brave men. *Bridaoine*, Gaelic, from *Bri*, dignity, and *daoine*, men. *Pryddain*, the fair and beautiful

4*

isle. *Brait* or *Briand*, extensive, and *in*, land. *Brit-tanc*, the land of tin.

BROCK. From the Saxon *Broc*, a badger. *Broch*, in Gaelic or Irish, Cor. Br. and Welsh, has the same meaning.

BROCKLESBY. Local. Derived from *Brockles*, a small town of that name in England, and *by*, near to; a village. Dutch, *Brock*, a marsh; also, broken land.

In a party in which the celebrated Porson was a guest, there was also a physician by this name, Dr. Brocklesby, a descendant of the eminent man who attended Dr. Johnson in his last illness. In addressing Dr. Brocklesby, Porson called him Dr. Rock—"Yes, Dr. Rock—no, Dr. Rock," etc.—a name rendered almost infamous by Hogarth, in his picture of the "March of the Guards." At length, Dr. Brocklesby became offended, and said, "Mr. Porson, my name is not Rock, it is Brocklesby," pronouncing the syllables distinctly, Brock-les-by. "Well," said Porson, "if *Brock-les-b* is not Rock, then I know nothing of Algebra.

BRODIE. (Gaelic.) Local. From the lands of Brodie, Co. Moray, Scotland. The name signifies a little ridge; a brow; a precipice. *Brody*, a town of Gallicia.

BRODT. Local. So named from a town in Sclavonia, settled by an ancient people who came from Scythia.

BROME or BROOME. The Earls of Anjou first took the surname of Brome or Broome after their pilgrimage to the Holy Land. Fulke, Earl of Anjou, having worn a sprig of the broom-plant as the symbol of humility.

BROMFIELD or BROOMFIELD. Local. The field abounding in broom.

BROMLEY. Local. From Bromley, a small town in England, so called from *brome* or *broom*, and *ley*, a field or common.

BROOME. The same as Brome, above.

BRONSON, BRUNSON. A contraction of Brownson, the son of Brown. *Briaunson*, local, a place in France. This name came into England with William the Conqueror.

OF FAMILY NAMES.

83

BROOKS. Local. Brooks, Becks, and Rundels are names for small rivers.

BROSTER. (Cor. Br.) Greatness, majesty.

BROTHERSON. The same as nephew.

BROUGHAM. Local. Originally *Burgham*. The village on a hill; a borough town. The name of a place in England.

BROUGHTON. Local. A town on the hill; a village in Flintshire, England.

BROWER. (Dutch.) From *Brouwer*, a brewer.

BROWN. A name derived from complexion, color of hair or garments, consequently, a very common name.

BROWNSON. The son of Brown.

BRUCE. (Nor. Fr.) Local. *De Bruys;* from Bruy or Bruys, a place in Normandy where the family originated. De Bruys was one of the followers of William the Conqueror, and fought at the battle of Hastings. From this ancestor, King Robert Bruce was descended.

BRUNNER. Local. From a town of that name in Switzerland.

BRUX. Local. A town in England.

BRUYERE. (Fr.) Local. A common or heath covered with shrubs.

BRYAN. The same as Brian or Brien (which see).

BRYN. (Welsh.) A mountain; a mountaineer.

BRYCE. (Welsh.) A contraction of Ap Rhys, the son of Rhys or Rhees. (See Rhees.)

BRYNE. Local. A river in Donegal, Ireland; in Welsh, a hill. *Bryne*, Saxon, a burning.

BUCHAN. Local. A district of Aberdeenshire, Scotland. The derivation of the name is uncertain. It may be from the Gaelic *boc, bocan,* deer; a place abounding in deer.

BUCHANAN. Local. A parish in the shire of Sterling, Scotland. The derivation of the name is uncertain. It is probably from the same root as *Buchan.*

84 ETYMOLOGICAL DICTIONARY

BUCHER. (Fr.) Pronounced *Booshay*. A wood-house; pile of wood; pyre; funeral-pile.

BUCK. Such names as Lyon, Bull, Buck, etc., may have been borrowed from armorial bearings, the shields and banners of war, or for a resemblance to those animals noted for courage, agility, or swiftness, or from signs and emblems over shops and inns.

BUCKBEE. Local. The town or village among the beech-trees, from *boc*, a beech-tree, and *by*, a village.

BUCKHOUT. (Dutch.) Local. The beech-wood; from *beuk*, a beech, and *houdt*, a wood.

BUCKINGHAM. (Sax.) Local. A shire and town in England, and so called either from *Bucen*, beechen, and *ham*, a village, from the abundance of beech-trees growing there, or from the Saxon *bucca*, deer—the deer-village.

BUCKLIN. (Gaelic.) Local. From *Bucklyn*, a town in Sterlingshire, Scotland. The name may be derived from *Boc*, plural, *Buic*, a roe-buck, deer, and *linne*, a pool or lake.

BUCKMASTER. A name probably given to one who had the care of herds of venison.

BUCKMINSTER. (Sax.) From *bucen*, beechen, or *bugan*, to bend, a bow, a corner, round; and *minster*, a church, a monastery.

BUCKSTON or BUXTON. (Sax.) Local. From *boc*, a beech-tree, and *ton*, a town—beech-town.

BUDD. (Welsh.) Thrift, gain, riches, victory; *bod*, a dwelling. *Bud*, in the Danish, signifies a messenger, courier, a sergeant.

BUDDINGTON. Local. The flourishing town, or *Boddington*, the dwelling town. *Buttington*, a place on the Severn, England, which may indicate the town on the limit, boundary, or extremity.

BUEL. (Welsh.) A herd of cattle; an ox. *Bueil*, local, a place in France.

OF FAMILY NAMES.

BULKELEY or **BUCKLEY**. Local. Derived from the manor of Bulkeley, in the County Palatine of Chester, England. A corruption of *Bullock-ley*, the bullock-field or pasture.

BULL. A well-known animal, powerful, fierce, and violent. The name may have originated from the sign of a shop or inn, as "John at the Bull." *Bul*, in Saxon, is a brooch, a stud, a bracelet.

BULLARD. Having the disposition of a bull.

BULLER. (Danish.) *Boler*, a gallant; an amorist.

BULLOCK. A full-grown ox. All the families of Bulls, Bullards, and Bullocks are noted for being firm and inflexible in their way.

BULLIONS. Probably local, from *Bolleyne*, a town in France, whence the family of Anne Boleyne took their name; or from the city of *Boulogne*, which was so called from *Beul*, Gaelic, the mouth, and *Liane*, the river, or the "*mouth of Liane*," it being situated at the mouth of that river.

BUN. (Gaelic.) A foundation; *Bunn*, a hill.

BUNNELL. Local. A corruption of *Bonhill*, a parish in the county of Dumbarton, Scotland.

BUNTING. A kind of bird.

BUNYAN. (Welsh, Celtic, and Gaelic.) From *Bunan*, a squat, short person.

BURR. (Saxon.) *Burh*, a wall, a fortress, a castle; a hill, a heap, the same as *burgh*.

BURBECK. Local. The beak or point of the hill; from *Burh*, a hill, and *bek*, Dutch, a point, a beak; or from *Burh*, a hill, castle, fort, or dwelling, and *beck*, a brook.

BURBY. (Saxon.) The house or village on the hill; from *Bur*, a hill, and *by*, a house or village.

BURD. Local. A river in France.

ETYMOLOGICAL DICTIONARY

BURDEN. Lower says this name is probably a corruption of *bourdon*, a pilgrim's staff,—a very appropriate sign for a wayside hostelry.

It may be local, derived from *Bour*, a house (from the Saxon *bure*, a bed-chamber), and *den*, a valley—the house in the valley.

BURDER. A bird-catcher or fowler.

BURDETT. A little bird, *ett* signifying young, small, tender.

BURG. In all the Teutonic languages signifies a hill, a fortification, tower, castle, house, city, and nearly so in the Armoric and Welsh.

BURGESS. An inhabitant of a borough; a freeman, citizen; a representative of a borough in parliament.

BURGOS. Local. A city of Spain, in Old Castile, situated beside a hill, on the river Arlanzon.

BURGOYNE. Local. From Bourgogne, now Burgundy, an old province of France. A name given to a native of that province.

BURKE. A corruption of (*De*) *Burgo*, as the name was formerly written, that is, from the fort, castle, hill, or city. This family went from Normandy into England with the Conqueror, and afterward into Ireland with Strongbow.

BURLASE. (Cor. Br.) Local. The green summit or top.

BURLEIGH. Local. *Burh*, Saxon, is the same as *burg*, a city, castle, house, or tower; in composition, it signifies defense; *leigh*, a low place, opposed to a place higher, the same as *ley*, a meadow, a pasture. *Burly*, swelled, bulky, boisterous.

BURNHAM. Local. Derived from *Burnham*, a town in Norfolk. also in Essex. England; in the old English, *Bourn* or *Burn*, signifies a river, and *ham*, a village or town—the village by the river. *Bourn*, *burn*, and *bern*, in the Cornish-British, is a hill, a heap; and *Burnham*, the house or town on the rising ground.

OF FAMILY NAMES.

BURNS. Local. A *burn*, in Scotland, is a small stream, the same as *Bourne*. *Biorn*, in the Danish and Swedish, signifies a bear, figuratively, a ferocious, valiant man.

BURNSIDE. Local. Beside the brook or burn.

BURRARD. Local. A high hill or top. *Boorard.* resembling a countryman; *Boer*, Dutch, a rustic, a farmer, and *ard*, nature, mode, kind.

BURRELL. *Borel* is used by Chaucer in the sense of *lay*, as *borel-clerks*—lay-clerks. It may be a corruption of *Borrail* (which see).

BURT. (Gaelic.) *Burt*, quizzing, joking; also, in English, a kind of fish. *Buurt*, Dutch, a hamlet, consisting only of a few houses; a neighborhood.

BURTIS. (Welsh.) *Burdais*, a burgess.

BURTON. Local. A town in Leicestershire, England. The name signifies either the town on the hill, or, as Bailey says, the Bur-town, from the abundance of burs growing thereabouts. There are several places by this name in England.

BUSHNELL. (Dutch.) *Bossen-hall*, a faggot or wood-market, or a hall or mansion in the wood.

BUSHWELL. Local. *Bushwild.* From *bush* and *well*, *wild*, *wold*, a wood, a lawn, or plain; an uncultivated bushy place; *Bushfeldt*, the bushy field.

BUSK. (Swed.) From *Busche*, a wood, a thicket.

BUSKIRK. (Dutch.) Local. From *Bos*, a wood, and *kerk*, a church—the church in the wood.

BUSSEY. (Fr.) Local. From the town of Bussey, in the province of Burgundy, France.

BUTLER. This family derive their origin from the old Counts of Briony or Biony, in Normandy, a descendant of whom, Herveius Fitz Walter, accompanied the Conqueror into England. His son, Theobold, went with Henry II. into Ireland, where, having greatly assisted in the reduction of

ETYMOLOGICAL DICTIONARY

the kingdom, he was rewarded with large possessions there, and made it the place of his residence. The king afterward conferred on him the office of chief *Butler* of Ireland, whence his descendants, the Earls of Ormond and others, took the surname of *De Boteler* or *Butler.*

BUTMAN. Local. Perhaps the man who lives at the *butt* or boundary; a marksman. *Botman,* one who gives a blunt answer.

BUTTS. *Butts* were marks for archery. In most parishes places were set apart for this necessary sport which were called " the Butts,"—hence, the name was given to a person residing near such a spot, as " John at the Butts." *But* signifies a promontory, as the Butt of Lewis, an isle of Scotland. Danish, *But,* blunt, rough.

BUXTON. Local. From the Saxon *boc,* a beech, German, *buche,* and *ton*—the beech-town. A village in Derbyshire, England.

BYFIELD. The village in the field, from *By,* Danish, a town, —or the place by or near the field.

BYGBY. (Danish.) Barley-town; from *byg,* Danish, barley.

BYINGTON. (Saxon.) From *Bying,* a habitation, and *ton,* a hill or inclosure.

BYRON. (Fr.) Local. Originally *De Biron,* from the town of Biron, in the province of Guienne, France.

CAD. (Gaelic and Welsh.) War, a battle-field.

CADE. An old word for a barrel or cask; probably taken from a sign at an ale-house or tavern—*"John at the Cade."* Shakspeare uses Cade in this sense:

> *"Cade.*—We, John Cade. so termed of our supposed father.
> *Dick.*—Or rather of stealing a *cade* of herrings!"
> HEN. VI., ACT IV., SC. II.

CADOGAN. (Welsh.) Terrible in battle; from *cad,* battle, and *gwg,* fierce.

OF FAMILY NAMES. **89**

CADELL. (Welsh.) Warlike. Gaelic, *Cathell.*

CADER. (Welsh.) A keep, fortress, or strong-hold.

CADWALLADER. (Welsh.) Derived from *cad*, battle, and *gwaladr*, a leader. a lord—the leader or lord of the battle. *Gwaladr* would seem to come from *gwal*, a wall or defense, and *adre*, signifying at home or abroad, everywhere.

CADWELL. Local. A village in South Wales; written Cydwell.

CADY. *Ca-dia*, in Gaelic, the house of God. There is a commonalty of Switzerland called Gotthespunt, or *Casdee*, i. e.. the house of God. *Cadie*, in the Scottish, is an errand-boy, a messenger.

CAETH. (Welsh.) A captive.

CAIN. (Welsh and Gaelic.) Chaste, beloved, fair, beautiful.

CAIRN. (Cor. Br.) Local. A circular mound of stones.

CALDER. Local. A river in Yorkshire, England. *Calduor*, Gaelic and Welsh, the water that incloses or shuts in.

CALDERWOOD. Local. The wood on the river Calder.

CALDICOTT, COLDICOT, and CALDECOTE. Local. (Welsh.) *Col-dow-cwtt, Colcoit*, the neck of the wood. · O'Connor derives Caldecott from *Cald-i-scot*, the inclosure of the Scot; a locality hemmed in by Glamorgan, the Wye, and high lands on the north. A village in Hertfordshire, England.

CALDWELL. Local. *Col-wold*, the wood of hazels; or it may be *Cold-well*, a cold spring.

CALHOUN. A corruption of *Colquhoun* (which see).

CALL. (Welsh.) Prudent, discerning, cunning, trickish Caill and *Cuil*, Gaelic, are the same.

CALLAGHAN. (Gaelic or Celtic.) From *Ciallach*, prudent, judicious, discreet.

ETYMOLOGICAL DICTIONARY

CAMERON. (Gaelic.) From *Cam*, crooked, and *sron*, nose, crooked or hooked-nose.

CAMPBELL. (Celtic and Gaelic.) Wry-mouth, the man whose mouth inclined a little on one side; from *cam*, crooked, distorted, and *beul*, the mouth. This ancient family may be traced as far back as the beginning of the fifth century, and is said to have been possessed of Lochore, in Argyleshire, as early as the time of Fergus II. Sir Colin Campbell, of Lochore, flourished toward the end of the thirteenth century, and was called Sir Colin More, or Colin the Great. His descendants were called by the Irish *McCallen*, that is, the descendants of Colin.

CAM. (Gaelic and Welsh.) Crooked, winding; injury, deceit, injustice.

CAMUS. (Gaelic.) A bay, a creek, a harbor. *Camoys*, one whose nose is turned upwards.

CAN or **CAIN.** (Gaelic.) Clear, white, fair, and hence, beloved, dear; *can*, a lake, a whelp.

CANN. (Gaelic.) *Ceann* and *Kin;* Welsh, *Ken* or *Cen*, the head; projection.

CANNING. (Saxon.) *Cyning*, a leader, a king. Germ., *König;* Dutch, *Koning;* Dan., *Konge;* Swedish, *Konung;* Welsh, *cun;* Irish, *cean*, which is the same as the Gaelic *Ceann*. and the oriental *Khan* or *Kaun*, all signifying head, a leader. Saxon *Connan* and *Cunnan*, to see, to know; hence *Cunning*, or *Canning*, *Kenning*.

CANON. (Welsh.) The river *Taf* is called in the interior the *Canon*, or the singing river. A rule, a law; a dignitary of the church.

CAPEL. An old word signifying a strong horse.

> " And gave him *caples* to his carte."
>
> CHAUCER.

Capel, Danish, an oratory, a chapel.

OF FAMILY NAMES.

CARACTACUS. (Gaelic.) From *Caer*, a castle or city; *eacht*, an exploit, and *cios*, a tribute, expressive of his abilities in conducting an offensive, as well as a defensive war; or, as O'Connor derives it, from *Cathreacteac-eis*, the leader of the host in battle.

CARD. A word used in some parts of Scotland to denote a traveling tinker. *Ceairde*, Gaelic, a tradesman.

CARDEN. Local. Assumed from the manor of Cawarden or Carden, near Chester, in England.

CAREW. (Welsh.) Derived from the castle of Carrw, in Wales. The castle by the water, from *Caer*, castle or fort, and *ew*, water.

CAREY or **CARY.** Local. From the manor of Cary or *Kari*, as spelled in the Doomsday Book, in the parish of St. Giles, near Launceston, England. *Cary*, in the British, signifies beloved, dear. This name may be the same as *Carew*.

CARMICHAEL. Local. Assumed from the lands and barony of Carmichael, in the shire of Lanark. The castle or stronghold of Michael, from *caer*, a castle or fortified place.

CARNE and **CARNES.** (Welsh.) Local. A rock, a heap of stones. This family claim descent from *Ithel*, King of Ghent, now Monmouthshire. Thomas o'r Gare, youngest son of Ithel, King of Ghent, was brought up at one of his father's seats called *Pencarne* (from *pen*, the head, and *carne*, a rock, a heap of stones), whence he was named *Carne*, which continues the surname of the family.

CARNIGAN. In the Gaelic, *Carneach* signifies a Druid or priest, and *Carnahan*, rocky or stony ground.

CARR. This name has several significations; *Caer*, Cornish-British, a city, town, a fort, a castle; *Carre*, French, a stout, broad-shouldered man; *Cawr*, Welsh, a giant.

CARTER. A name of trade, one who drives a cart. *Cairtear*, Gaelic, a tourist, a sojourner.

92 ETYMOLOGICAL DICTIONARY

CARSON or **CORSON.** The son of Car; *Curson*, the stock of a vine.

CARTERET or **CARTRET.** (Gaelic and Welsh.) Local. The place or town of the castle.

CARWIN. (Cor. Br.) Local. The white castle; from *caer*, a castle, and *win* or *gwin*, white.

CARY. The same as *Carey* (which see).

CASE. (French.) *Case.* A hut, a hovel; Gaelic, *cass, caise*, steep; quick, hasty, passionate.

CASS. (Gaelic.) *Cas*, a verb, to turn against, to thwart, oppose; a difficulty, a trying situation, a cause. *Cas*, a castle, the primary sense is to separate, drive off, or hate; the radical sense of hatred is driving off.

CASSIDY. (Gaelic.) From *casaideach*, apt to complain or accuse. *Casadow*, in the Cor. Br., signifies an offender.

CATHCART. (Gaelic.) Local. From the parish of Cathcart, in Lanark and Renfrew, Scotland. The river Cart runs through it, whence the name is derived. *Caeth-Cart*, from *caeth*, a strait, the river here running in a narrow channel.

CATHERWOOD. (Gaelic.) Local. A fenny-wood, wet ground, from *Cathar*, soft, boggy ground; or the fortified place in a wood, from *Cathair*, Gaelic, a town, a fortified city, a guard, a sentinel.

CAVAN. (Welsh and Gaelic.) Local. The ridge of a hill.

CAW. Local. Gaelic, *Ca*, a house, a place fortified, inclosed, surrounded. *Caw*, Welsh, whatever defends or keeps together; *Cawr*, an old English word for a king. *Caw* or *Cu*, an ancient king of North Britain whose capital was Dumbarton.

CAXTON. Local. Derived from Caxton, a small town in England.

OF FAMILY NAMES.

CAY. *Kea*, in the Cornish-British and Welsh, is an inclosure; that which fastens or secures; a landing for vessels; French, *quai*; Dutch, *kaai*; Gaelic, *ceithe*.

CAYLY. Local. From *Calais*, a sea-port of France; *Cala*, Gaelic, a harbor, port, haven, bay, a road for ships.

CHADWICK. Local. The cottage by the harbor, or sheltered place; from the Saxon *Cyte* and *wick*; *Cyte* signifies a cottage, and *wick*, a harbor, a sheltered place. It may be so called from the shad fisheries.

CHAFFEE. (Fr.) *Chafe*, to heat, to grow warm or angry; Fr., *chauffer*, to warm, to cannonade, attack briskly.

CHALK. A well-known earth; a locality. *Chalk*, Saxon, a servant or attendant.

CHALLIS. A cup or bowl; taken perhaps from the sign of a house or shop.

CHALLONER. Local. Derived from a town in France of the same name. This family derive their origin from Macloy Crum, of the line of chiefs in Wales, who resided several years in Challoner.

CHALMERS or CHAMBERS. One of the clan Cameron of Scotland, going to France, put his name in a Latin dress, as was customary in those times, styling himself *De Cameraria*, which was called in French, *De la Chambre*, and upon his return to Scotland, he was again, according to their dialect, called *Chambers*. *Chalmers* is a corruption of the same.

CHAMPE. (Fr.) Local. From *champ*, a field.

CHAMPION. A soldier, one that fought in public combat in his own or another man's quarrel.

CHAMPLIN or CHAMPLAIN. The same as champaign, a flat, open country; from *Champ*, an open, level field or plain, and *lean*, a meadow; *laine*, Gaelic, full; *leathann*, wide; Cor. Br., *laun*; Welsh, *llann*, full, wide.

CHAMPNEY. (Fr.) Local. From *Champ*, a field, and *ey*, water—the wet country or country near the water.

ETYMOLOGICAL DICTIONARY

CHANDLER. A name of trade; a maker and seller of various wares, originally of candles.

CHANNING. (Saxon.) *Cyning*, knowing, wise; Dutch, *Koning*, whence king; the same derivation as Canning.

CHAPEL. Local. A private oratory; a place of public worship.

CHAPIN. A corruption of Chapman; a trader, a shopman.

CHAPMAN. The same as Chipman, a trader, a shopman; from the Saxon *ceapan* or *cypan*, to buy or sell. Sax., *ceap*, a bargain, a price; one who cheapens, asks the price, buys.

CHARLES. (Ger.) From *carl*, strong, stout, courageous, and valiant. The Hungarians called a king by the general name *Carl*, and Scaliger makes Carl-man the same as the Greek ἀνδρέας.

CHARNOCK. (Nor. Fr.) Local. Derived from the town of *Chernoc*, in Normandy.

CHATHAM or **CHETHAM.** Local. From a town in Kent, England, on the Medway, so named from the Saxon *cyte*, a cottage, and *ham*, a village, signifying the village of cottages. A paragraph to the following effect went the round of the papers not many years since:

Two attorneys in partnership had the name of the firm, "Catcham and Chetum," inscribed, in the usual manner, upon their office-door; but as the singularity and ominous juxta-position of the words led to many a coarse joke from passers-by, the men of law attempted to destroy, in part, the effect of the odd association, by the insertion of the initials of their Christian names, which happened to be Isaiah and Uriah; but this made the affair ten times worse, for the inscription then ran:

"*I. Catcham and U. Chetum !*"

CHATSEY or **CHADSEY.** Local. From the Saxon *cyte*, a cottage, and *sey*, near the water.

OF FAMILY NAMES. 95

CHATSWORTH. Local. Derived from a village of that name in Derbyshire, England, and signifying the cottage-farm; from *cyte*, a cottage, as above, and *worth*, a place or estate.

CHATTERTON. Local. *Chadderton*, Saxon, *cete-doir-ton*, the cottage-town in the wood; from *cete* or *cyte*, a cottage, hut, cabin; *doir*, a wood, and *ton*, a town.

CHEDSEY. Local. From *Chertsey*, a town in Surrey, England, near the Thames, pronounced by the natives, *Chedsey*, meaning "Cerot's Island."

CHEESEMAN. A dealer in cheese.

CHEEVER. (Fr.) *Chevir* signifies to master or overcome; and *Chevre* is a goat.

CHENEY. (Fr.) Local. From *Chene*, an oak; *Chenaie*, a grove, a plantation of oaks.

CHESEBROUGH. Local. The cheese-borough or town. *Chessbro*, the hill or town on the river Chess.

CHESTER. Local. From the city of Chester, the capital of Cheshire, England, founded by the Romans. The name is derived from the Latin *Castrum*; Saxon, *ceaster*, a fortified place, a city, a castle or camp, it being a Roman station where the twentieth legion was quartered. The Roman stations in England were generally so called, being sometimes varied in dialect to *Chester*, *Chaster*, or *Caster*, the termination of many English towns, as Colchester, the camp on the river Coln; Doncaster, on the Don; Lancaster, on the Lon or Lune, etc.

CHICHESTER. Local. From the city of Chichester, Sussex, England, whose Saxon name was *Cissanceaster*; from *Cissa*, the son of Aella, who settled the kingdom of the South-Saxons; and *ceaster* or *chester*, a city, from *castrum*, a Roman station.

CHICKERING. (Cor. Br.) Local. The stone house, a house on a rock, a fortress; from *chi*, a house, and *cairne*, a rock or stones.

CHILDS. Child, Page and Varlet were names given to youths from seven to fourteen years of age, while receiving their education for knighthood.

CHILTON. Local. From a town of the same name in Wiltshire, England, signifying the chalk-hills; from the Saxon *cylt*, clay or chalk.

CHIPMAN. A trader. (See Chapman.)

CHITTENDEN. (Cor. Br. and Welsh.) The lower house on the rising or fortified ground; from *Chy-tane-din—Chy*, a house, *tane*, lower, and *din* or *dun*, a hill.

CHOLMONDELEY. (Norman.) Local. The place at the gorge or neck of the mountain; from *Col*, a strait or defile, and *mond* or *mont*, a hill. This name is pronounced *Chumley*. An English gentleman meeting the Earl of Cholmondeley one day coming out of his own house, and not being acquainted with him, asked him if Lord *Chol-mond-e-ley* (pronouncing each syllable distinctly) was at home. "No," replied the peer, without hesitation, "nor any of his pe-o-ple."

CHUBB. From the Saxon *cob*, a great-headed, full-cheeked fellow. The fish called *chubb* was so named from its having a large head.

CHURCH. Local. A house of Christian worship, derived from the old English *chirch*, and Scottish *Kirk*, Latin *circus*, and this from the Gaelic *cearcal*, a temple, a round building. The root of *Church* is from the Gaelic *car*, roundness, from which we have *cirke* or *kirke*.

CILLY. Local. A town in Germany.

CLAGET. (Ger.) From *klugheit*, good sense, wisdom, prudence, dexterity. The Danish *klegt* signifies the same.

CLAPP. (Cor. Br.) Full of chat, tonguey; from the Cornish-British *clap*, prating.

CLARE. (Fr.) *Clair*, from the Latin *Clarus*, pure, renowned, illustrious.

OF FAMILY NAMES.

CLARK. Clerk, a clergyman, a scholar, one who can read and write.

CLAUSON. Local. A town of Germany, near Pozen; derived from *klause*, a mountain defile.

CLAVERING. Local. First assumed by the proprietors of the barony of Clavering, in Essex, England, near the spring-head of the river Tort. Derived from the Anglo-Saxon *clœfer*, or Belgic *klaver*, both denoting clover; and *ing*, a meadow, a pasture—the clover-fields.

CLAY. Local. A town of France in Seine. A lake on the isle of Lewis, Scotland. *C'lee*, hills in Wales. *C'le*, left-handed, a place lying to the left, in relation to another place. *C'ledh, cloid*, and *cladd*, in the Gaelic, Welsh, and British, signify a ditch, a trench, a wall; *cladh*, a church-yard; *cledd*, Welsh, a sword; Gaelic, *claiheamb*, from which we have *C'laymore*, a large sword. The same word in Welsh and Gaelic that signifies a river is often applied to a sword, from their resemblance in glittering brightness.

CLAYTON. Local. The clay-hill.

CLEARY or **CLERY.** From the Gaelic *Cleireach*, a clerk, a clergyman, a writer. A noted family of historians whose estates were in the county of Donnegal, Ireland.

CLEAVER. English, one who cleaves; a dweller on a cleave or cliff.

CLEMENT. From the Latin *Clemens*, mild, meek, gentle.

CLEVELAND. Local. Derived from a place by that name in Yorkshire, England; a corruption of Cliff-lane, and so called from its being steep and almost impassable with cliffs and rocks.

CLIFF. Local. A steep bank, a precipice; a town in Northamptonshire, England.

CLIFFORD. Local. The ford or way by the cliff.

CLIFTON. Local. A small village in England; the town on the cliff.

CLING. (Danish.) *Klinge*, a blade, a sword.

CLINGMAN. (Danish.) A swordsman, fencer, fighter.

CLINTON. (Dano-Norman.) Local. *Klint*, a promontory, brow of a hill, cape; and *ton*, a town. Colonel Charles Clinton, the progenitor of the distinguished family of Clinton, and his associate emigrants from Ireland, settled, in 1722, in " Little Britain," Orange County, New York.

CLOSSON. (Dutch.) The son of *Klaas*, the abbreviation of Nicholas among the Dutch. *Klaas-son*, the son of Nicholas. So Santa Klaas for St. Nicholas.

CLOUGH. (Anglo-Saxon.) Local. A small valley between hills, a breach; from the past of the Anglo-Saxon participle *cleofian*, to cleave, divide.

CLOWES. (Anglo-Saxon.) Local. A cliff or cleft in a hill; from *Clough*, as above.

CLUM. Local. A place in Germany, the ancient residence of the Knight of Clum, the friend of John Huss.

CLUTE. *Kluit*, Dutch, a lamp; " hij heeft kluiten," he has got the chink, he is rich.

COATES. Local. The side, the shore, coast, border.

COBERN. Local. A town in Germany; the high or united hill.

COBB. Local. A harbor; as the Cobb of Lyme-Regis, County Dorset, England.

COCHRAN. Local. *Cocrinn*, Gaelic, a point or promontory in open sight; from *Coc*, manifest, plain, and *rinn*, a cape or promontory.

COCKBURN. Local. The brook by the hillock; from *cock*, a hillock, and *burn*, a brook.

OF FAMILY NAMES.

COE. The primitive word *Co* is an elevation, exalted. *Koh*, in the Coptic, is a rock; *koh*, Persic, a hill; *Coey*, Gaelic, a hero, literally, a dog. Lower says that *Coe* is a Norfolk provincialism to designate "an odd old fellow."

COOEY. Gaelic, *Cu-maighe*, figuratively, the hero or swift warrior; literally, the "*dog of the plain.*"

COEYMAN. (Dutch.) The cow-man; from *koey*, a cow. *Kooiman*, a man who decoys ducks.

COFFIN. Local. *Cyffin*, in Welsh, signifies a boundary, a limit, a hill; *cefyn*, the ridge of a hill. This name has its origin from *Co*, high, exalted, and *fin*, a head, extremity, boundary. This family settled early in this country, on the sland of Nantucket, near Cape Cod, where the name is very common. The following humorous lines, descriptive of the characteristics of the different families residing on that island, were written by one Daniel Allen, a native of the island, more than a hundred years ago:

> "The hasty COFFIN, fractious, loud,
> The silent *Gardiner*, plotting,
> The *Mitchells* good, the *Barkers* proud,
> The *Macys* eat the pudding;
> The *Rays* and *Russels* coopers are,
> The knowing *Folger* lazy,
> A learned *Coleman* very rare,
> And scarce an honest *Hussey*."

COGGESHALL or COGSWELL. Local. Derived from the town of Coggeshall, in Essex, England; *Cog*, a small boat, and *shoal*, a place where the water is shallow, and where fish abound, a fishing-place.

COHEN. (Heb.) A bishop or priest.

COIT. Local. A wood.

COLBERN. *Colbrin*, Welsh, the hazel-hill; from *Coll* (plural), hazel, and *bryn*, a hill.

COLBURN. (Cor. Br.) The dry well, or the well on the neck of the hill.

COLBY. Local. Kolbye, a town in Denmark; *Col*, with or near, the "*by*" or town.

COLE. An abbreviation of Nicholas, common among the Dutch.

COLEMAN and **COLMAN.** A dealer or workman in coals. Gaelic, *Colman*, a dove.

COLLAMORE. Local. From *Coulommier*, a town in France. This family originally came into England with William the Conqueror. *Colmar*, Gaelic, a brave man; *Collmor*, the great wood.

COLLEY. Local. *Coll-lle*, in Welsh, denotes the place of hazel; *Cil-lle*, the place on the back or neck of the hill; from *cil* or *col*, the back or neck. *Coille*, Gaelic, a wood.

COLLIER. A name of occupation, a dealer or workman in coals.

COLLINE. (Fr.) Local. A hill that rises by degrees.

COLLINS. (Gaelic.) From *Cuilein*, darling, a term of endearment applied to young animals, as *Catulus*, in Latin. In the Welsh, *Collen* signifies hazel—a hazel-grove.

COLQUITE or **COLQUOIT.** Local. From *col*, the neck, and *coit*, a wood. *Col*, in the Cor. Br., signifies the neck of a hill, a promontory.

COLQUHOUN and **CALHOUN.** According to tradition, the progenitor of this family was a younger son of *Conach*, King of Ireland, who came to Scotland in the reign of Gregory the Great, and obtained lands in Dumbartonshire, to which he gave the name of *Conachon*, corrupted into *Colquhoun*. I am inclined to think the name is from the Gaelic, denoting one who is brave, lively, quick, and furious in battle; from *Colg*, and *chuoin*, the genitive of *Cu*, a hound, a war-dog.

COLSON. The son of *Col* or *Cole* (which see).

OF FAMILY NAMES.

COLT. A name given to one of a sportive disposition, or may be taken from the sign of an inn. " Will at the Colt."

COLTON. Local. The town at the neck of the hill, from *Col*, the neck of a hill, and *ton*, a town. *Caltuinn*, Gaelic, hazel.

COLVER. From the Dutch *kolver*, one who plays at *kolf*, a favorite game in Holland.

COLVILLE. (French.) Local. From *Col*, a neck, strait, or defile; a pass between hills; and *ville*, a town, the place in the gorge or pass of the dell.

COLVEN and COLVIN. Local. From Colvend, a town in Kircudbrightshire, Scotland, the ancient name of which was *Culwen*, derived from Joannes De Culwen.

COLWELL or COLVILLE. The village on the neck of the hill, or near the hazel-wood; *Col*, Gaelic, hazel; and *ville*, a village, changed into *well*. *Coldwell* denotes the quality of the water, a cold spring; *Colwold*, the hazel-wild, or bushy place of hazels.

COLY. Local. A little river in Devonshire, England.

COMEYN, or DE COMINGES, as it was anciently written; from *Cominges*, a town in France, anciently called *Lugdunum Convenarum*, situated on a hill near the banks of the river Garonne, so named because people of diverse countries assembled together to dwell in that place. Comeyne or De Cominges went into England with William the Conqueror.

CONANT. (Welsh and Gaelic.) *Conan*, a river. *Counant*, a cataract in North Wales, from *cau*, a chasm, a deep hollow, shut up, and *nant*, a rivulet.

COMSTOCK. (Dutch.) From *kom*, a dock or harbor, and *stock*, a stick or timber—the wharf or dock of timber.

CONN. (Gaelic.) Strength, according to O'Donovan; it is also the genitive plural of *cu*, a dog. *Cond*, signifies protecting, keeping.

CONDE. May be a local name from the town of Conde, in the French part of Hainault, which gave its name to a branch of the royal family of France, the Princes of Conde. *Kundig* or *kundy*, Dutch, signifies knowing, skillful, expert.

CONDER. Conders were persons stationed upon high places near the sea coast to watch the shoals for fishermen, at the time of herring-fishing. The name is derived from the French *conduire*, to conduct.

CONE. (Heb.) A bishop or priest; *koen*, in the Dutch, signifies bold, daring, intrepid.

CONKLIN. (Dutch.) From *Con*, bold, wise. knowing, and *klein*, little or son, *i. e.*, the son of Con. *Konkelen*, in Dutch, signifies to plot, intrigue, conspire. *Ceangleann*, Gaelic, the head of the valley.

CONNELL or **CONNELLY.** (Celtic and Gaelic.) From *conal*, love, friendship.

CONNOR or **CONOR.** (Celtic and Gaelic.) From *Conchobar*, the chief of men, powerful among men, a leader. O'Donovan derives this name from *Conn*, strength, and *cobhair*, aid, assistance. *Con-na-fir*, the head of men.

CONRAD. (Ger.) Able counsel.

CONRY. Local. "Gauir *Gonrigh*," a high mountain near Tralee, County of Kerry, Ireland.

CONSTABLE. A name of office. Roger de Lacey first assumed this surname from being constable of Chester, in England. A commander of the cavalry.

CONTIN. Local. From *Contin.* a parish in Rosshire, Scotland, derived from the Gaelic *Con-tuinn*, signifying the meeting of the waters, alluding to the forking of the river Rasay, which here form an island.

CONWAY. (Br. and Celtic.) Local. From a river of that name in Wales, which issues from a lake in Merionethshire, and flows through a fertile vale of the same name, and enters the Irish Sea, at Aberconway; from *Con*, head, chief, and *wy*, a river.

OF FAMILY NAMES.

CONYERS. Local. From *Coigniers*, in Normandy, their ancient residence; came into England with William the Conqueror.

COOEY or COE. (Gaelic.) A hero; literally, the dog of the plain, from *cu*, a dog, and *magh*, a plain. The names of various animals were given anciently to heroes, to denote power, swiftness, or courage.

COOKE. One whose occupation it is to prepare victuals for the table.

COOKSON. The son of Cook; originally from Settle, in Yorkshire.

COOMBS. (Cor. Br.) A place between hills, a valley; in the Welsh, *Cwm*.

COONS. Dutch, *Koen*, bold, daring, audacious. *Coon*, Saxon, bold.

COOPER. A name of occupation or trade. The name is also local, from *Cupar*, a town in Fifeshire, Scotland, which is derived from *Cu-pyre*, the inclosed fire, or *Co*, high, a beacon fire, or signal on the coast for ships. *Pyre*, a beacon fire, on a high place, is the origin of the word *pier*, a wharf or landing-place for ships; Danish, *pyr* and *fyr*, a lantern; $\pi\bar{v}\rho$, Greek, a fire; the whole landing-place in time was called the *pier*.

COORTAN. (Anglo-Saxon.) A band of soldiers.

COOTE. Local. Welsh, *Coed*, a wood; Cor. Br., *Coit* and *Cut*. *Coot-hill* or *Coit-hayle*, the wood on the river.

COPP. (Sax.) Local. A hill.

CORBET or CORBIE. (Fr.) A raven.

CORBIN. Local. The name of a place in Glencreran, Scotland, signifying a *steep hill*, from the Gaelic *Cor-beann* or *Cor-beinn*.

CORDLAN. Welsh, *Corddlan*, a hamlet, same as Cortlan.

104   ETYMOLOGICAL DICTIONARY

CORKIN. (Gaelic.) Local. The head of the dale; from *coire*, a dell, a circular hollow, and *ceann*, the head.

CORMAC. (Celtic.) The son of the chariot; first given, it is said, to a prince of Leinster who happened to be born in a chariot, while his mother was going on a journey.

CORNELIUS. From the Latin *cornu*, a horn (Greek, κέρας); and ἥλιος, the sun—the horn of the sun.

CORNELL. In the British it signifies a corner, a place shaped like a horn (from the Latin *cornu*). *Corneille*, in the French, signifies a crow.

CORNING. Local. Welsh, *cornyn*, a small horn, or the place of winding or turning.

CORNISH. Local. Belonging to Cornwall, indicating the place from which the family came.

CORNWALLIS. Local. A native of Cornwall; Cornwall is derived from *cornu*, a horn; Welsh, *corn* and *Galwys*, the Gauls, the ancient people of France; a term indicating the circular form of the coast. O'Connor derives Cornwall from *carna*, altars, and *Gael*, i. e., the altars of the Gael.

CORRIE. Local. A town in the Isle of Arran, Scotland. *Coire*, Gaelic, a circular hollow surrounded with hills; a mountain dell.

CORWIN. (Cor. Br.) Local. The white castle; from *caer*, a castle, and *win* or *gwin*, white; or the white *choir*.

CORSE. (Welsh.) A fen, a wet meadow. *Carse*, Armoric and Gaelic, a level tract of fertile land.

CORY. *Correy*, local, a town in Scotland. The word conveys the idea of roundness, bending, turning, the winding of a stream. Gaelic, *car;* Welsh, *cor*, a circle, a dell, a glen; *caire*, a circular hollow surrounded by hills.

COSTAR or COSTER. (Dutch.) From *koster*, a sexton; also, a cunning, sly fellow.

OF FAMILY NAMES.

105

COTTRELL.   A cottage, or a cottager.

COTESWORTH.   Local.   The estate or place in the wood; from *coit*, a wood, and *worth*, a place or possession.   If from the French *cote*, the sea-shore, the estate on the shore.

COTTON.   This name affords several derivations.   Local, Welsh, *Coedton*, the woody hill; *Coiton, Cuiton*, Cor. Br.; *Cwtton*, Welsh, the cottage hill.   *Cotden*, Saxon, the cot in the valley; *Cwthen*, Welsh, the ancient cottage or dwelling.

COURT.   A place inclosed, protected, cut off; that which excludes access.   Saxon, *curt;* Arm., *court;* Fr., *cour;* Gaelic, *cuairt*, a circle; Welsh, *cor* and *cwr*, a circle.

COURTLANDT.   (Dutch.)   Local.   From *kort*, short, little, and *land* or *landt*, from the short or narrow land, properly *Van Courtlandt*.

COURTENAY.   Local.   A town of France which stands on a hill on the banks of the small river *Clairy*, about fifty-six miles south of Paris.   This small town has imparted its name to several princes, whose actions are celebrated in French history.   The name signifies " The court near the water."

COVERT.   Local.   A sheltered place.

COVENTRY.   Local.   A city in Warwickshire, England; from *Coven*, a convent, and *tre*, British, a town—the town of the convent; Welsh, "*Cyfaint-tre.*"

COWAN.   (Gaelic.)   *Gobhainn*, a smith; *Gowan*, a Scottish word for a wild flower.

COWDRAY or COULDRAY.   Local.   The grove of hazels.

COWLEY.   Local.   The cow-pasture.

COX.   *Cock*, little—a term of endearment, a diminutive, the same as *ot* or *kin*, used as a termination, as *Willcox*, little Will; *Simcox*, little Sim, etc.   The word is also often used to denote a leader or chief man.   Addison says: " Sir Andrew is the *cock* of the club."

5*

COWLES. A monk's hood or habit.

CRADOCK. A corruption of the old British name *Caradoc*, which is said to signify "dearly beloved."

CRAIG. (Cor. Br. and Welsh.) A rock, a crag, a stone; Gaelic, *carraig*, a rock, *creag*, a rock.

CRAM. (German.) From *kram*, a retail shop.

CRAMER. (German.) From *kramer*, a retail dealer.

CRANDELL. (Welsh.) Local. From *kren*, round, or *cran*, wood; and *dal*, or *dol*, a vale—the round or woody vale. *Crandal*, in Irish, signifies the woody vale.

CRANSTON or **CRANSTOUN.** Local. The town of *Crans*, a Danish leader who invaded England; a parish in Edinburgshire, Scotland.

CRAPO. (Fr.) From *crapaud*, a toad, an ugly man.

CRAVEN. One who begs for his life when conquered; from *crave*, a word used formerly by one vanquished in trial by battle, and yielding to the conqueror. *Craven* is also the name of a place in Yorkshire, England, very stony, derived from *craig*, Cor. Br., a rock, and *pen*, a head.

CRAWFORD. Local. First assumed by the proprietor of the lands and barony of Crawford, in Lanarkshire, Scotland. The extreme ancestor of the ancient family of Crawford, in Scotland, was Reginald, youngest son of Alan, the fourth Earl of Richmond. He seems to have accompanied David the First to the north, and to have received extensive grants of land in Strath Cluyd, or Clydesdale, whence his immediate descendants adopted the name of Crawford, then forming one of the largest baronies in Scotland, and signifying in Gaelic "*The pass of blood*," from *cru*, bloody, and *ford*, a pass or way, as commemorative, probably, of some sanguinary conflict between the Aborigines and the Roman invaders. The name has been derived by others from *crodh* and *port*, pronounced *cro-fort*, signifying "a sheltering place for cattle."

OF FAMILY NAMES.

CRAYFORD. Local. A town on the river Cray, in Kent, England. The ford over the Cray.

CRESSY. Local. From a town in France by that name.

CRICHTON. In the Gaelic, *criochton* signifies a boundary hill, end, limit, landmark; *creachton*, the hill or castle of plunder, or the ruined, pillaged place.

CRIGAN. The same as Crogan; *creagan*, Gaelic, a little rock.

CRITTENDEN. (Cor. Br. and Welsh.) Local. The cot on the lower hill; from *cru*, a cot; *tane*, lower, and *dun* or *din*, a hill; or it may be the chalk hill, from *krit*, Saxon, chalk.

CROCKER. A maker of coarse pottery. The word *crock* signified a large barrel-shaped jar. Chaucer says: "Spurn not as doth a *crocke* against a wal."

CROCKET. *Kroget*, Danish, crooked, bowed, bent.

CROFT. Local. A town of the same name in England; a small field near a dwelling.

CROGAN. (Gaelic.) A lean little person; literally, a shell, a pitcher, from *krogan; Crogan*, a castle in North Wales. It may signify a little rock.

CROMWELL. (Br.) Local. From *crom*, crooked, and *hal* or *hayle*, low, level land bordering on the river or sea. Lowlands on the bend of a river.

CRONAN. (Gaelic.) A mournful tune or murmuring sound.

CRONKHITE. (Ger.) From *krankheit*, sickly, rickety.

CROOKSHANKS. A name descriptive of bodily peculiarity.

CROSIER. A bishop's staff, with a cross on the top in the form of a crutch or T. A sign over a shop.

CROSS. Local. A place where a cross was erected, or where two ways, roads, or streets intersected each other.

CROSSWELL. Local. A cross erected near a well. John at the *Cross-well* became John Crosswell.

108 ETYMOLOGICAL DICTIONARY

CROTHERS and CROWTHER. (Welsh.) A harper, a musician; from *crwth*, a harp, a Scandinavian fiddle. Gaelic, *cruit.*

CROUCH. A cross; from the Latin *crux.*

CROUNSE. Dutch, *kruin,* the top or crown; *krans,* a wreath or garland; *Krantz,* local, a town in the Duchy of Bremen from which the family may have come.

CROWELL. Local. From a town in England by that name.

CUDNEY. (Br.) From *Cud* or *Coit.* a wood, and *ey,* water —the wood near the water.

CUDWORTH. From *Cud* or *Coit,* a wood, and *worth,* a place, a dwelling—the farm or dwelling in the wood.

CULLEN. Local. From the town of Cullen, in Banffshire, Scotland. The derivation is uncertain. It may be from *Cuillean,* holly, a place of holly-trees; or *Cullin,* the place at the neck of the lake, from *Cul,* a neck, the back of any thing, and *lin,* a lake, a pond.

CULBERT. (Gaelic.) From *Culbheart,* craft, cunning.

CULBERTSON. The son of Culbert.

CULVER. A pigeon, a dove.

CUMMINGS. Local. A corruption of *Comeyn,* anciently written *De Comminges;* from Comminges, a place in France, whence they came. (See Comeyn.)

CUNNINGHAM. Local. A district in Ayrshire, Scotland. The name signifies the dwelling of the chief or king, from the Saxon, *cyning,* Dutch, *koning,* a leader or chief, and *ham,* a house or town.

CUPAR. Local. A borough in Fifeshire, Scotland; the inclosed or fortified hill, from *Cu,* Gaelic, inclosed, and *bar,* a top, a hill. *Cu,* a hero, a chief—the chief's hill or fortress.

CURTIS. An abbreviation of *courteous.* It may be from *Curthose,* a name given for wearing short hose, as the name *Curtmantle* was given to Henry the Second of England, from his introducing the fashion of wearing shorter mantles than had been previously used.

OF FAMILY NAMES.

CURE. (Dutch.) From *Keur*, an elector; as *Keursaxen*, the elector of Saxony.

CUSICK. *Kessoch*, a town near the Moray Frith, Scotland; *casach*, Gaelic, an ascent going up by steps. *Casag*, in Gaelic, signifies a long coat or *cassock*, formerly a cloak or gown worn by the clergy over the other garments. The name may be local, from the place, or from the peculiar dress worn by the individual.

CUTTER. A boat; a name probably taken from the sign of an inn, as "John at the Cutter." *Coutier*, French, a weaver or seller of ticking.

CUTTING. (Saxon.) *Cuth*, well known, famous; and *ing*, equivalent to the Latin *ens*, expressing the existence of the quality or action of the word to which it is affixed; or *Cuthing*, the son of Cuth. *Ing*, *inge*, or *inger*, in most of the Teutonic languages, denotes *offspring*, a descendant.

CUYLER. (Ger.) From *Keiler*, a wild boar; figuratively, a powerful man.

CYNCAD or **KINCADD.** (Welsh.) The front of the battle. In Gaelic, *Ceanncath*, the chief or commander of the battle; from *Ceann*, the head, commander, or chief, and *cath* or *cad*, battle, war.

DABNEY. (Nor. Fr.) Local. A corruption of D'Aubigne; from Aubigne, a town in the department of Cher, France.

DAG. (Dutch.) The same as Day—the time between the rising and setting sun; a dagger, a hand-gun, a pistol; a sign over a shop or inn.

DAGGETT. Local. Probably a corruption of *Dowgate*, a place in London, so called from *dow*, British, water—the water-gate.

DALE, DELL, or DEAL. Nearly synonymous; a bushy vale; low ground, with ground ascending around it.

110 ETYMOLOGICAL DICTIONARY

DALLAS. (Welsh.) From *Deallus*, knowing, skillful.

DALRY. (Gaelic.) Local. A parish in Ayrshire, Scotland; derived from *Dal*, a valley, and *righ*, a king—the valley of the king.

DALRYMPLE. Local. Taken from the lands and barony of Dalrymple, in Ayrshire, Scotland. The name is said to be a corruption of the Gaelic *Dale-roi-milleadh*, which signifies "the valley of the slaughter of kings," and the place was so called from a battle fought there before the Christian era, in which two kings, Fergus and Coilus, were slain. According to others, it signifies "the valley of the crooked pool." I think the name signifies "the valley on the margin of the pool," from the Welsh *Dol*, a valley; *rhim*, the edge or border, and *pwll*, a pool. It is very nearly the same in Gaelic; *Dail*, a vale, *troimh*, by, along the whole extent, and *poll*, a small lake.

DALTON. Local. Lerived from the town of Dalton, in Lancashire, England; a corruption of *Dale-ton*, the town in the dale; or *D'Alton*, abbreviated to Dalton, that is from the high or rocky hill.

DALZIEL or **DALYELL.** (Gaelic.) Local. Taken from the parish of Dalziel, in Lanarkshire, Scotland. The parish is said to have received its name from the old parish church which stood near the Clyde, which was probably so called from *Dal*, a dale or valley, and *cille*, a church—the church in the valley. There is the following tradition, told by Nisbet, of the origin of the name:

"A favorite of Kenneth II. having been hanged by the Picts, and the King being much concerned that the body should be exposed in so disgraceful a situation, offered a large reward to him who should rescue it. This being an enterprise of great danger, no one was found bold enough to undertake it, till a gentleman came to the king, and said, *Dalziel*, that is, 'I dare.' In memory of this circumstance his descendants assumed for their arms a man hanging on a

OF FAMILY NAMES.

111

gallows, and the motto 'I dare.'" The Dalziels afterward became Earls of Carnwath. Unfortunately, there is no such word as *Dalziel* in either the Gaelic or Celtic, which signifies "I dare." The name is local, as given above.

DAN. (Gaelic.) Bold, daring, intrepid.

DANA. (Celtic.) From *Dana*, bold, daring. The chosen successor of a king, among the Celts, was so called; a poet.

DANFORTH or DANFORD. Local. A place in England; the way or ford of the Danes.

DANGAN. (Celtic.) Strong, secure.

DANGER. A corruption of *D'Angier*, that is, from Angier, a town in France. Lower says, a person named Danger kept a public house near Cambridge on the Huntingdon road. On being compelled to quit his house, he built an inn on the opposite side of the road, and placed beneath his sign "*Danger* from over the way," whereupon his successor in the old hotel, inscribed over *his* door, "There is no *Danger* here now."

DANGERFIELD. (Fr.) A corruption of *D'Angerville*, that is, from Angerville, a town in the province of Orleans, France.

DANIELS. (Heb.) Daniel signifies, the judgment of God, the *s* added, being a contraction of *son*—the son of Daniel.

DANSEREAU. (French.) A dancer.

DANVERS. (Fr.) Anciently written *D'Anvers* or *De Anverso*, that is, from the town of Anvers, in France.

DARBY. Local. A corruption of Derby, a shire of England, so called from *doire*, a forest, a woody, hilly country abounding in deer; or it may be *Deerby*, the town of deer.

DARLEY. (Fr.) A corruption of *D'Erle*, from the town of Erle in France.

DARLING. A name of endearment, a darling; *ing*, denoting child, progeny, offspring.

DARRELL. (Nor. Fr.) A corruption of *De Orrell*, so called from a castle and family of Normandy.

DART. Local. A river in England. Duart, a town in Scotland.

DARWIN. (Welsh.) From *Derwin*, an oak; local, *Derwent*, a river in England.

D'AUBIGNE. (Fr.) From *Aubigne*, a town in France, in the department of Cher.

DAUBY. A corruption of *De Auby* or *D'Auby*, that is, from *Auby*, a town in the Netherlands, near the borders of France.

DAUCHY or DAUCHE. A Dutchman; an old form of the word Dutch or Dutcher, a name given in France to an emigrant from Holland.

DAUTRY. (Fr.) A corruption of *De Autry* or *D'Autry*, that is, from Autry, a town in Champagne, France.

DAVENPORT. Local. Derived from the town of Davenport, in Cheshire, England, so called from the river *Dan* or *Daven* (which name signifies a *river*), and *port*, a haven or harbor.

DAVIDS. (Heb.) Beloved, dear; the *s* added, being a contraction of *son*.

DAVIS. A corruption of *Davids;* the son of David.

DAW. (Welsh.) A son-in-law. The name of a species of birds.

DAWES. Local. *D'Awes*, from the river, fountain, or water.

DAWNAY. (Nor. Fr.) *De Aunay* or *D'Aunay*, from the town of Aunay, in Normandy.

DAWSON. Said to be a corruption of the Nor. Fr. *D'Ossone*, from the town of Ossone, in Normandy. Camden, however, thinks it a contraction of *Davison*, the son of David, which is the more probable derivation.

OF FAMILY NAMES.

DAY. The Celtic and Gaelic word *deag* or *dagh* signifies good, excellent, the same as *Da*, in Welsh. Camden supposes the name to be a contraction of David. *Dai, Du*, in the Welsh, signifies dark, in allusion to the complexion or color of the hair. *Dhu*, in Gaelic, the same, dark color, black. *Deah*, Anglo-Saxon, dark, obscure.

DEACON. A servant or minister in the church.

DEALTRY and **DAUTRY.** A corruption of the Latin *De Alta Ripa*, from the high bank or shore; Radulphus De Alta Ripa, Archdean of Colchester died at the siege of Acre in the Holy Land, during the Crusades.

DEARBORN. (Saxon.) *Dear-boren*, noble, well-born.

DEARDEN. Local. A corruption of *Du-er-den*, as still pronounced by the natives of Lancashire, England, where branches of the family reside, and which signifies, "A thicket of wood in a valley." "*Doir-den*."

DECKER. From the German *Decher*, the quantity of ten; probably a name given to the tenth child. It may be one who *decks* or covers ships or vessels.

DE GRAFF. (Dutch.) *De Graaf*, the count or earl, the great man; *de*, the, and *graaff*, count.

DE GROOT. (Dutch.) The great, tall, large man; or if local, from the town of Groot, in Holland, which signifies the great or large place; from *de*, the, and *groot*, great.

DELAFIEDD. (Fr.) *De La Field*—from the field.

DELAFLOTE. (Fr.) "From the fleet" or ships. It is said, that not long since, in London, a certain Mr. Delafloat had his name undergo a singular mutation, in consequence of the indistinct manner in which his name was announced. The porter understood the name to be *Helaflote*, and so proclaimed it to the groom of the chambers, and the luckless visitor—a quiet, shy, reserved young man—was actually ushered into the midst of a crowded drawing-room, by the ominous appellation of *Mr. Helafloat !*

114　　ETYMOLOGICAL DICTIONARY

DELAMATER. (Fr.) *"Le maitre,"* the master, overseer, landlord, preceptor.

DELANCY. (Fr.) Local. *De Lancy*, from the town of Lancy, in the province of Burgundy, France.

DELANY. Anciently *O'Dulainy.*

DELAUNEY. (Fr.) Local. *De Launey*, from Launey, a town in the province of Champagne, France.

DELMAR. (Spanish.) *Del Mare*, " of the sea."

DE LORME. (Fr.) From the town of Lorme, in the province of Livernoi, France.

DELVEN. (Fr.) *De Elven* or *D'Elven*, from Elven, a town in Brittany, France.

DE MEER. (Dutch.) From the sea; the same as *Delmar.*

DEMPSTER. Anciently an arbitrator or officer of justice in the Scottish courts.

DENIO. Local. *Denia*, a city of Valencia, in Spain; *De Noyon*, from Noyon, a town of France.

DENMAN. A denizen; in Welsh, *Dinman*, the place of a fortress, from *din*, a fortress, and *man*, a place. *Denman*, Saxon, the man of the valley; a dweller in the vale.

DENNIS or DENIS. A corruption of the Greek name *Dionysius*, which is derived from δῖος, divine, and νōυς, mind. *Dinas*, Welsh, a fort, a stronghold.

DENTON or DINTON. (Sax.) Local. A town in the county of Buckingham, England. From *den*, a valley, and *ton*, a town.

DERBY. Local. From *Derby*, in England. *Deer-by*, the town or county abounding in deer. (See Darby.)

DERING. (Saxon.) From *Dearran* or *Darran*, to dare, bold, daring; a name given to an old Saxon chieftain.

DERMOD, DIARMAID, DERMOND, and DERMOT. (Celtic and Gaelic.) Signify a free man, one having amiable qualities.

OF FAMILY NAMES. 115

DESHON. (Fr.) Local. *Dijon*, a town in France.

DEVENISH. Local. Signifies deep water. This surname was given to an ancestor of the family who was early settled at the confluence of the rivers Isis and Thames, near Oxford, England. *Dwfn*, Welsh, deep; *uisge*, Gaelic, water.

DEVENPECK. (Dutch.) Local. From *Diepen*, deep, and *beck*, a brook—the deep brook.

DEVEREUX. (Fr.) *D'Evereux*, from Evereux, a town in Normandy.

DEVILLE. (French.) *De Ville*, from the village or town. Some write this name *Devil!*

DEVINE or DEVIN. (Fr.) A soothsayer, a cunning man.

DEVLIN. Local. The Norman spelling of Dublin. In the great charter of King John, Henry, Archbishop of Dublin, is written *Henri de Diveline*.

DEWEES. (Dutch.) *De*, the, and *wees*, orphan—the orphan.

DEWEY. *Dewi*, in the Welsh, is a contraction or rather a corruption of David.

DEWSBURY. Local. A town on the river Calder, England.

DE WILDE. Local. Wildau, called by the Germans Die Wilde, is a town of Poland, situated near the confluence of the rivers Wilia and Wiln, from whence its name is derived. *Wild*, a wilderness.

DEXTER. A contraction of *De Exeter*, from the city of Exeter, in Devonshire, England; anciently written *Excester*, from *Exe*, the name of the river on which it is situated, and *cester*, a camp or town, for the derivation of which see *Chester*.

DIBDIN. (Welsh.) Local. From *Dib*, a slope, sloping ground, and *din*, a fortified hill—the fortress on the slope of the hill.

DIBIN. (Welsh.) Local. A clough, a cleft in a hill; from *dibyn*.

DICK. The familiar abbreviation of Richard. It may come from the Dutch *Dyck*, a bank or dike, a bulwark thrown up in the Low Countries against the sea or rivers to prevent inundation.

DICKENS. *Dickings*, the son of Dick or Richard.

DICKSON. The son of Dick or Richard.

DIE. Local. A town in the province of Dauphiny, France.

DIEFENDORF. (Ger.) Local. Derived from a small town of that name in Germany, and so called from *Diefen*, thieving, and *dorf*, a village—the thieving village.

DIGBY. Local. From Digby, a town in the county of Lincoln, England, so named from the Danish *Dige*, a dike, ditch, or trench, and *by*, a town—the town by the dike.

DILLINGHAM. (Saxon.) Local. A place in the county of Cambridge, England; the town of the market; the buying and selling place; of paying out or telling money. Saxon, *Daelan*, to divide, separate, throw off, pay over; and *ham*, a village.

DILLON. From the Welsh *Dillyn*, handsome, gallant, brave, fine.

DIMOCK or DYMOCK. (Welsh.) A corruption of *Dia Madoc*, that is, David, the son of Madoc, *Dia* being the diminutive of David among the Welsh. *Madoc* is derived 'from *mad*, good, with the termination *oc* affixed, which has the same effect as our English termination "y."

DINSMOR. Local. *Dinas*, in Welsh and Cor. Br., is a fort, city, or walled town, and *mawr*, great, large.

DISNEY. (Nor. Fr.) Anciently written *D'Isney* or *D'Eisney*, and originally *De Isigney*, from *Isigney*, a small village near Bayeaux, in Normandy.

DIX. The same as Dicks or Dickens, the *s* being a contraction of son—the son of Dick or Richard.

OF FAMILY NAMES.

117

DIXIE. (Sax.) Local. From the Saxon *Dic*, a ditch, dike, or fosse, and *ea*, water, or *ig*, an island.

DOBBIN, DOBBS, and DOBSON. The son of Dob or Robert.

DOBNEY. A corruption of D'Aubigne (which see).

DODD or DOD. (Ger.) A god-father. *Dod*, in Gaelic, signifies "the pet;" peevishness, one who is peevish.

DODSON. The son of Dod.

DODGE. To evade by a sudden shift of place; one who evades, or quibbles.

DOLBEER. Local. *Dolbyr*, Welsh, the short vale; from *dol*, a dell, a valley, and *byr*, short. *Dalbyr*, local, a town in North Jutland, from which the family may have originated.

D'OILY. Local. From *Oily*, a place in France; the same as Doyle.

DOLE. Local. A town in France; *Dowyll*, Welsh, shady, dark.

DONALD, DONELL, or DONELLY. (Gaelic and Celtic.) A great man, a proud chieftain, from *Domhnull*. These names appear to have their root in the Gaelic noun *Dion*, a defense, shelter, protection. The verb *Dion* signifies to defend, to protect. *Dun* has nearly the same meaning, a heap, a hill, or mount, a fortified house or hill, a castle. Surnames compounded of *Dion*, *Don*, or *Dun*, were figuratively used to denote persons of courage, and who were not easily subdued.

DONKIN. The same as Duncan (which see).

DONNACH. The same as Duncan. *Diongnach*, Gaelic, strong, fortified.

DONOVAN. (Celtic.) The brown-haired chief; from *Dondubhan*.

DORAN. The son of Dorr. *Doran*, Gaelic, an otter; *Doran*, grief, depression of spirits. *Dorran*, Gaelic, vexation, anger.

118   ETYMOLOGICAL DICTIONARY

DORLAN, or DORLAND. (Dutch.) Local. From *Dor*, sterile, barren, and *land*, unproductive soil.

DORN. (Dutch.) A thorn-tree.

DORR. This name may have several significations, according to the language in which it was first given. *Dorr*, Gaelic, difficult, easily vexed. *Dur*, Gaelic, persevering, earnest, obstinate. *Dorr*, Icelandic, a spear. *Dor*, Cor. British, the earth; also *dorre*, to break. *Doir*, local, a woody place. *Dar*, Welsh, oak.

DORSET. Local. A county in England. *Dorsette*, Anglo-Saxon, mountaineers.

DOTY. Welsh, *Diotty*, an ale-house.

DOUAY. (Fr.) Local. Derived from the town of Douay, in the province of Artois, France.

DOUGALL. (Gaelic and Celtic.) The black stranger, from *Dhu*, black, and *gall*, a stranger, a term used by the Celts to denote a Lowlander, a foreigner. not one of them. The Danes, Swedes, and Norwegians were called by the Irish Fionne Gael, or fair-haired, and the Germans " Dubh Gail," or the black strangers.

DOUGHTY. Strong, brave, noble.

DOUGLASS. (Gaelic.) Local. The dark green river, from *Dhu*, black, dark, and *glass*, green. A river of Scotland which flows into the Clyde. A town of Lanarkshire. The tradition of the origin of the name is this: in the year 770, a man of rank and figure came seasonably to the assistance of Solvatius, King of Scotland, whose territory was then invaded by Donald Bain, of the Western Isles. The victory being obtained, the King was desirous to see the man who had done him so signal a service, and he was pointed out to him in these words, in the Gaelic, " Sholto Dhuglass," " behold that dark, or swarthy, man."

DOUGREY. (Gaelic.) *Dugharra*, stubborn.

OF FAMILY NAMES. 119

DOWNS. A term applied, in England, to a tract of poor, sandy, hilly land, used only for pasturing sheep.

DOWELL. (Welsh and Gaelic.) *Dowyll*, Welsh, shady, dark. *Ynis Dowyll*, the shady island.

DOYLE. A corruption of *D' Oily*, from *Oily*, a city in France.

DRAKE. (Gaelic.) *Drak*, a drake; *drac*, a route, a way, a footstep; one who draws or leads, a leader.

DRAIN. (Gaelic.) *Droigheann*, a thorn.

DRAPER. One who sells cloths.

DRENNON. Local. *Draenon*, Welsh, a thorn-tree or bush.

DRISCOL. (Celtic and Gaelic.) Local. From *dreas* and *coill*, a thicket of briars, the place of wild roses.

DRIVER. A drover, one who compels or urges any thing else to move.

DROVER. One who drives cattle.

DRUMMER. One who, in military exercises, beats the drum.

DRUMMOND. (Gaelic.) Local. From *Druim*, the back, and *monadh*, mountain, a name of place—the back of the mountain.

DRURY. A jewel. [Camden.]

DRYDEN. From the Welsh *Drwydwn*, broken nose. According to Evans, Jonreth, surnamed *Drwydwn*, the father of Llywelyn, was the eldest son of Owain Groynedd, but was not suffered to enjoy his right on account of that blemish.

DUDLEY. Local. A town in Worcestershire, England, so called from the old English *Dode-ley*, the place of the dead, a burying-ground. *Dodelig*, in the Danish, signifies pale, death-like, mortal; so also the Dutch *Doodelijk*, and German *Todlich*.

Duv-da-lethe, in the Gaelic and Celtic, which has been corrupted to Dudley, has the same signification.

120 ETYMOLOGICAL DICTIONARY

DUFF. In the Gaelic, signifies black, but in the Cor. Br. and Welsh, a captain.

DUFIELD. *Du feldt*, from the field.

DUGAN. *Dugan*, Gaelic, the son of *Dhu*, or the dark-haired.

DUMAN. *Du*, from, and *man*, an elevation, something grand or admirable. In the ancient languages, *man* signifies the sun, and *mon*, the moon.

DUMFRIES. Local. A town in Scotland on the river Nith, and said to be so called from the Gaelic *Dun*, a castle, and Dutch *vrows*, women—the castle or retreat of the women, a nunnery. I think rather it is derived from *Dunfrith*, the castle in the forest; Gaelic, *Dun*, a castle, and *frith*, a deer-forest.

DUMMER. From the Danish *Dommer*, an arbiter or judge.

DUMONT. (Fr.) *Du Mont*, from the hill or mountain.

DUN. Local. From the parish of Dun, Forfarshire, Scotland, derived from the Gaelic *Dun*, a hill or rising ground, a fort or castle.

DUNBAR. Local. From the town of Dunbar, at the mouth of the Frith of Forth, Scotland. *Dunabar*, Gaelic, signifies the castle, town, or fort on the height or summit. The town was so called from its situation on the rock which at this place projects into the sea.

DUNCAN. (Gaelic.) A powerful chieftain, From *Dun*, a fortress, and *ceann*, head or chief. *Duncean* or Duncan, strong-headed.

DUNCANSBY. Local. Duncan's Bay.

DUNDAS. (Gaelic.) Local. The south hill, fort, or castle; from *dun*, a hill or fort, and *deas*, south.

DUNHAM. Local. A small village in England, so called from *dun*, a hill, and *ham*, a village.

DUNIPACE. Local. From the Latin *Duni-pacis*, hills of peace.

OF FAMILY NAMES.

121

DUNKELD. (Gaelic.) Local. The hazel-hill.

DUNLEVY. (Cor. Br. and Gaelic.) Local. From *Dun,* a hill, *ley,* green, and *vy,* a river or stream—the green hills by the river. *Dunlamh* or *Dunlavy,* in Gaelic, signifies the strong-handed. *Dunalamhas, mh* having the sound of *v,* is the hill or castle of warriors.

DUNLOP. (Gaelic.) Local. A parish in the district of Cunningham, Ayrshire, Scotland; from *Dun,* a castle, fort, or hill, and *lub,* a curvature, a bending of the shore—the castle or hill at the bend.

DUNN. Gaelic, *Dun,* a heap, hill, mount; a fortress, a castle, fastness, a tower. *Dunn,* Saxon, brown, of a dark color, swarthy.

DUNNING. The brown offspring, from the Saxon *Dunn,* brown, and the termination *ing,* which, among the Saxons, signified offspring, as *White-ing,* the fair offspring, *Cuth-ing,* the son of Cuth. *Dunning* has retained its original orthography since the days of the Saxons.

DUNSTAN. (Sax.) From *Dun,* a hill, and *stan,* a stone—the stone-hill, or the strong, enduring *dun* or fortress.

DUPPA. Local. A corruption of *D'Uphaugh,* "from the high or upper *haw;*" *haugh,* Scottish and North English, a low-lying meadow, a green plot in a valley. *Du Pau,* local, from *Pau,* a town of France.

DUR. In the Gaelic, signifies dull, stubborn, obstinate; also, steady, earnest, persevering.

DURANT. From the Latin name *Durandus,* enduring, strong, inured to hardships, from *duro,* to harden, to inure to hardships, to make strong.

DURBAN. Local. *D'Urbin,* a province of Italy. *Urbin* or *Urbino,* a city situated nearly in the middle of the province or Duchy of Urbin, near the source of the river Foglia.

DURDEN. Local. An old English word signifying a coppice or thicket of wood in a valley.

6

ETYMOLOGICAL DICTIONARY

DURHAM. Local. According to Bailey, this word is derived from the Saxon *Dun* and *holm*, a town in a wood. It seems rather to come from the British *Dour*, water, and *holm*, land surrounded mostly by water. It may be derived from *Doire*, which, in the British and Celtic, signifies a woody place, abounding in oaks; hence Doireholm or Dourham, that is, the place or town surrounded by woods.

DURKEE or DURGY. In the Gaelic, *Duirche* is the comparative of *Dorch*, dark, cloudy, hence dark-complexioned. It may come from *Durga*, Gaelic, surly, sour, repulsive. *Durgy*, in the Cor. Br., signifies a small turf hedge.

DURWARD. A porter or door-keeper—*Door-ward.*

DUSTIN. Welsh, *Dysdain*, a steward of a feast.

DUTCHER. (Dutch.) Local. From *Duitscher*, a German.

DUTTON. Local. A village in Cheshire, England, and may have several derivations. *Dut-ton*, i. e., Dutch-town. *Du-ton*, from *Du*, Cor. Br., side, and *ton*, the same as *dun*, a hill, that is, the side of the hill; or *Du-ton*, the two hills, from *Du*, two, and *ton*, a hill. *Dhu-ton*, Gaelic and Welsh, the black hill.

DWYRE. (Gaelic.) Local. From *Do-ire*, a woody place, uncultivated.

DYER. One whose occupation it is to dye cloth.

DYKE. Local. A name given to one who lived near a ditch, bank, or entrenchment, as "John at the dyke."

DYKEMAN. One who makes dykes or entrenchments; a dweller near a dyke or embankment.

DYSART. (Gaelic.) Local. A parish in Fifeshire, Scotland; from *Dia*, God, and *ard*, high—the temple of the highest. *Dysart* was a place of ancient Druidical or Gaelic worship.

EAGER. Sharp-set, vehement, earnest. The name may be local, from the river Eger, in Bohemia, or Egra, a city on the river Eger.

OF FAMILY NAMES.

EASTCOTE. Local. The *east-cote* or house; so Westcott, the west-cote.

EATON. (Sax.) Local. From *ea*, water, and *ton*, a town. There are several parishes in England by this name.

EBERLEE. Local. *Eabar*, in the Gaelic, is a marshy place, a place where two or three streams meet. Welsh and Cor. Br., *Aber-lle*.

EBERLY. (Ger.) From *eber*, a boar, and *ly*, like; indicating courage, fierceness, bravery.

ECCLES. A church, from the Greek ἐκκλησία, an assembly, a church, Gaelic *eaglais*, Cor. Br., *Egles* and *Eglas*.

EDDY. In the Gaelic, *Eddee* signifies an instructor. The name may be local from the Saxon *Ed*, backwards, and *ea*, water—a current of water running back, a whirlpool. *Edd*, Welsh, signifies motion, going; *Eddu*, to go, to move.

EDGAR. (Sax.) From *Eadigar*, happy or blessed; honor.

EDGECUMBE. Local. From the manor of Edgecumbe, in Devonshire, England. The name signifies, "*the edge of the valley.*"

EDIKER. (Sax.) From *Eadigar*, happy.

EDMOND. (Sax.) Happy peace.

EDWARD. (Sax.) Happy keeper.

EGBERT. (Sax.) Always bright, famous.

EGGLESTON. (Welsh or Br.) From *Egles*, a church, and *tun* or *dun*, a hill—the church on the hill.

EIGINN. (Gaelic.) Strong-handed.

ELDRED. (Sax.) All reverent fear.

ELI. (Heb.) The offering or lifting up.

ELIAS. (Heb.) Signifies Lord God.

ELLET. Little Elias, the diminutive *ette* being added, as Willett, Hallett.

124 ETYMOLOGICAL DICTIONARY

ELLIOT. Supposed to signify the son of *Elias; Heliat*, Welsh and Cor. Br., a huntsman, a pursuer.

ELLIS. Contracted from Elias.

ELPHINSTONE. Local. From the lands and barony of Elphinstone, in Scotland, and derived from the Anglo-Saxon *Elfenne*, a fairy or spirit, and *stone*. These *elfenne* or *elf*-stones are a peculiar hard flint, and in the olden times were supposed to be shot by the fairies or elfs. The place is so named from this kind of stone being found on the land.

ELTON. There are many places of this name in England; it is impossible to decide from which the family appellation is derived. The derivation is from the Saxon words *ael*, an *eel*, and *ton*—a town abounding in eels.

ELWY. Local. A river in Wales.

ELY. Local. From Ely, a city in Cambridgeshire, England, and signifies the place of willows, from *Helig*, Cor. Br. and Welsh; Latin, Salix. Greek ἕλιξ, *Ealig*, an island; land in waterland. Greek, Ἕλος, a marsh.

EMERSON. (Sax.) *Emar*, from *Ethelmar*, noble, and *son*— the son of the noble.

EMMET. Local. The name of a river; "*Eimot*," Gaelic. the quick river, from *eim*, quick. *Emmet*, Saxon, *aemet*, an ant.

ENNIS, ENNES, or INNIS. (Celtic or Gaelic.) Local. An island or peninsula, made so either by a fresh water river or the sea. *Ynys* in the Welsh.

ENOS. (Heb.) Fallen man, mortal, sickly.

ERRICK. " There is a tradition," says Dean Swift, " that the ancient family of the Ericks or Herricks derive their lineage from Erick the Forrester, a great commander who raised an army to oppose the invasion of William the Conqueror." Erick is derived from *Ehr*, German, honor, and *rick*, rich— rich in honor.

OF FAMILY NAMES.

ERSKINE. Some writers deduce this family from a noble Florentine who came to Scotland in the reign of Kenneth II. It is said, in the reign of Malcolm II., a Scotchman of high distinction having killed with his own hand Enrique, one of the Danish generals, at the battle of Murthill, cut off his head, and with the bloody dagger in his hand showed it to the king, and in the Gaelic language said *Eriskynĕ*, "upon the knife," alluding to the head and dagger; and in the same language also said, "I intend to perform greater actions than what I have done." Whereupon, King Malcolm imposed upon him the surname of *Eriskine*, and assigned him for his armor-bearings a hand holding a dagger, with "Je pense plus" for a motto, which has continued to be the crest and motto of this family.

ERWIN. Welsh, *Erwyn*, very fair, white. *Urfionn*, Gaelic, beautiful, fair.

ESHAM. Local. From a town by that name in Worcester-shire, England, formerly *Eoves-ham*, so called from one Eoves Egwins, a shepherd, who was afterward Bishop of Worcester, and *ham*, a village.

ESTLEY. Local. The east field or pasture—*East-ley*.

ETHELBERT. (Sax.) Noble, bright, from *Ethel* or *Adel*, noble, and *bert*, bright, famous.

ETON. Local. *Awtwyn*, in Welsh, is the hillock near the waters, from *Aw*, water, and *twyn*, a small hill. In Saxon, *Ea* and *ton* have the same signification, i. e., "the hill or town near the water."

EURE. Local. From the lordship of *Eure*, in Buckingham-shire, England. *Eure*, in the Cor. Br., signifies a goldsmith.

EUSTACE. From the Greek Εὐσταθής, standing firm.

EVANS. The Welsh for John, the same as Johns. *Evan*, *eofn*, fearless, bold.

EVELYN. Local. From Evelyn, in the county of Salop, England.

126   ETYMOLOGICAL DICTIONARY

EVERARD. (Sax.) The same as Εὔδοξος in Greek, that is, *well reported, ever honored;* or from *Eberhardt,* ever hard or enduring. Some writers are of opinion that we have *Ebers, Everard, Evered,* and *Everet,* from *Eber,* a boar.

EVERETT and EVERTS. A corruption of *Everard.*

EVERLY. Local. A place in Wiltshire. England.

EWELL. Local. A town in England. *Ewhill,* Cor. Br., signifies high, tall.

EYRE. The same as *Ayres* or *Ayre* (which see).

EYTINGE. (Saxon.) Local. From *Ey,* Saxon, *ig,* an island, a watery place, and *ing,* a meadow—the meadow on the island or near the water.

FAAL. (Gaelic.) A rocky place; *Fells,* Saxon, crags, barren and stony hills. *Fales* has the same signification. *Falaise,* a town in France, takes its name from the rocks which surround it.

FABER. (Latin.) A workman, a smith.

FABIAN. Derived from the Latin *Fabius, Faba,* a bean—the bean-man, so called from his success in cultivating beans.

FACET. French, *Facette,* a little face. *Facete,* from the Latin *Facetus,* gay, cheerful.

FADEN. (Gaelic.) *Feadan,* a fife, flute, chanter of a bagpipe, a musical instrument. *Fudan,* the son of Fad.

FAGAN. (Gaelic.) A beech-tree. The Fagans were descended from Patrick O'Hagan, living A.D. 1180. O'Hagan, the posterity of *Agan. Ogan, Ogyn,* or *Hogyn* signifies, in the Welsh, young, a youth. Gaelic, *Og,* a young man.

FAGG. (Saxon.) *Fag,* variable or many colored; may be bestowed on the first possessor from his variable disposition. *Fag,* a laborious drudge.

FAIRBAIRN. The same as Fairchild—a fair, handsome bairn or child.

FAIRFAX. (Sax.) Fair-hair; *Faex,* hair.

OF FAMILY NAMES.

127

FAIRHOLM. Local. The fair island, or fair lands bordering on water; also, where a fair or market is held.

FAKE or FALKE. (Ger.) A falcon or hawk; figuratively, daring or enterprising.

FALES. Local. *Fale*, a river of Cornwall, England; also, a rough, rocky place.

FALKLAND. (Sax.) From *Folck*, the common people, and *land*—the land of the common people, in the time of the Saxons.

FALUN. Local. A town of Sweden. *Falan*, Gaelic, the son of Fale.

FANE. From *Fane*, a temple, a church. Gaelic, *Fann*, faint, weak, feeble.

FANNING. The son of Fann.

FANSHAW. Local. *Fane*, a temple or church, and *shaw*, a small wood or grove, a thicket—the church in the grove.

FAR. *Fawr*, same as *Mawr*, Gaelic and Welsh, great.

FARMAN. (Ger.) *Fahr-mann*, master of a ferry-boat.

FARNHAM. Local. From a town in Surrey, England, "so called from the Saxon *Fearn*, fern, and *ham*, a habitation or village—the village in the place overgrown with fern."

FARQUHAR. (Gaelic.) From *Fear*, a man, and *còir*, just, honest, good, or *car*, friendly; *Fearciar*, from *Fear* and *ciar*, dark-gray—a dark-gray man.

FARQUHARSON. The son of Farquhar.

FARRADAY. (Gaelic.) From *Farraideach*, inquisitive, prying, curious.

FARRAR. A corruption of *Farrier*, a name of trade. *Pfarrer*, in German, a minister.

FASSET and FAUCET. (Fr.) *Fausette*, falsehood, cheat, forgery.

FAULKNER. (Ger.) A catcher or trainer of hawks.

ETYMOLOGICAL DICTIONARY

FAY. (Spanish.) *Fe*, faith. In Normandy, plantations of beech were called *Faye*, *Fayel*, and *Fautlaie*.

FEARAN. (Gaelic.) An estate.

FELCH. Probably a corruptiou of *Welch;* Filch means to pilfer.

FELL. *Fel*, in the Dutch, signifies fierce, furious, violent; also local, a rocky place, barren and stony hills; any uninclosed place; a moor, a valley. A short time since, a tradesman named James Fell migrated from Ludgate Hill to Fleet-street, and announced the event in the following manner: "I. Fell, from Ludgate Hill;" under which a wag wrote, "Oh what a fall was there, my countryman!"—LOWER.

FELTON. Local. A small town in England; the rocky or stony hill.

FENSHAW. Local. The *shaw* or grove in the *fen*.

FENTON. (Welsh or Br.) A well.

FERDINAND. (Ger.) From *Fred*, peace, and *rand*, pure—pure peace.

FERGUS. (Gaelic and Celtic.) A fierce or brave chieftain, from *Fear*, man, and *guth*, a voice or word, that is, the man of the word, a commander of an army. Some suppose the first Fergus was so named from *Fairghe*, the sea, on account of his large navy; others, from his raging like the sea iu battle. *Feargach*, fiery.

FERGUSON. The son of Fergus.

FERRER or **FERRERS.** Local. From *Ferrieres*, a small town of Gastinois, France, so called from the iron mines with which the country abounded; or the name may have originated from the occupation of a farrier or iron-dealer.

FERRIS. A corruption of Ferrers (which see). *Fferis*, in the Welsh, signifies steel.

FERROL, FIROL. (Gaelic.) Famous men.

OF FAMILY NAMES.

FIELDING. This family trace their descent to the Earls of Hapsburgh, in Germany. Geffery, a son of Edward of Holland, served with Henry III. in the wars of England, and because his father had dominions in Lauffenburgh and Ren*felden,* he took the name of *Felden* or *Fielding.*

FIFE. Local. A shire or county of Scotland; lands held in *fief.*

FIFIELD. Local. Has the same signification as Manorfield. Lands held in *fee* or *fief,* for which the individual pays service or owes rent.

FILEY and **FILLEY.** Local. From a town in England by that name. *Filid,* Gaelic, the *d* silent, a poet, a bard.

FILO. *Filea,* in the Gaelic, is a bard, poet, or historian. Φίλος, in the Greek, a friend.

FILMUR and **FILMORE.** This name, in all probability, arose from a residence near a lake or a fertile piece of ground; *Fille,* Sax., denoting fullness or plenteousness, and *mere,* a lake or moist piece of ground. The name has been spelled at different times *Fylmere, Filmour,* and *Filmore.* Several other derivations may be found for the etymology of this name. From *Filea,* Celtic and Gaelic, a bard, a historian, and *mor,* great, that is, the famous bard. The *Fileas,* among the Gauls, or Celts, were held in great esteem, and their office was honorable. They turned the tenets of religion into verse, and animated the troops before and during an engagement with martial odes, and celebrated the valorous deeds of the chieftains and princes who entertained them.

FINCH. A small singing bird.

FINNEY. *Finne,* Gaelic, the genitive of *Fionn,* fair, sincere, true; bringing to an end, wise, a head, chief. The name may be local from *Fines,* a place in France.

FIRMAN. *Ferdmon,* a soldier.

FISK. (Fr.) From *Fisc,* revenue, public funds.

6

130   ETYMOLOGICAL DICTIONARY

FISTER. (Dan.) A fisherman.

FITZ GERALD. (Nor. Fr.) The son of Gerald, *Fitz*, a son, *Gerald* (Teutonic), all-surpassing, excellent.

This ancient and honorable family is traced from Otho or Other, a Baron in Italy, descended from the Grand Dukes of Tuscany. Walter, son of Otho, came into England with William the Conqueror, and afterward settled in Ireland.

Maurice Fitz Gerald assisted Richard Strongbow in the conquest of that kingdom.

FITZ GILBERT. (Nor. Fr.) The son of Gilbert; Fitz, a son, *Gilbert*, gold-like bright, or bright or brave pledge, from *gisle*, Saxon, a pledge. (See Gilbert.)

FITZ HAMON. The son of *Hamon*, Hebrew, faithful, *i. e.*, the son of the faithful.

FITZ HARDING. The son of Harding (which see).

FITZ HATTON. The son of Hatton (which see).

FITZ HENRY. The son of Henry (which see).

FITZ HERBERT. The son of Herbert (which see).

FITZ HERVEY. The son of Hervey (which see).

FITZ HUGH. The son of Hugh (which see).

FITZ JOHN. The son of John (which see).

FITZ MORICE. The son of Morris (which see).

FITZ ORME. The son of Orme (which see).

FITZ PARNELL. The son of Parnell (which see).

FITZ PATRICK. The son of Patrick (which see).

FITZ RANDOLPH. The son of Randolph (which see).

FITZ ROY. The son of Roy (which see).

FITZ SWAIN. The son of Swain (which see).

FLACK. Local. (Dutch.) "*Vlak*," flat, low ground.

OF FAMILY NAMES. **131**

FLAHERTY. (Celtic.) A man of chieftain-like exploits. From *flaith*, a lord or chief, and *oirbheartach*, noble-deeded; the man of noble deeds.

FLANDERS. Local. A name given to a native of Flanders, a County or Earldom of the Low Countries, or Netherlands. It took its name either from *Flandrina*, the wife of Liderick II., Prince of Buc, or from *Flambert*, the nephew of Clodion, King of France.

FLANNAGAN. (Gaelic.) From *flann*, ruddy complexion.

FLEMING. Local. A native or inhabitant of Flanders. See Flanders.

FLETCHER. A maker of arrows, or superintendant of archery. From the French *flèche*, an arrow.

FLINT. Local. Derived from a market town of that name, near the sea, in Flintshire, Wales, which gives name to the county.

FLOOD. Originally *Fludd* or *Floyd* (which see).

FLOYD. The same as *Llwyd*, Welsh, brown, gray, hoary.

FOLGER. Camden defines the name, "*Foulgiers*, Fearne" (fern). *Fougeres*, local, a town of France, near the frontiers of Normandy. This town has given its name to a noble family. Raoul de Fougers fortified the town, and built the castle.

FOLJAMBE. Full James, Fool James?

FOLLET or **FOLLIOT.** (Fr.) Frolicksome, merry, gay. "Rightly named was Richard Folioth, Bishop of Hereford, who, when he had incurred the hatred of many for opposing himself against Thomas Becket, Archbishop of Canterbury, one cried with a loud voice at his chamber window at midnight: '*Folioth, Folioth, thy god is the Goddess Azaroth.*' He suddenly and stoutly replied: '*Thou liest, foul fiend, my God is the God of Sabaoth.*"—Camden.

FONDA. Spanish, *Fonda*, bottom, foundation, the source or beginning. *Fondi*, a town of Naples, in Italy, so called from the Latin *fundus*, the bottom.

FOOTE. Local. A place at the bottom of a hill or mountain, the base.

FORBES. Local. Lands free from military service, called *Saor Forba*, or free lands. The name of a parish in Aberdeenshire, Scotland.

FORBISHER. A polisher of armor or weapons.

FORDHAM. Local. So named from a town in England; the house or village at the ford.

FORRESTER and **FORSTER.** A woodman.

FORSYTHE. (Gaelic.) From *Fear*, a man, and *Syth*, upright, honest, stiff.

FORTESCUE. Strong shield. Sir Richard Le Forte (the brave), one of the leaders in the army of William the Conqueror, who had the good fortune to protect his chief at the battle of Hastings, by bearing before him a massive shield, hence acquired the addition of the French word *escue*, a shield, to his name.

FOSDYKE. Local. The name of a canal, cut by the order of Henry VIII., from the great marsh near Lincoln, England, to the Trent. *Fosse-dyke.*

FOSGATE. From *fosse*, a ditch, moat, or trench, and *gate*.

FOSS. (Cor. Br.) The entrenchment, moat, or ditch. *Fos*, Danish, a waterfall, cataract.

FOSTER. Probably a corruption of *Forrester* or *Forster*.

FOTHERBY. Local. The town of provisions, food and fodder, from *Fother*, the same as *fodder*, Saxon *fodre*, food for cattle, and *by*, a town.

FOTHERGILL. Local. From *Fother*, as above, and *gill*, a brook.

OF FAMILY NAMES.

FOTHERINGHAM. Local. The house or town supplying food for man and beast, from *Fother*, as above, and *ham*, a village.

FOULIS. The surname of Foulis is of Norman extraction. Their first British ancestor came into England either at or before the Conquest, and his armorial bearings were *three leaves*, called "*Feuilles*" in the old Norman; it is certain that the name was either given to the family while residents of South Britain, or else assumed by him who first settled in Scotland in the reign of Malcom Canmore, when surnames were then first adopted.

FOUNTAIN. Originally De Fonte or De Fontibus (Fountain), from the springs or fountains near which they resided.

FOWLER. A sportsman who pursues wild fowl.

FOX. A name taken from the cunning animal; about the year 1333 the *Shanachs* in Ireland anglicised their name to Fox.

FRAME. (Gaelic.) *Freumk* or *Freamk*, a root, stem, stock, lineage.

FRANK. A native of France, free; a name given by the Turks, Greeks, and Arabs, to any of the inhabitants of the western part of Europe, whether English, French, or Italians.

FRANCIS. From the Saxon, *Frank*, free. The Franks were a people who anciently inhabited part of Germany, and having conquered Gaul, changed the name of the country to France.

FRANKLAND. A name given by the Saxons to the land of the Franks.

FRANKLIN. Anciently, in England, a "superior freeholder," next below gentlemen in dignity, now called country Squires. Fortescue says (De Leg. Ang.), "Moreover England is so filled and replenished with landed menne, that therein the smallest thorpe can not be found wherin dwell-

ETYMOLOGICAL DICTIONARY

eth not a knight or an esquire, or such a householder as is there commonly called a *Franklin*, enriched with great possessions, and also other freeholders. and many yeomen, able for their livelyhood to make a jury in form aforementioned." So Chaucer, in his Canterbury Tales;

> " A *Franklin* was in this companie,
> White was his beard, as is the dayesie."

FRASER. *Fraischeur*, French, freshness, coolness, bloom; *Friseur*, a hairdresser, from *friser*, French, to curl.

FREDERICK. (Germ.) Rich peace, or peaceable reign.

FREEMAN. One who enjoys liberty, or is entitled to a franchise, or peculiar privilege, as the *freeman* of a city or state.

FREER. French, *Frere*, a friar, a monk, a brother.

FREIOT. (Dutch.) *Fraaiheid*, signifies prettiness, neatness.

FREMONT. Local. From *Framont*, a place in France, near Lorraine, meaning the *Franc* or *free* mount, the *battel* hill; or the fresh, blooming, beautiful hill, from *frais*, French, blooming.

FRENCH. Originally coming from, or belonging to France.

FRERY. Contracted from Frederick (which see).

FRIAR. (French.) From *Frère*, a brother, a member of a religious order; a monk who is not a priest, those friars who are in orders being called *fathers*.

FRISBY. Local. (Danish.) The new, or fresh town; Welsh, *fres;* French, *frais*, fresh, new, recently built; Danish *frisk*, and *by*, a town.

FRISKIN. (Gaelic.) From *Fear*, and *skein*, a sword; the man with the ready sword or hanger.

FROBISHER. The same as Forbisher (which see).

FROST. (Welsh.) *Ffrost*, a brag.

OF FAMILY NAMES.
135

FROTHINGHAM. Local. A house or village situated near a *strait* or arm of the sea. *Frithingham*, the house or village among the hawthorns; *frith*, Cornish British, a hawthorn, white thorn. *Frith*, Gaelic, a forest, a place of deer.

FRY. (Cornish British.) Local. A hill, a town or house on the most prominent part of a hill or eminence. German, *Frei*, free, Dutch, *Vry*, or *Fry*, free.

FULHAM. Local. A village on the Thames, England, and derives its name from the Saxon *Fullen*, fowl, and *ham*, that is, the house or village of fowl. Either from the house noted for its good living, or from the neighborhood producing good poultry.

FULKE. Dutch, *Valk*, a hawk; German, *Falke*.

FULKINS. The son of Fulke.

FULLER. One who fulls cloth; a clothier.

FULLERTON. Local. The town where cloth is dressed.

FULSOM. Local. From *Foulsham*, a town in England, where, perhaps, were raised plenty of fowl, or the streets foul, or the population full and crowded. Saxon, *Fullen*, foul.

FURBUSHER. The same as *Forbisher* (which see).

GADSBY. (Dan.) From *gade*, a street, and *by*, a town, *i. e.*, street-town; or the gate-town, if Webster is correct in giving *gade* the Danish for gate.

GAIRDEN. (Gaelic.) An inclosed or fortified place; the beacon hill or hill of alarm, from *gair*, an *outcry*, an alarm and *din*, a hill or fortress.

GALBRAITH. A compound of two Gaelic words, *Gall* and *Bhreatan*, that is, strange Briton, or Low Country Briton. The Galbraiths in the Gaelic are called *Breatannich*, or *Clann-a-Breatannich*, that is, the Britons, or the children of the

136 ETYMOLOGICAL DICTIONARY

Britons, and were once reckoned a great name in Scotland, according to the following lines :—

> " Bhreatanuich o'n Talla dhearg,
> Hailse sir Alba do shloinneadh."

> " Galbraith's from the Red Tower,
> Noblest of Scottish surnames."

The "*Talla dhearg*," or " Red Tower," was probably Dumbarton, that is, *Dun Bhreatain*, the hill or stronghold of the Britons, whence it is said the Galbraiths came. *Galbraith*, Welsh, the diversified plain.

GALE. A Gael or Scot; a stranger. Fingal, the white stranger, Dugal, the black stranger, alluding to the complexion or color of the hair. The root of Gall, or Gaul, is *Hal*, the sun, from which we have *Gal*, *Gel*, *Gl*, brilliant, bright, glorious. Greek, ἥλιος ; Welsh, *haul*, Cornish British, *houl*, the sun. *Ge*, brilliant, and *haul; Gehaul*, Gaul, the ancient name of France—still called "*sunny* France."

GALGACHUS. In the chronicle of the kings of Scotland Galgachus is called *Galdus*, of which name and its etymology Gordon gives the following account :

Galgachus was Latinized by the Romans, from the Highland appellations *Gald* and *cachach :* the first, *Gald*, being the proper name, and the second, *cachach*, being an adjection to it from the battles he had fought; it signifies the same as *præliosus; Gald the fighter of battles*, which kind of nicknames are still in use among the Highlanders. *Colgach*, Gaelic, fierce, furious, and *ach*, battle, skirmish.

GALL. A native of the Lowlands of Scotland; any one ignorant of the Gaelic language; a foreigner, stranger. *Gal*, Gaelic and Cor. Br., battle, evil warfare; *Gal*, Welsh, clear.

GALLAGHER. (Gaelic.) From *Gallach*, valiant, brave, and *er* put for *fear*, a man. *Air* is a common termination of nouns, and changes into *eir*, *ir*, *or*, *oir*, and *uir*, its etymon being *fear*, a man.

OF FAMILY NAMES.

137

GALLIGAN. (Gaelic.) From *Gealagan*, white.

GALLUP. (Ger.) A corruption of *Gottlieb*, from *Gott*, God, and *lieb*, love or praise—God's praise.

GALT or GUALT. A bush of hair. Welsh, *Gwallt*.

GAINNES. Gaelic, *Gainne*, a dart, an arrow, a shaft; given because of expertness in the use of these weapons of war.

GANESVOORT. (Dutch.) From *Gans*, a goose, and *voort*, advanced, forward, that is, the forward goose or the gander; figuratively, a leader.

GANO. Local. Welsh, *genau*, an opening of a lake, river, dale or valley; a place admitting entrance. *Genau*, in Ger., signifies short, alluding to stature.

GARDENER and GARDNER. A name derived from the occupation.

GARDINER. This name may be derived from the same roots as *Gairden*. It is probably, however, the same as *Gardener*, the orthography having been changed. Camden says, "Wise was the man that told my Lord Bishop (Stephen Gardiner, Bishop of Winchester) that his name was not Gardener as the English pronounce it, but Gardiner, with the French accent, *and therefore a gentleman*."

The principal family of the Gardiners in this country derive their descent from Lion Gardiner, a native of Scotland, who served under General Fairfax in the Low Countries as an engineer. He was sent to this country in 1635, by Lords Say and Sele, Brooke, and others, to build a fort, and make a settlement on their grant at the mouth of the Connecticut river. He built the fort at Saybrook, which name he gave to it after the names of his patrons Lords Say and Brooke. His eldest son, David, born at Fort Saybrook, in 1636, was the first white child born in Connecticut. He afterward bought from the Indians the island in Long Island Sound, called by them Monchonack, and by the English the Isle of Wight, paying for it as the old records say, a black dog, a

138 ETYMOLOGICAL DICTIONARY

gun, and some Dutch blankets. He removed there with his family, and gave it the name of Gardiner's Island. The island still remains in the possession of the family, having descended in a direct line from Lion Gardiner.

GARENNIER. (Fr.) A warrener, a keeper of a warren.

GARFIELD. Local. Sax., *Garwian*, to prepare; German and Dutch, *gar*, dressed, done, ready prepared, and *field*, a place where every thing is furnished necessary for an army.

GARNET. Local. *Garnedd*, Welsh, a tumulus; an ancient place of Druid worship. *Carnedd*, a cairn. *Garnet*, a precious stone.

GARNIER. Fr., *Garnir*, to summons, warn, call out, furnish, supply. Italian, *Guarnire;* Norman, *Garner*, to warn, to summon. to fortify.

GARRAH. (Cor. Br.) Local. The top of the hill; *Garw*, Welsh, rough.

GARRET. A corruption of Gerard (which see).

GARRISON. Local. A place where troops are stationed, for the defense of a town or fort, or to keep the inhabitants in subjection.

GARROW, GAROW, and GARO, in the British, signifies fierce, keen, sharp, rough, a rough place; Gaelic, *Garbh*, rugged, mountainous.

GARRY. Local. A town in Scotland.

GARTH. (Welsh.) Local. A hill or promontory; *Gart*, Gaelic, a head.

GASKELL. (Gaelic.) From *Gaisgeil*, valorous.

GASTON. Local. From Gastein, a town in Bavaria. Also a brave or valorous man, from *Gais*, Gaelic, bravery, valor, and *duin*, a man.

GATES. Local. *Gate*, in Scotland, means a road or way.

OF FAMILY NAMES. 139

GAVET. Local. A town in Savoy or Dauphiny, an old province of France.

GAYER. A gray-hound; a swift dog.

GAYLOR. That is, *Geller*—loud-voiced.

GEAR and GEER. *Gear* signifies all sorts of wearing apparel and equipments for horses and men, from the Saxon *gear-rian*, to make ready; and the name was probably given to one who took charge of and superintended the *gear*. *John of the Gear, John O' Gear,* and at length *John Gear.*

GEDDES or GETTY. Local. *Gaeta,* a town of Italy, and signifies a stronghold. Gaelic, *Caetigh ;* Welsh, *Caety,* from *Cae,* surrounded, defended, shut up, and *tigh or ty,* a house. *Geddes,* the son of Gideon.

GEOFFREY. (Belgic.) From *gau,* joyful, and *fred,* peace— joyful peace,

GEORGE. (Greek.) A husbandman, a farmer, from Γεωργὸς.

GERARD. (Teut.) From *Gar,* all, and *ard,* nature; apt, docile; one ready to do or learn, amiable.

GERMAIN. (Ger.) A name given to a native of Germany. German is derived from Werr-man, *i. e.,* war-men, a name assumed by the Tungri, in order to strike terror into their Gaelic opponents. The Romans, for want of a W, for *Werr-man* wrote *Gerrman.* Vonhammer derives the word from the land of *Herman,* now Chorasin.

GERRY. A corruption of Gerard (which see). *Gairdeach,* the *d* silent, from *Gairde,* Gaelic, festive, joyful.

GERVAS. (Ger.) Steadfast, honorable.

GETMAN. (Ger.) The same as *Ketman,* from *kette,* a chain, and *mann*—a chain-man, one who used or carried a chain; a surveyor; a maker of chains.

GIBBON. (Welsh.) *Guiban,* a fly. *Gibean,* in Gaelic, signifies a hunch-back; *Gibb-ing,* the son of Gilbert.

140　　ETYMOLOGICAL DICTIONARY

GIBBS. From *Gib*, a nickname for Gilbert.

GIBSON. The son of Gib or Gilbert.

GIDDINGS. The son of Gid or Gideon.

GIFFORD or GIFFARD. (Sax.) Liberal disposition; the giver. The name is also local, a town on the water of Gifford, Haddington Co., Scotland, from *Gaf*, Celtic, a hook, a bend, and *ford*.

GIHON. Local. *Gien* or *Gihen*, a town of France, in the province of Orleans.

GILBERT. (Ger.) Bright pledge, from *Gisle*, a pledge; or gold-like, bright, from the Saxon *Geele*, yellow.

GILCHRIST. (Gaelic.) From *gille*, a servant, and *Chriosed*, Christ—the servant of Christ.

GILKINSON. The son of *Gilkin*. *Gilkin* is the child of *Gil* or Gilbert, *kin* meaning child or offspring.

GILL. Local. A valley or woody glen; a narrow dell with a brook running through it; a small stream.

GILLAN. Local. A town in Scotland.

GILLESPIE. The Gaelic for Archibald, from *Gille*, a youth or servant, and *speach*, a word expressive of quickness and sharpness in battle; *spuaic*, Gaelic, to break the head, to knock.

GILLETT. From *Guillot*, the French diminutive for William. The family may have come with William the Conqueror into England, from *Gillette*, a town in Piedmont, France. *Gillette*, the son of *Giles*.

GILLIES. (Gaelic.) *Gill-Iosa*, the servant of Jesus.

GILLPATRICK. (Gaelic.) From *gille*, a servant, and Patrick —the servant of Patrick.

GILLY. (Cor. Br.) The wood or grove of hazel; Gaelic, *Coille*.

OF FAMILY NAMES.

GILLMAN. The Gillmans are said to have come from the province of Maine, in France, into England with William the Conqueror, and to have settled in Essex, England. Whether a *Gaulman*, a *Gael*, or *Brookman*, from *gill*, a brook, the same as *kill* in Dutch, is uncertain.

GILMOUR. *Gillemore*, Gaelic, the henchman or follower of the chief, one who carried the chief's broadsword, from *gille*, a servant, and *mor*, large, great.

GILROY. *Gile-roimh*, a running footman attendant on a Highland chieftain; from *gille*, a servant, and *roimh*, before, in respect of situation or place; or *Gille-righ*, the servant of the king.

GILSON. The son of Gil or Gilbert.

GIRDWOOD. Local. The green wood, from the Welsh *gwyrdd;* or the inclosed wood, from the Danish *gierde*, a hedge; *girds*, shoots of trees.

GIRVAN. Local. From the river and town of Girvan in Ayrshire, Scotland. In the Welsh, *Gearafon* or *Gwyrddafon*, implies the river flowing through the green flourishing place, from *afon* or *avon*, a river, and *Gwyrdd*, green, flourishing.

GIVENS. (Welsh.) A smith, the same as *Gove;* Gaelic, *gobhain.*

GLANVILLE. Local. A house or castle on the shore of a river or the sea; Welsh, *glan*, a shore, bank of a river; old French or Gaelic, the same; as *Glandeve*, in France, on the banks of the *Var*. *Glan* or *glen* signifies also a narrow valley or dell.

GLASGOW. (Gaelic and Cor. Br.) Local. From the city of Glasgow, Scotland. The green, fruitful place, from *glas*, green, and *geu* or *gew*, a " choice field," the stay or support of the estate.

GLASS. (Gaelic.) Gray, pale, wan; *glas*, Welsh, green.

GLENTWORTH. Local. From *Glyn*, a valley, and *worth*, a habitation, dwelling, or farm.

142 ETYMOLOGICAL DICTIONARY

GLISTON. Local. *Glaston*, the green hill; *Gliston*, the shining hill, the mineral or *mica* hill.

GLOUCESTER. Local. From the city of Gloucester, England, the ancient *Gleva*, from the Welsh *Glo*, coal, coal-mines, and *castrum*, Latin, a Roman fort or camp; Saxon, *ceaster*, a city,—the city of coal.

GLYN. (Br.) The woody vale.

GOADBY. Local. This name is derived from the Danish word *Gode*, that is, good, fair, rich, fine, and *by*, the Danish for a town—meaning the fair or handsome town. If the word is of British origin, it signifies the *town by the wood*, from *Goed*, in the Cor. Br., a wood.

GODARD. (Ger.) God-like disposition. The name may be local, from *Goddard*, a mountain in Switzerland.

GODENOT or GODENO'. (Fr.) "*A Jack in the box*," a puppet, a little ugly man. The name may be local, and come from *Gudenaw*, a town on the Lower Rhine, Germany.

GODFREY. (Ger.) God's peace, godlike peace, from *God* and *frid* or *frede*, peace, or from *Gau-fred*, joyful peace.

GODOLPHIN. (Cor. Br.) A little valley of springs; from *Godol*, a little valley, and *phin* or *phince*, springs.

GODWIN. Same as Goodwin or Gooden, derived from *God* or *good*, Sax., and *win*, conqueror, that is, a conqueror in God, converted or victorious in God.

"In one of those battles fought between Edmund the Anglo-Saxon, and Canute the Dane, the Danish army being routed and forced to fly, one of their principal captains named Ulf lost his way in the woods. After wandering all night, he met at daybreak a young peasant driving a herd of oxen whom he saluted, and asked his name. 'I am Godwin, the son of Ulfnoth,' said the young peasant, 'and thou art a Dane.' Thus, obliged to confess who he was, Ulf begged the young Saxon to show him the way to the Severn, where the Danish ships were at anchor. 'It is foolish in a

OF FAMILY NAMES. 143

Dane,' replied the peasant, 'to expect such a service from a
Saxon; and besides, the way is long, and the country people are all in arms.' The Danish chief drew off a gold ring
from his finger, and gave it to the shepherd as an induce-
ment to be his guide. The young Saxon looked at it for an
instant with great earnestness, and returned it, saying, 'I
will take nothing from thee, but I will try to conduct thee.'
Leading him to his father's cottage, he concealed him there
during the day; when night came on, they made prepara-
tions to depart together. As they were going, the old peasant said to Ulf, 'This is my only son, Godwin, who risks his
life for thee. He cannot return among his countrymen
again; take him, therefore, and present him to thy King,
Canute, that he may enter into his service.' The Dane
promised, and kept his word. The young Saxon peasant
was well received in the Danish camp, and rising from step
to step by the force of his talents, he afterward became
known over all England as the great *Earl Godwin.*"

GOFF. (Welsh.) *Gof,* a smith.

GOLBURN. (Cor. Br.) Local. The holy well.

GOLDSMITH. A name of trade; formerly in England, a
banker.

GOLLY or GOLLAH. Local. (Cor. Br.) The bottom, or
low place.

GOODALL. *Good-hall,* a fine hall or mansion; or *good-ale.*

GOODENOUGH. The same as *Godenot* or *Godeno'* (which
see).

GOODHUE. Compounded of good and Hugh. *Good-Hugh.*

GOODRICH. (Saxon.) *Goderick,* from *God,* God or good,
and *ric,* rich; rich in God, or in goodness.

GOODYEAR, GOODSIR, GOODSIRE. It is not difficult to
derive these.

GOOKIN. (Gaelic.) From *Gugan,* a bud, flower, a daisy.

144 ETYMOLOGICAL DICTIONARY

GORDON. *Gurtduine*, Gaelic, a fierce man; *Gwrddyn*, Welsh, a strong man; *Cawrdyn*, Welsh, a hero, a giant.
Some have derived the Gordons from *Gordinia*, in Thessaly; others say they are descendants of the Gorduni mentioned by Cæsar in his Commentaries. The name appears to be local, and may be derived from a town in France of that name, in the Department of Lot. It signifies in Gaelic the round hill, or the hill that surrounds, from *Gour*, round, and *dun*, a hill or fort.

GORING. Local. A battle field, a bloody place, from *gore*, bloody, and *ing*. A place in Sussex, England; an angle, a corner.

GORMAN. A native of Germany, the same as Germain (which see).

GORTEN. Local. (Gaelic.) From *Gairtean*, a garden, a small piece of arable land enclosed. *Gortan*, signifies a hungry, stingy, penurious fellow.

GOSPATRICK. Corrupted from the Latin "*Comes Patricius*," "Count Patrick," a title given to the Earl of March, of Scotland.

GOSS. (Saxon.) A goose, from *Gos*, a goose.

GOUDY. Local. From *Gouda*, a town in the Netherlands, in South Holland.

GOUPIL. (Fr.) An obsolete French word for *fox*.

GOW or GOWAN. (Gaelic.) A smith. The Gowan or smith of a Highland clan was held in high estimation. His skill in the manufacture of military weapons was usually united with great dexterity in using them, and with the strength of body which his profession required.
The Gowan usually ranked as third officer in the chief's household.

GOWER. Local. (Welsh.) *Gwyr*, a place in Glamorganshire, a place inclosed round, encircled. This peninsula is mostly surrounded by the sea and rivers.

OF FAMILY NAMES. 145

GRACE. Originally *Le Gros* ["the fat or large"], a name given to Raymond, one of the adherents of Strongbow, who was the ancestor of the family in Ireland.

GRAHAM, GRÆME, GRIMES. From the Anglo Saxon *Grim*, Dutch, *Grim*, Germ., *Grimm*, Welsh, *grem*, Gaelic, *gruaim*, surly, sullen, dark, having a fierce and stern look, courageous.

GRANGER. (Saxon.) One who superintended a large farm or Grange.

GRANT. On this name Playfair remarks that it may be derived from the Saxon, Irish, or French.
"In the Saxon, Grant signifies *crooked* or *bowed*. Thus *Cambridge*, the town and University in England so called, signifies a crooked bridge, or rather a bridge upon Cam River, or the crooked and winding river.
"The Saxons called this town *Grant Bridge, Cam* in the British, and *Grant* in the Saxon, being of the same signification, *crooked*.
"So *Mons Gramphius*, the Grampian Hill, was called by the Saxons *Granz Ben*, or the crooked hill, but we can not see how from this Saxon word the surname should be borrowed.
"In the old Irish, *Grandha* signifies ugly, ill-favored. *Grande* signifies dark or swarthy. *Grant* and *Ciar* signify much the same thing, or are synonymous words, and there being a tribe of the Grants called *Clan Chiaran*, it is the same as Clan Grant. Thus the surname might have been taken from a progenitor that was *Chiar* or *Grant*, that is to say, a swarthy or gray-headed man, and, though, in time, Grant became the common and prevailing surname, yet some always retained the other name, *Chiaran*, and are called *Clan Chiaran*. In the French *Grand* signifies great, brave, valorous, and from thence many are inclined to think that the surname *Grant* is taken from *Grand*, which in the Irish is sounded short, and thereby the letter *d* at the end of the word is changed into *t*, and thus *Grand* into

7

146   ETYMOLOGICAL DICTIONARY

Grant. The surname, it seems, was thus understood in England about five hundred years ago, for Richard Grant was made Archbishop of Canterbury in the year 1229, and is, in Mr. Anderson's Genealogical Tables, as well as by others, expressly called Richard Grant. But the English historians of that time, writing in Latin, call him *Richardus Magnus*, which plainly shows that they took *Grant* to be the same with the French *Grand*, and the Latin *Magnus*. To which let us add, that in the old writs, the article *the* is put before the surname *Grant.*"

GRANVILLE. Local. (Fr.) A town in France on the English channel, *Grande-ville*—the great town or city. *De Grandville.*

GRASSE. Local. From *Grasse*, a town in Piedmont, France. *De Grasse.*

GRAY. Local. A town in Burgundy, France, on the banks of the Saone. Rollo, Chamberlain to Robert, Duke of Normandy, received from him the castle and honor of Croy, in Picardy, whence his family assumed the name of *De Croy*, afterward changed into *De Gray.*

GREELY. Local. Probably the same as *Grelley* or *De Grelley*, from *Greilly*, in France. Leland, in his Roll of Battel Abbey, includes this name with those who came into England with William the Conqueror. *Grele*, French, slender, slim, delicate.

GREENOUGH and GREENO'. Local. The green hill.

GREER. A corruption of *Gregor*. Gilbert McGregor, second son of Malcom, Laird of McGregor, who settled at Nithesdale, Dumfries Co., Scotland, in 1374, left issue, who assumed the short appellation of *Greer*. Welsh, *Grewr*, a herdsman.

GREGOR. (Gaelic.) From *Greigh* a herd (Latin *Grex*), and *fear* a man, a herdsman. In the Cornish British *Gryger* or *Gruger* signifies a partridge.

OF FAMILY NAMES.

GREGORY. From the Greek Γρήγορος, watchful. It may be derived from *Gregor*, as some of the Clan M'Gregor changed their name to *Gregory*, when the clan was proscribed and outlawed.

GREIG. (Welsh.) From *Cryg*, hoarse.

GREY. See Gray.

GREW. (Br. and Welsh.) A crane.

GRIER. A contraction of Gregor, the same as *Greer* (which see).

GRIERSON. The son of Greer or Gregor; the same as McGregor.

GRIFFIN. A name given to a noted man, whose qualities or disposition, in some respects, resembled this fabulous creature. *Griffwn*, in Welsh, is applied to a man having a crooked nose, like a hawk's bill. *Gryffyn*, in the Cornish British, signifies "*to give.*" It may be the same as *Griffith*.

GRIFFITH. (Welsh and Cor. Br.) One who has strong faith, from *Cryf*, Welsh, strong, and *ffyd*, faith.

GRIMSBY. Local. A borough in Lincolnshire, England, on the Humber, so named from the appearance of the place or the character of the people. *Grim*, Saxon, fierce, rough, ugly, and *by*, a town—or the village or town of *Grimm*, the owner or founder.

GRINELL. (Fr.) Local. From *Grenelle*, a town in France.

GRISSELL. *Grisyl*, in the Cor. Br., signifies sharp, keen; *Grüs* or *Grys*, in the Dutch, is gray; *grissel*, gray-haired. *Grizzle* is the old familiar abbreviation of the name *Griselda*.

GROESBECK. (Dutch.) Local. Derived from the town of Groesbeck in Holland, so called from *Groot*, great, and *beck*, a brook.

GROOT or **GROAT.** (Dutch.) Local. Large, great, the great man. *Groot* is also a name of a town in Holland, whence the surname may be derived—the great town, *De Groot*.

148 ETYMOLOGICAL DICTIONARY

GROSCUP. (Ger.) From *gross*, big, and *kopf*, head—big-head.

GROSVENOR. A great hunter or the grand huntsman, from the French *Gros veneur*. The ancestor of the family assumed the name from holding the office of grand huntsman to the Dukes of Normandy.

GROVER. *Groover*, *Graver*, one who carves or engraves.

GUELPH. A wolf; the surname of the present Royal Family of England. We have the following amusing tradition of the origin of the royal house of *Guelph:*

" It is told in the chronicles that as far back as the days of Charlemagne, one Count Isenbrand, who resided near the Lake of Constance, met an old woman who had given birth to three children at once, a circumstance which appeared to him so portentous and unnatural that he assailed her with a torrent of abuse. Stung to fury by his insults, she cursed the Count, and wished that his wife, then enciente, might bring at a birth as many children as there are months in the year. The imprecation was fulfilled, and the countess became the mother of a dozen babes at once. Dreading the vengeance of her severe lord, she bade her maid go drown eleven of the twelve. But whom should the girl meet while on this horrible errand but the Count himself, who, suspecting that all was not right, demanded to know the contents of the basket. '*Welfen*,' was the intrepid reply (*i. e.,* the old German term for puppies or young wolves). Dissatisfied with this explanation, the Count lifted up the cloth, and found under it eleven bonny infants nestled together. Their unblemished forms reconciled the scrupulous knight, and he resolved to recognize them as his lawful progeny. Thenceforward, their children and their descendants went by the name of *Guelph* or *Welf*."

GUEY. Welsh, *Gwiw*, good, excellent.

GUIAR. (Spanish.) A guide.

GUIOT. The son of Guy; a guide.

OF FAMILY NAMES.

149

GUISCHARD or GUISCARD. (Nor.) A wily or crafty man, a shifter.

GUNTER. Supposed to be the same as *Ingulphus*, from *In* and *golpe*, Belgic, to swallow down, to devour. The name may be local, and given to a native of Gaunt or Ghent.

GUNN or GOON. (Br.) Local. From *Gun*, a plain, a down or common; Welsh, *gwaen*.

"A person whose name was *Gunn* complained to a friend that his attorney, in his bill, had not *let him off easily*. 'That's no wonder,' said his friend, '*as he charged you too high!*' But this is not so good as an entry in the custom-house books of Edinburgh, where it appears that '*A*,' meaning Alexander—'*A. Gunn was discharged for making a false report!*'"—LOWER.

Lower also tells us of a German named *Feuerstein* (fire-stone—the German for flint) who settled in the West when the French population prevailed in that quarter. His name, therefore, was changed into French *Pierre à Fusil*, but in the course of time, the Anglo-American race became the prevalent one, and *Pierre à Fusil* was again changed into *Peter Gun*.

GUNNING. Belonging to Gunn, the son of Gunn.

GUNSALUS. *Goncalez*, the son of Goncale, the supposed founder of Castile. *Gonzales*, Spanish; *Gonsalves* (Port.), consolation, in safety, in salvation.

GURDIN. (Welsh.) A strong man, from *gwrdd*, strong, and *dyn*, a man; also, *gwyrdd-din*, the green hill or inclosure.

GURNEY. Local. From the town of *Gournay*, in Normandy.

GURR. *Gur*, in Welsh, signifies a man or husband.

GUTHRIE. Warlike, powerful in war, from *guth*, Saxon, war. *Guthmor*, Gaelic, loud-voiced. Guthrie, a town in Scotland. *Gutric*, *Gotric*, *Gotricus*, rich in goodness, rich in God.

150   ETYMOLOGICAL DICTIONARY

GUY. A term given in Gaul to the mistletoe, or cure-all; also a guide, a leader or director, from *Guia*, Sp. and Port.

GWYNNE, GUINEE, and WINNE. (Welsh.) From *Gwyn*, white.

GY. Local. A town of France. *Gye*, to guide.

HACKER. (Dutch.) A chopper, a cleaver, hewer; figuratively, a brave soldier. Danish, *Hakker*, to cut in pieces, to chop, to hoe. *Hekker*, a hedge, from *hekke*, a hedge, a protection, place of security.

HADLEY. Local. A town of Suffolk, and also of Essex, England, from *houdt*, a wood, and *ley*, a place or field.

HAFF. (Ger.) A sea, bay, or gulf; in Cor. Br., *Haf*, summer. *Hof*, Ger., a court; *Hoff*, Welsh, dear, beloved.

HAGADORN. (Dutch.) Local. Hawthorn.

HAGAR. *Hagar*, Hebrew, a stranger; one fearing. *Hygar*, in the Welsh, is amiable, pleasing. *Hegar*, Cor. Br., lovely; also, a bondman, a slave. *'Aigher*, Gaelic, gladness, joy, mirth.

HAINEAU. Local. From *Haineau*, a city of Hesse Cassel, Germany.

HAINES or HAYNES. Camden derives the name from *Ainulph*, and that from *Ana*, alone, and *ulph*, Sax., help, that is one who needs not the assistance of others. *Haine*, a river in Belgium. *Haine*, Fr., signifies malicious, full of hatred. *Hain*, German, a wood, forest, thicket, grove.

HAINSWORTH and **HAYNSWORTH.** (Anglo-Saxon.) Local. The farm or place in the forest or grove, from *haine*, German and Saxon, a wood, and *worth*, a place inclosed, cultivated. British and Welsh, the estate on the river.

HALDEN. Local. A contraction of *Haledon*, a place in Northumberland, England, from the Saxon *halig*, holy, and *dun*, a hill; a place where Oswald got the victory of Cad-

OF FAMILY NAMES.   **151**

wallader, the Briton, and from this circumstance was called
the Holy Hill, and also *the Heavenly Field.*

HALE, HAYLE, or HAL.   (Welsh.)   A moor; also, *Hayle,* a
salt-water river.

HALES.   Local.   From a village in Gloucestershire, and also a
town in Norfolk, England.   In Cor. Br., it signifies low,
level lands washed by a river or the sea; a moor.   Playfair
says, "The word Hales is a compound one, being formed of
the Saxon *Hale* or *Heile,* strong, healthy, and *ley,* etc.
Others derive it from *Halig,* Saxon, holy.

HALIFAX.   (Sax.)   Local.   From the city of Halifax, in Yorkshire, England, so called from *Halig,* holy, and *faex,* hair—
holy hair; from the sacred hair of a certain virgin whom a
clerk beheaded because she would not comply with his de-
sires.   She was afterward canonized.   From this circumstance, the village was also called *Horton,* from *Haer,* Sax.,
hair, and *ton,* a town.

HALKETT.   The name of Halkett, in the writs of the family,
is promiscuously written "*de Hawkhead*" and "*de Halkett.*"
It is territorial or local, and was assumed by the proprietor
of the lands and barony of Hawkshead, in Renfrewshire, as
soon as surnames became hereditary in Scotland.

HALLAM.   From *Hall,* Welsh, salt, and *ham,* a house or village, from its manufacture in that place, or being situated
near the salt water.   It may be derived from *Hal* or *Hayle,*
a moor, and *ham,*—the house on the moor.   *Halham,* the
house on the hill, from *Hal,* Cornish British, a hill.

HALLER.   (Ger.)   From *Haller,* a man belonging to a salt-
work.

HALLETT.   Little Hal, or Henry, the diminutive termination
ett being added, as Willett, Ellett.

HALLIDAY.   "Holy-day."   It is said this name had its ori-
gin in the *Slogan,* or war-cry of a Gaelic clan residing in
Annandale, who made frequent *raids* on the English border.
On these occasions they employed the war-cry of "A holy-

152   ETYMOLOGICAL DICTIONARY

day," every day, in their estimation, being holy, that was spent in ravaging the enemy's country.

HALLOWELL. Holy well.

HALPEN. (Welsh.) The head of the moor or salt river. Gaelic, *Alpin*, the highest land, peak of a mountain, from *Alp* and *ben*.

HALSE. Local. (Dutch.) *Hals*, the neck, a narrow tract of land, projecting from the main body.

HALSEY. Local. From *Hals*, and *ey* or *ig*, Saxon, an island, water, the sea; the neck on the water, or running into the sea. The island neck.

HALSTEAD. Local. A town in Essex, England, from *Hals*, as given above, and *sted*, a place. Holsted, a town in North Jutland, that is, the *low place; Hol*, Dutch, *hollow*, and *stead*, a place: a house or town in a hollow place.

HAM. Local. A house, borough, or village, the termination of many names of places in England; German, *heim*, a home; France.

HAMILTON. Originally *Hambleton*, from the manor of Hambleton, in Buckinghamshire. William, third son of Robert, third Earl of Leicester, took that surname from the place of his birth, as above. He was the founder of the family of that name in Scotland, whither he went about the year 1215. The name is derived from *Hamell*, a mansion, the seat of a freeholder, and *dun*, an enclosure, a fortified place, a town.

HAMLIN. Local. A corruption of *Hammeline*, which was taken from *Hamelen*, a town on the river Weser, Germany. Hamelin, a town in Scotland, so called from *Ham*, a house or village, and *lin*, a waterfall, a small lake or pond.

HAMMEL. (Armoric.) A house, a close, a place of rest, a home. *Hamle*, a river in Brunswick, Germany.

HAMMOND. *Ham-mount*, the town or house on the elevation. It may come from *Hamon*.

OF FAMILY NAMES.

HAMON. (Heb.) Faithful.

HAMPTON. Local. The town on the hill; a village in Middlesex, England.

HANNA. Local. From *Hanan*, a strong city in Hesse Cassel, Germany. *Hana*, Saxon, a cock; figuratively, a leader, a chief man.

HANDEL. (Danish.) Trade, commerce; to trade, traffic; *handel*, Dutch, traffic, commerce, mechanic art, profession, business, or employment.

HANDSEL. (Danish.) To deliver into the hand. An earnest money for the first sale. A New Year's gift.

HANFORD. Local. (Welsh.) From *hen*, old, and *ford*, a way; "the old way."

HANHAM. (Welsh.) *Hen*, old, and Saxon, *ham*, a town; that is, the old town.

HANKS. A nurse-name, or an abbreviation of John, the "*s*" being added for "son;" so "Sims," and "Gibbs," etc.

HANLEY. Local. From the town of Hanley, in Shropshire. The old place or field, from *Hen* or *Han*, old, and *ley*, a place, a common.

HANSEL. Local. (Saxon.) A free market or hall, from *haunse* or *hanse*, a society, *hansa*, Gothic, a multitude, and *sel*, a hall.

HANSON. The son of *Hans* or John, same as Johnson. Bailey derives it from *Han*, the diminutive of Randall, the son of Randall.

HANWAY. A native of *Hainault*, which country was called *Hanway*, in the time of Henry VIII.

HARCOURT. Local. From the lordship of Harcourt, in Normandy. *Har*, from Saxon *Here*, an army, and *court*.

HARDING. Local. *Har*, from *here*, an army, and *ing*, a meadow or common. The place where an army was encamped.

154   ETYMOLOGICAL DICTIONARY

HARDY. (Fr.) Bold, free, noble.

HARGILL. Local. Hartgill, a small river in England. "The deer-brook."

HARGRAVE. Saxon. The provider or commissary of an army, from *Here* or *Har*, an army, and *grave*, a steward or disposer.

HARLEY, HARLEIGH, and HARLOW. Local. From a town in Essex, England; the place of the army. From *Here*, Saxon, an army, and *ley*, a place, a field.

HARMAN, says Verstegan, "should rightly be *Heartman*, to wit, a man of heart and courage." Probably the same as *Herman*, from *Here*, an army, and *man*, a soldier.

HAROLD. In old Anglo Saxon, signifies "The love of the army." From *Har*, an army, and *hold*, love.

HARRINGTON. Local. From the parish of Harrington, in Cumberland, corrupted from Haverington, so called from *Haver*, Dutch, *Haber*, Teut., oats. *ing*, a field, and *ton*. The town in or surrounded by oat fields.

HARRIS, HARRISON, and HERRIES. The son of Henry.

HARROWER. The subduer; from the French *harrier*, to harrass;—and this, perhaps, from the Anglo Saxon, *hergian*, to conquer or subdue;—one who harrows the ground.

HARTFIELD. Local. The deer field.

HARTGILL. Same as Hargill (which see).

HARTSHORN. The horn of the hart or male deer; an emblem or sign over a shop or inn, whence the name, "*Will at the Hartshorn.*"

HARTWELL. Local. From a village in Buckingham, England, noted for being some years the residence of Louis XVIII. The well or spring frequented by deer.

HARVEY. (Sax.) From *here*, an army, and *wic*, a fort.

OF FAMILY NAMES.

155

HASBROUCK. Local. Derived from the town of *Hazebrouck*, in the province of Artois, France.

HASCALL or **HASKELL.** (Welsh.). From *hasg*, a place of rushes, or sedgy place, and *hall* or *hayle*, a moor. "The sedgy place." *Asgall*, in the Gaelic, signifies a sheltered place, a retreat, and with the addition of the aspirate "H," might make the name.

HASWELL. (Dutch or Germ.) *Hasveldt*, from *Hase*, a river in Westphalia, and *veldt*, a field, corrupted into *well*; or from *Wald*, German, a wood or forest,—the forest on the Hase. The name may also signify the *misty* place, or the *Wild* or field of *hares*, from *Haas*, Dutch, a hare.

HASTINGS. Local. Derived from the borough of *Hastings*, in Sussex, England, which is memorable for the landing of William the Conqueror, and defeat and death of Harold II., in 1066.

Camden derives this name from one Hastings, a Dane, a great robber, who either seized, or built, or fortified it. Somnerus derives it from the Saxon *haeste*, heat, because of the bubbling or boiling of the sea in that place; but as *haste* applies rather to voluntary beings, as men and other animals, the name more correctly signifies one who hurries, presses, drives; vehemency, quickness of motion.

HATCH. Local. A kind of door or floodgate. These ancient *stops* or *hatches* consisted of sundry great stakes and piles erected by fishermen in the river Thames or other streams, for their better convenience of securing fish. Also, a term for gates leading to deer-parks or forests.

HATHAWAY. Local. Derived from Port Haethwy, in Wales.

HATFIELD. Local. From a town in Hertfordshire, also in Essex and Yorkshire, England. Bailey says it is from *Hat*, hot, Sax., and *field*—from the hot sandy soil. *Houtfield*, the

156 ETYMOLOGICAL DICTIONARY

field in the wood, from *hout*, Dutch, a wood. Perhaps the same as Heathfield.

HATHORN. Local. A dwelling near hawthorns.

HATTON. Local. A town in Warwickshire, England. The town on the height; *haut*, Fr., high. *Haughton*, the town in the meadow or vale. *Houdt-ton*, Dutch, the town in the wood. Shortly after the Conquest, Hugh Montfort's second son, Richard, being Lord of Hatton in Warwickshire, took the name of Hatton.

HAUGH. Local. A little meadow lying in a valley.

HAVEMEYER. (Danish and Dutch.) A garden-master.

HAVENS. From *Haven*, a harbor.

HAVERILL. Local. Derived from the town of Haverill, in Suffolk, England, so named from the Dutch *Haver;* Teut., *Haber*, oats, and *hill*.

HAW and HAWES. (Sax.) *Haeg*, a small inclosure near a house, a haugh, a close. The name of a town in England.

HAWLEY. From *Haw*, a hedge, Saxon, *haeg*, a small piece of ground near a house, a close, a place where hawthorns grow, and *ley*, a field or meadow.

HAY. A hedge, an inclosure, to inclose, fence in, a protection, a place of safety. In Dutch, *Haag;* Sax., *Hege;* Ger., *Heck;* Danish, *Hekke;* Swedish, *Hagn;* Fr., *Haie;* Welsh, *Cae;* Gaelic, *Ca;* Cor. Br., *Hay*.

"In the reign of Kenneth III. (says Douglass), about 980, the Danes having invaded Scotland, were encountered by that king, near Loncarty, in Perthshire. The Scots at first gave way, and fled through a narrow pass, where they were stopped by a countryman of great strength and courage, and his two sons, with no other weapons than the yokes of their plows. Upbraiding the fugitives for their cowardice, he succeeded in rallying them; the battle was renewed, and the Danes totally discomfited. It is said, that after the victory was obtained, the old man, lying on the ground

OF FAMILY NAMES. 157

wounded and fatigued, cried '*Hay, Hay,*' which word became the surname of his posterity. The king, as a reward for that signal service, gave him as much land in the Carse of Gowrie as a falcon should fly over before it settled; and a falcon being accordingly let off, flew over an extent of ground six miles in length, afterward called Errol, and lighted on a stone still called *Falconstone* or *Hawkstone.*"

HAYCOCK. A name probably given to a foundling exposed in a hayfield.

HAYDEN and HAYDYN. Local. Heyden, a town of Denmark; a place built, made, inclosed, or cultivated, from *daane,* Danish, to form, to fashion, to make, cultivate.

HAYFORD. *Hay,* an inclosure, and *ford,* a way—the road or way inclosed, or the way through the inclosure or park.

HAYMAN. (Sax.) A high man, or may be the same as Hayward (which see).

HAYNE or HAYNES. (See Haine.)

HAYNER. (Ger.) From *Hech* or *Hohe,* high, and *narr,* a fool, a jester, a merry fellow, king's fool. Perhaps, like George Buchanan, who was so called, a wise and learned man.

HAYNSWORTH. (See Hainsworth.)

HAYWARD. Anciently in England the keeper of the common herd or cattle of a town, from the Saxon *hieg,* hay, and *ward,* a keeper.

HAZARD. (Br.) From *ard,* nature, and *has,* high—of high disposition, proud, independent.

HAZELRIGG. Local. The hazel-ridge.

HAZELWOOD. Local. A wood where hazel-nuts grow.

HAZEN or HASEN. (Dan.) A hare.

HEAD. Anciently written *Hede* or *Hide.* Probably from the place written Hede or Hide in Doomsday Book, now *Hithe,* in Kent, England, where the earliest traces of the Head family are found. From the Anglo-Saxon *Hithe,* a harbor, a shelter for boats.

158 ETYMOLOGICAL DICTIONARY

HEATON. (Saxon.) Local. The high town or hill, from *Hea*, high, and *ton*.

HEBER. (Heb.) Derived either from *Heber*, one of the ancestors of Abraham, or from the Hebrew word *eber*, which signifies "from the other side," that is, foreigners.

HECKER. (Dan.) *Hekker*, a hedger, from *hekke*, a hedge, a protection.

HEDD. (Welsh.) Peace; *haidd*, barley.

HEDGES. Local. A fence of thorn-bushes; a thicket of shrubs; an inclosure of shrubs or small trees.

HEDON. Local. From a town in England of the same name —the high town.

HELLIER or **HILLIER.** In the dialect of Dorsetshire, England, signifies a thatcher or tiler.

HELLING. Local. *Hellan*, in the Welsh, signifies the elms— the place of elms. *Helling*, in the Dutch, means a slope or declivity.

HELMER or **ELMER.** Contracted from Ethelmer, noble, renowned. *Holmer*, the low, shallow pond or lake, from *Hol*, Sax., low, and *mer*, a pond. *Halemer*, Cor. Br., the lake in the moor, or the salt water.

HENDERSON. The son of Hendrik or Henry.

HENLEY. Local. From a market-town in Oxfordshire, also a town in Warwickshire, England. From *Hen*, old, and *ley*, a field or common.

HENRY. Verstegan derives this name from *Einrick*, ever rich; others from *Herrick*, rich lord or master; Camden, from the Latin *Honoricus*, honorable. Kilian writes it *Heynrick*—Heymrick, *i. e.*, rich at home.

HERBERT. (Sax.) From *Here*, a soldier, and *beorht*, bright —an expert soldier, or the glory of an army; famous in war.

OF FAMILY NAMES. 159

HERIOT. A provider of furniture for an army. A fine paid to a lord at the death of a landlord.

HERISSON. Local. From a town by that name in France.

HERMAN. (Sax.) From *Here*, an army, and *man*. A man of the army; a soldier. *Here* and *Hare* signify both an army and lord.

HERMANCE. (Germ.) A ruler. *Heermensch*, Dutch, a master, from *Heer*, a master, lord, or ruler, and *mensch*, a man.

HERNDON. Local. From *Herne*, a cottage, and *den*, a valley. The cottage in the valley.

HERNE. May come from the Saxon *Hern*, a cottage.

HERNSHAW. Local. From *hern*, a kind of fowl, a hern, and *shaw*, a shady inclosure, a place where herns breed.

HERON. (Welsh.) A hero.

HERR. (German.) Sire, lord, master.

HERRICK. The same as Erick or Erricks (which see).

HERRING. *Hirring*, a town in the Diocese of Alburg, Denmark.

HERSEY. Local. From *Herseaux*, in the Netherlands.

HEYDEN. Local. From a town in Westphalia, also a town of the same name in South Jutland, Denmark.

HEYMAN or **HAYMAN.** (Sax.) A high man.

HEWER, HUER, and **EUER.** A person stationed on the sea-shore, to watch and notify the fishermen of the shoals of fish; from the Saxon, *Earian*, to show.

HEWIT. The son of Hugh.

HIBBARD. Same as Hubbard and Hubert (which see).

HICCOCK. The son of Hig or Hugh; *cock* signifying *little*,—

6*

160 ETYMOLOGICAL DICTIONARY

little Hig. It may be a corruption of *Haycock* (which see).

HICKS. Hig(s) or Hick(s). The son of Hugh. Hig or Hick being a common nick-name for Hugh. *Hick,* in the Dutch, signifies a simpleton.

HICKEY. The *Huicci, Gwychi,* a word signifying valiant men, anciently possessed Warwickshire, Worcestershire, and a part of Gloucestershire, England.

HIERNE. (Dan.) Local. An angle, a corner.

HIGGINBOTTOM. A corruption of the German name, *Ickenbaum,* that is, oak-tree.

HIGGINS. Little Hig or Hugh; the son of Hugh; from *Hig,* and the patronymic termination *ings;* belonging to, or the son of.

HILDYARD and HILYARD. Anciently Hildheard. *Hild,* in Saxon, is a hero or heroine, as *Hildebert,* illustrious hero, and *heard,* in the same language, a pastor or keeper.

HINCKLEY. Local. From Hinckley, a town in Leicestershire, England.

HINDMAN and HINMAN. A domestic, a servant; one who has the care of herds.

HINDON or HINTON. Local. A borough in Wiltshire, England. Welsh, *Henton,* the old town, from *Hen,* old.

HIPPISLEY. Local. From the Saxon *Hiope,* a hip-berry, or wood-rose, and *ley,* a field.

HIPWOOD. Local. The wood where sweet-briars or roses grow.

HITCHENS. Local. A town in Hertfordshire, England.

HOAG. (Welsh.) Low in stature, small.

HOARE. White, hoar, gray.

HOBART. The same as Hubert (which see).

OF FAMILY NAMES. **161**

HOBBS. From *Hob*, the nick-name for Robert.

HOBBY. (Dan.) Local. From *hob*, a herd, and *by*, a town; the town of herds or flocks.

HOBKINS. From *Hob*, Robert, and the patronymic termination *kins;* the same as Robertson or Hobson.

HOBSON. The son of Hob, or Robert.

HODD. From the Dutch *Houdt*, a wood; the same as Hood.

HODGE. The same as *Roger*, which signifies quiet or strong counsel.

HODGES. From Hodge, a nick-name of Roger, the "s" being added for son.

HODGEKINS. From Hodge, as above, and the patronymic termination *kins*:—changed now to *Hotchkiss*.

HODSON. The son of Hod or Hodge.

HOE. (Welsh.) A state of rest, a stay; ease, quiet. *Hoh*, Saxon, the heel. Local, *Haut*, Fr., high, the top, summit, noisy, proud, haughty.

HOFF. (Danish and Dutch.) A court, residence, palace.

HOFFMAN. (Dutch.) From *Hoofdman*, a captain, a director, head or chief man. *Hofman*, from *Hof*, a court—the man of the court.

HOGAN. In the Cornish, *mortal*, in the Gaelic, a young man, from "*Og*," young. *Hogyn*, Welsh, a stripling.

HOGARTH. (Dutch.) From *hoogh*, high, and *aerd*, nature or disposition.

HOGG. Same as Hoag (which see).

HOGGEL. From the Norman, *Hugel*, a hill.

HOLBECH. Local. A place in the county of Lincoln, England; the low brook, or the brook in the ravine or hollow. *Holzbeck*, the brook in the wood.

HOLCOMBE, or HOLTCOMBE. Local. (Saxon.) A woody vale, from *Holt* or *Hultz*, a wood, and *combe*, a valley.

162 ETYMOLOGICAL DICTIONARY

HOLDEN. (Danish.) Safe, entire, wealthy; a safe place held, protected, defended.

HOLLAND. Local. A name given to a native of that country, which was so called from *Hollow-land*, because it abounds with ditches full of water. Bailey is of opinion that the Danes who conquered Holland, so called it from an island in the Baltic of the same name, from *ol*, beer, drink. Why not from *Hold land*, the land taken and kept, held, governed?

HOLLENBECK. From Hollenbach a town on the Rhine, Germany.

HOLMAN. A corruption of *Allemand*, a German, that is, a mixture of all men, *Alle-mann.*

HOLME and HOLMES. Local. Meadow lands near or surrounded by water, grassy plains; sometimes an island.

HOLSAPPLE. Local. From *Holz*, German, a wood, an apple, or *apfel*, an orchard; apple-trees in or near a wood.

HOLT. Local. A small hanging wood, from *Hultz*, Dutch, a wood; a peaked hill covered with wood; a grove of trees around a house.

HOLYWELL. Local. A place of importance in Flintshire, Wales. Geraldus Cambrensis says that there was formerly near this place a rich mine of silver. Wenefride's Well, from which the name of Holy Well was given to this place, springs from a rock at the foot of a steep hill. The well is an oblong square about twelve feet by seven.

HOME and HUME. Same as Holmes (which see).

HOMER. Greek, Ὅμηρος, a hostage, a pledge or security.

HONE. Welsh. *Hoen*, joy. *Honan*, the son of Hone.

HOMFRAY. From the French *Homme-vrai*, a true man.

HOOD. (Sax.) Local. From *houdt*, the wood.

OF FAMILY NAMES.

163

HOOGABOOM. (Dutch.) High-tree, from *Hoog*, high, and *boom*, tree, either local or expressive of stature.

HOOPER. A cooper.

HOOGSTRATEN. (Dutch.) Local. High-street.

HOPE. Local. The side of a hill, or low ground between hills.

HOPKINS. Little Robert, or the child of Robert. The same as Hobkins (which see).

HOPPER. (Sax.) *Hoppere*, a dancer.

HORE. *Hoar*, white, gray. *Horr*, Local a ravine.

HORNBLOWER. A musician, one that blows a horn.

HORTON. Local. A town in Yorkshire England—the *horrible* town, or the town in the ravine, from *Horr*, a ravine.

HOSFORD. Local. From *Ouseford*, in England, the "o" being aspirated—that is, the ford or way of the river *Ouse*.

HOSKINS or **HASKINS.** (Cor. Br.) From *Heschen* or *Hoskyn*, the place of rushes, the sedgy place.

HOTCHKISS. The same as *Hodgkins* (which see).

HOTHAM. Assumed from the place of residence, Hotham in Yorkshire, probably derived from the Saxon word *Hod*, a hood or covering, and *ham*, a house, farm, or village, or a piece of ground near a house or village, both of which terms are applicable to the situation of Hotham. *Houtham* signifies a place at or near a wood, from the Dutch *Hout*, a wood.

HOUGH. Local. A place so named in the county of Lincoln, England. Saxon and Dutch, *Hoch*, *Hoog*, and *How*, high.

HOUGHTAILING. (Dutch.) From *Hoofd*, head or chief, and *telling*, counting or telling, that is, head clerk or account-ant; a money-master, a money-collector. *Hough*, *hauff*, *haife*, a pile, a lump; *dell*, to pay, give over. Sax., *daelan;* Dutch, *deelen;* Ger., *theilen*, to separate, give, pay over.

164   ETYMOLOGICAL DICTIONARY

HOUGHTON. Local. A town in Lancashire, England. Sax., from *hoog*, or *hoch*, high, and *ton*, a hill, castle, or town.

HOUSE. A covering, a dwelling place, a mansion.

HOUSTON. Local. From the parish of Houston, in Renfrewshire, Scotland. There is an old tradition, that in the reign of Malcolm IV., A.D. 1153, Hugh Padvinan obtained a grant of the barony of Kilpeter, from Baldwin of Biggar, sheriff of Lanark, and hence called Hughstown, corrupted into Houstoun. These Houstons were of great consideration in Renfrewshire.

HOWARD. William, son of Roger Fitz Valevine, took the name of Howard from being born in the Castle of Howard, in Wales, in the time of Henry I. Spelman derives Howard from *Hof-ward*, the keeper of a hall; Vestegan, from *Hold-ward*, the keeper of a stronghold; Camden, from *Hoch-ward*, the high keeper.

HOWE or HOO. A high place, a hill; critically, a hill in a valley. *De La Howe*, "from the hill," was originally the name of the family. They came to England with William the Conqueror. (See Athill.)

HOWELL. (Cor. Br.) From *Houl*, the sun; Greek, Ἥλος, *Euhill*, high, exalted.

HOWLETT. A night-bird, an owl.

HUBAND. Anciently *Hubaude*, from *Hugh*, and *baude*, bold— bold Hugh.

HUBBARD. (Anglo-Saxon.) A corruption of Hubert, *i. e.*, bright form, fair hope.

HUBBELL. Local. From *Hubba*, a Danish chief, and *hill*— Hubba's-hill or Hubhill. *Hub* means a heap or a lump, and may indicate a small round hill on the summit of another.

HUBERT. Bright form, fair hope; Saxon, *hiewe*, color, form, beauty, and *beort*, bright.

OF FAMILY NAMES.

HUCKSTEP. A corruption of *De Hoghstepe*—"from the high steep."

HUDDLESTON. Local. From a small parish by that name in the West Riding of Yorkshire.

HUDSON. The son of Hod or Roger.

HUGET. Little Hugh, the son of Hugh.

HUGGINS. The same as Higgins, from *Hug*, the nickname for Hugh, and the patronymic termination *ings*, belonging to, or the son of.

HUGHES. The son of Hugh. Aventinus derives Hugh from *Hougen*, that is, slasher or cutter. Alfred, in the year 900, used Hugh to denote comfort. Hugh in the Gaelic, is *Aoidh*, which signifies affability, a guest, a stranger. *Hu* suggests the idea of elevation; *Ho*, *Hu*, highness.

HULET or **HOWLET.** A small owl. *Heulaidd*, Welsh, sun-like; *heuledd*, sunshine.

HULL. Local. From the city of *Hull*, in Yorkshire, England, which comes from the Teutonic or Saxon *Hulen* or *Heulen*, to howl, from the noise the river Hull makes when it meets there with the sea. *Hull* is an old word for a hill; *Hull*, Welsh, a rough, uneven place.

The city of Hull was anciently famous for its good government, whence arose this old saying, called the Beggars' and Vagrants' Litany:

> "From Hell, Hull, and Halifax,
> Good Lord deliver us!"

From *Hull*, because of the severe chastisement they met with there, and from *Halifax*, for a law there instantly beheading with an engine, without any legal proceedings, those who were taken in the act of stealing cloth—either being probably more terrible than *Hell* itself.

HULSE. From the town and manor of Hulse, in Great Budworth, Cheshire, England. *Holtz*, Ger., a wood.

166   ETYMOLOGICAL DICTIONARY

HUMPHREY. (Anglo-Saxon.) From *Humfred*, that is, house-peace—a lovely and happy name.

HUNGERFORD. Local. A market-town in Berkshire, England, on the Kennet. *Hunger's pass* or *way*, so called from Hunger, a celebrated Danish leader who invaded England.

HUNN. A native of Hungary, or from the German *Hune*, a giant; a Scythian.

HUNT or HONT. It occurs in Chaucer for huntsman.

HUNTINGTON. (Sax.) *Hunter's-don*, the mount of hunters; the name of a shire and town in England.

HUNTLEY. Local. A town in Aberdeenshire, Scotland; the hunting field.

HURD. (Welsh.) From *Hurdh*, a ram.

HURST. (Saxon.) Local. A wood, a grove; fruit-bearing trees.

HUSTED. Local. *Hus*, Sax., a house, and *sted*, a fixed place.

HUTCHINS. The child of Hugh. (See Hitchins.)

HUTCHINSON. The son of Hitchins or Hutchins.

HUTTON. Local. A town in England; the high town. Camden defines the name to signify a mutineer. *Hutain*, in French, is haughty, proud.

HYDE. Local. A farm; as much land as can be cultivated with one plow; a town of Cheshire, England. *Hyd*, or *Hithe*, a landing place, a haven, harbor.

IDE. The same as Hide or Hyde (which see), the "*H*" being dropped in the pronunciation. *Iden*, a small town in England.

ILSLEY. Local. *Isle's-ley*, the place on the island.

INCLEDON. Local. *Ingleton*, the beacon hill, the fire-hill, or hill of alarm, so named from an ancient custom of kindling a fire on an eminence, as a signal of invasion or danger.

OF FAMILY NAMES.

167

INGE. *Ing*, Saxon, a pasture, a meadow or watering place, low ground. Danish, *Eng*, a meadow, meadow ground, pasture; a place near a river. Welsh, *Ing*, narrow, a strait.

INGLEBY or **INGOLDSBY.** Local. *Inglesby*, the town of the English, or Angles; perhaps the town was first named at the time the Angles first invaded Britain. *Ing-gil-by*, Saxon, the town near the brook in the narrow valley. A town in Lincolnshire, England.

INGLIS or **INGLES.** The name was given in Scotland, to distinguish the family of some English settler. The Englishman. In the ancient records of the family the name *Anglicus* is often mentioned.

INGHAM. Local. The town on the low ground, meadow or pasture.

INGRAHAM or **INGRAM.** (Ger.) Camden derives this name from *Engelramus*, from *Engel*, Saxon, angel, and *rein*, purity. Pure as an angel.

INNIS or **INNES.** The same as *Ennis* (which see). This family is of great antiquity in Scotland, and derives its surname from the lands of *Innis*, a word supposed to be derived from the Gaelic *Inch*, an island, part of that barony being an island, formed by the two branches of a stream running through the estate.

IPRES. Local. A town in the Netherlands, and has its name from the small river Yperlee on which it stands.

IRELAND. A name given to a native of that island. Ireland signifies West-land, from the Gaelic *Iar*, the West, and the Teutonic *land*, Welsh, *Llan*, a clear place, a lawn.

IRETON. Local. From Ireton, a manor in County Derby, England. In Gaelic, the west town or hill.

IRISH. A native of Ireland, the country from which the nominal founder of the family came.

168   ETYMOLOGICAL DICTIONARY

IRON. A name taken from the mineral kingdom.

IRVING or IRVINE. Local. From a river and town of the same name in Ayrshire, Scotland.

ISAAC. (Heb.) Laughter.

ISHAM. Local. *Isis-ham*, that is, the town on the river Isis, in Northamptonshire, England.

ISLIP. Local. A village near Oxford, England; the name signifies a place on the edge or brink of the water; an island.

ISRAEL. (Heb.) Prevailing in the Lord; a name given to the Patriarch Jacob.

IVES. Local. From a town named St. Ives, in the county of Huntingdon, England. O'Connor derives *Ive* from *Iber*, the place of *Er*, the land of heroes, now pronounced Ive or Hy. Gaelic, *Ives*.

IVER. (Gaelic and Welsh.) A chief or leader. *Iver*, Danish, zeal, fervor; *ivre*, to speak or act with zeal. Gaelic, *Ian Vhor*, a hero; Welsh, *eon*, brave, and *mawr*, great.

JACK. The same as John.

JACKSON. The son of Jack, or John.

JACOB. (Heb.) He that supplants.

JACOBSON. The son of Jacob.

JAMES. (Heb.) The same as Jacob, he that supplants.

JAMESON or JAMIESON. The son of James.

JANES. The son of Jane.

JANEWAY. A Genoese.

JASON. (Greek.) Healing.

JEFFERS or JEFFREY. Corrupted from Geoffrey or Godfrey, German, from *God* and *fried*, God's peace, or from *Gau* and *fried*, joyful peace. This name was borne by the chief of the royal house of Plantagenet.

OF FAMILY NAMES.

JEMSE. Local. A town in Sweden.

JENKINS. From Jenks or John, and the patronymic termination *ings*, belonging to, or son of John.

JENKINSON. The son of Jenkins.

JENKS. The same as Johns; the son of John.

JENNER. An old form for *Joiner*.

JENNINGS. The same as Jenkins.

JEROME. The same as Jeremiah.

JESSUP. *Giuseppe*, Italian, the same as Joseph.

JETTER. (Fr.) *Jéter*, to overthrow; *Jouteur*, a tilter, fencer, a swordsman.

JEW. A contraction of *Judah*, Hebrew.

JEWELL. Joy, mirth, precious; a jewel, a precious stone; a name expressive of fondness.

JEWETT. The little Jew, the son of a Jew; *Jouet*, French, toy, sport.

JOB. (Heb.) Sorrowful; patient.

JOBSON. The son of Job.

JOHN. (Heb.) Gracious; God's grace.

JOHNSON. The son of John.

JOLLIE. ((Fr. and Sax.) Full of life and mirth.

JONADAB. (Heb.) Liberal, one who acts a prince.

JONAH and JONAS. (Heb.) A dove.

JONATHAN. (Heb.) The gift of the Lord.

JONES. (Heb.) The same as John or Johns, and signifies gracious.

JORDAN or JORDEN. (Heb.) The river of judgment. *Jardain*, Gaelic, the western river, with respect to the Euphrates. The name is derived from its two spring-heads, *Jor* and *Dan*.

170   ETYMOLOGICAL DICTIONARY

JOSEPH. (Heb.) Increase, addition.

JOSSELYN and JOSLIN. Local. Jocelin, a town in France.

JOY. Gladness, exhilaration of spirits; to shout, rejoice.

JOYCE. Joyous.

JUDD. (Heb.) From *Juda*, praise, confession, and signifies the *confessor* of God. *Jode* or *Jood*, in the Dutch, means *Israelite*, a Jew; *Jute*, a native of Jutland.

JUDSON. The son of Judd.

KAUFMAN. (Ger.) A merchant, a trader.

KAVANAGH. (Celtic or Gaelic.) *Coamhanach*, mild, benevolent, merciful; a friend, a companion. Mr. John O'Donovan says, that Donnell Cavanagh was so called from having been fostered by the Coarb of St. Cavan, at Kilcavan, in the present county of Wexford, Ireland.

KAY. Local. In Cor. Br., signifies a hedge, inclosure, a place of security, a fortified place. *Kai*, German, is a quay, a wharf.

KAYNARD or KINNARD. Local. (Gaelic.) From *Kinnaird*, a place in Perthshire, Scotland, so called from *Ceann*, the head, the end, and *aerd*, a height or promontory, from its high situation.

KEACH. *Keech*, a mass, a lump; a short, thick-set man.

KEAN. (Gaelic.) *Ceann*, the head, the top, a chief, a commander.

KEBBY, KIBBY. Local. (Danish.) *Kiob-by*, a market town, the place of buying, from *Kiob*, buying, purchase, bargain, and *by*, a town.

KEEL. A low, flat-bottomed vessel used in the river Tyne, to convey coals; an inn-sign; a harbor. *Kiel*, local, a town in Denmark, a corner, wedge, a ravine.

KEELER. One who manages barges and vessels.

OF FAMILY NAMES.
171

KEEN. Bold, eager, daring; bright, fair; or may be the same as Kean.

KEESE. (Dutch.) An abbreviation of *Cornelius*, among the Dutch. Keys, called Taxiaxia, were officers of justice, in olden times, in the Isle of Man.

KEIGWIN. (Cor. Br.) White dog, from *kei*, a dog, and *gwyn*, white; figuratively, a hero.

KEITH. Local. From the parish and lands of Keith, in Banff-shire, Scotland. The name *Keith* is said to be derived from the Gaelic *Gaoth*, wind, pronounced somewhat similarly to Keith. The old village and kirk are called *Arkeith*, which may be a corruption of the Gaelic *Ard Gaoth*, signifying "high wind," which corresponds to its locality, which is peculiarly exposed to gusts of wind. In some old charters, Keith is written *Gith*, which still more resembles *Gaith*. I think the name is derived from the Welsh *Caeth*, a place surrounded, shut up, inclosed, a deep hollow, a strait. The root of the word is the Welsh *Cau*, to close, to shut up. Concerning this family, the traditional account is, that they came from Germany in the reign of the Emperor Otho, and from the principality of Hesse, from which they were ex-pelled in some revolution.

The first person of this family of whom our oldest historians take notice, is Robert De Keith, to whom Malcom II., King of Scotland, gave the barony of Keith, in East Lothian, as a reward for killing Camus, a Danish general, who then in-vaded Scotland with a numerous army. The battle was fought at Barry, seven miles from Dundee, where an obelisk, called *Camus' stone*, still preserves the memory of the vic-tory, and it is said the king, dipping his three fingers in the blood of the general, stroked them along the field of the Scotch champion's shield, to whom, besides the landed es-tate before mentioned, he gave the dignity of Great Mar-shal of Scotland.

172 ETYMOLOGICAL DICTIONARY

KELLOGG. From *Chelioc*, or *Kulliag* (Cor. Br.), a cock, *coil-each*, in Gaelic, and *ceiliog*, in Welsh, the C having the sound of K.

KELLY. (Gaelic and Welsh.) A grove, generally of hazel. *Kill* or *Cille*, in the Gaelic and Celtic, denotes a church.

KELSO. Local. Derived from the town of *Kelso*, in Roxburghshire, Scotland. Kelso was originally written *Calchow*, a corruption of *Chalkheugh*, the chalk-hill.

KELSEY. Local. A town in Lincolnshire, England. *Kelsey*, in Cornish British, signifies the "*dry neck*," from *Kel*, a neck, and *syck*, dry.

KEMBLE or KIMBLE. The same as Campbell, of which it is a corruption.

KEMP. In old English, a soldier, one who engaged in single combat.
The name Kemp is derived from the Saxon word to *kemp*, or combat, which in Norfolk is retained to this day; a foot-ball match being called a *camping* or *kemping*; and thus in Saxon a Kemper signifies a combatant, a champion, a man-at-arms. In some parts of Scotland the striving of reapers in the harvest-field is still called *kemping*.

KEMPENFELT. Local. The camping or kemping-field.

KEMPHALL and **KEMPSHALL.** The soldiers' quarters.

KEMPSTER. From the Dutch *kampen*, to fight, or *kamper*, a champion.

KEMPTON. The camp town; place of the army.

KEMYSS. (Gaelic.) *Camus*, "nez retroussé," a person whose nose is turned upwards: crooked, from *cam*, Gaelic, crooked, not straight.

KENNAN. Gaelic, *Ceanann* or *Ceanfhionn*, white-headed, bald.

OF FAMILY NAMES.

173

KENDALL. Local. Derived from the town of Kendal, in Westmoreland, England, and was so called from the river *Ken*, on which it is situated, and *dale ;* the dale on the river *Ken*.

KENDRICK. From the Saxon *Kenrick*, from *Kennen*, to know, and *ric*, rich—rich in knowledge. Bailey derives this name from *cene*, bold, and *rick*, a kingdom—a valiant ruler.

KENNARD. (Gaelic.) From *Ceannard*, a chief, a chieftain, a leader, a commander-in-chief, from *Ceann*, head, chief, and *Ard*, high, lofty.

KENNEDY. From the Gaelic or Celtic words *Kean-na-ty ;* the head of the house, or chief of the clan. *Ceannaide* signifies also a shopkeeper, a merchant.

KENNICOT. (Cor. Br.) From *Chennicat*, a singer ; Welsh, *canu*, to sing.

KENT. Local. From the County Kent, in England. Camden derives this from *canton*, a corner, because England in this place stretches itself into a corner to the north-east. *Cant*, in Welsh, signifies, round, circular, which is probably the true signification.

KENWARD. (Saxon.) A cow-keeper, *Kine-ward*.

KENYON. (Welsh.) *Ceinion*, beautiful ; *Cyndyn*, stubborn, *Concenn* or *Kynan*, strong head, powerful, a leader.

KERR. (Gaelic, Welsh, and Cor. Br.) *Kaer*, a castle ; figuratively, strong, valiant ; *car*, dear, a kinsman, a friend ; Danish, *Kier*, dear, lovely.

KERSWELL. Local. The well where water-cresses grow.

KETMAN. (Ger.) From *Kette*, a chain, and *mann*,—a chainman.

KETTLE. Local. From the parish of *Kettle*, in Fifeshire, Scotland.

KEVIN. (Celtic.) From *Coemhghin*, the beautiful offspring, *aoibhinn*, pleasant, comely. *Caomhan*, a noble, kind, and friendly man.

KEYS. Probably from *Keyus*, an old Roman word for a warden or keeper.

KEYSER. (Ger.) An emperor.

KID. A young goat; also, *Kid*, from the Saxon *Cythan*, to show, discover, or make known.

KIDDER. A dealer in corn, provisions, and merchandize; a traveling trader.

KIEF. (Dan.) Brave, valiant, stout, bold.

KIEL. (Ger.) Local. Derived from the town of *Kiel*, in Lower Saxony.

KERCHER. Gaelic, *carcar;* Welsh, *carchar*, a prison; Anglo-Saxon, *cark*, a prison; *carker*, a jailor.

KIERNAN or **KIRNAN.** *Carnan*, Gaelic, a heap; figuratively, a strong man, a thick-set, stout man. *Cearnan*, local, a square, a quadrangle.

KIERSTED. (Danish.) Local. The place near a marsh, from *Kier*, a marsh, and *sted*, a dwelling, a town.

KILBURNE. Local. Derived from the village of *Kilburne*, in Middlesex, England, famous for its fine well of mineral water. *Kil*, Dutch; *kilde*, Danish, a channel or bed of a river, and hence a stream; *bourne*, a fountain, a spring-well.

KILGOUR. (Gaelic.) Local. The ancient name of a parish in Fifeshire, Scotland, so called from *kill*, a church, and *gour*, a hill—the church on the hill, or surrounded by hills.

KILHAM. Local. A town in England, from *Kil*, as above, and *ham*, a house or town.

KILLIN. (Gaelic.) Local. A place in Perthshire, Scotland, from *Cill-lin*, that is, the church or burying-place on the pool.

OF FAMILY NAMES. **175**

KIMBERLEY. *Kemperlike*, kemper, a veteran, a stout, war-like man, from the Dutch *kamper*, a champion, a fighting-man. The name may apply to the qualities of the person, or to the place of a camp or battle, that is, *Camper-ley ; Cumberley* indicates a place among hills in a narrow valley, from *Cum*, a vale, a dell.

KINCADE. (Gaelic.) From *ceann*, head, and *cath* or *cad*, battle—the head or front of the battle.

KING. The primary sense is a head or leader. Gaelic, *ceann ;* Welsh, *cun* and *cwn*, a head, a leader. Saxon, *cyng*, and nearly the same in all the Teutonic dialects.

KINGHORN. Local. A borough in Fifeshire, Scotland. The name is derived from the Gaelic *Cean-gorn* or *gorm*, " the blue head," from the adjoining promontory. It is fancifully suggested by one writer that as the Scottish kings long had a residence in the neighborhood, the name may have been suggested by the frequent winding of the king's horn when he sallied out to the chase in this neighborhood.

KINGSTON. Local. The name of several towns in England —the king's town.

KINLOCH. Local. From lands in Fifeshire. *Kian Loch*— " *the head of the lake.*"

KINNAIRD and **KENNARD.** (See Kaynard.)

KINNEAR. (Gaelic.) A head man or chief. *Ceanneir*, from *Ceann*, head, and *eir*, an abbreviation of *fear*, a man.

KINNEY. Gaelic, *Cine*, kindred, a clan, a tribe. *Keny* and *Cany*, seeing, knowing; Welsh, *cenio*, to see.

KINSLEY. (Gaelic.) From *Ceannsallach*, authoritative, commanding, ruling. Walker, in his Historical Memoirs of the Irish Bards, relates the following story: Eochaidh, the then monarch, was defeated by Ena, King of Leinster, at the battle of Cruachan. In this engagement Ena killed Cetmathch, laureate bard to the monarch, although he fled for

176　　ETYMOLOGICAL DICTIONARY

refuge under the shields of the Leinster troops. For this base deed the ruthless king was stigmatized with the epithet *Kinsealach*, that is, the foul and reproachful head, which name descended to his posterity.

KIPP. *Kippe*, in the German, denotes a situation on or near a precipice. *Kip*, Dutch, a hen, a chicken.

KIRBY. Local. The name of several small towns in England, whence the surname is derived; so called from *Kirk*, a church, and *by*, a village or town.

KIRK. (Teut.) *Kirche*, a church. Gaelic, *cearcall*, a circle, the primitive places of worship among the Celts were round, a symbol of eternity, and the existence of the Supreme Being, without beginning or end.

KIRKALDY. Local. From *Kirkcaldy*, a town in Fifeshire, Scotland, from *Kirk*, a church, and *culdee*, the worshipers of God, the first Christians of Britain, who were said to have had a place of worship there in ancient times.

KIRKHAM. Local. From *Kirk*, a church, and *ham*, a village. The name of a small town in England, whence the surname originated.

KIRKPATRICK. Local. A parish in Dumfriesshire, Scotland, *i. e.*, Patrick's Church.

KIRTLAND. A corruption of Kirkland, that is, the church land, from *kirk*, a church.

KIRWAN. The name was *O'Quirivane* until the time of Queen Elizabeth, when they, with many Irish houses, were compelled to drop the "O," and Quirivane was corrupted into *Kirwan*.

KISKEY. (Cor. Br.) Blessed, happy, to bless.

KITSON. The son of Christopher or Kit.

KITTS. The son of Kit or Christopher, "s" being added for son.

KLING. German *Klinge*, a blade, a sword.

OF FAMILY NAMES.

KNAPP. (Ger.) *Knappe,* a lad, boy, servant, workman; a squire, whence Knave and Knapsack.

KNEVETT. A corruption of the Norman name *Duvenet.*

KNICKERBACKER. (Dutch and Ger.) Cracker-baker, from *knacker,* a cracker, and *backer,* a baker.

KNIGHT. A term originally applied to a young man after he was admitted to the privilege of bearing arms, by a certain ceremony of great importance called *knighting,* which was generally conferred by the king.

KNIGHTLEY. From *Knight,* and *ley,* a place or field.

KNOWLES or **KNOLL.** The top of a hill. *Knowl,* in Cor. Br., is a promontory, hill, or eminence, a projection of hilly ground.

KNOX. Local. Gaelic, *Cnoc,* a little hill; figuratively, a stout man.

KREBS. Local. A town in Upper Saxony, Germany.

KYLE. Local. From a district of the same name in Ayrshire, Scotland. Gaelic, *Coill,* a wood. The river *Coyle* runs through the district, whence, perhaps, the name.

LACKEY. A person sent, an attendant servant.

LACY. Local. Derived from a place in France by that name. Sire De Lacy came into England with William the Conqueror. The Lacys afterward settled in Ireland.

LADD. (Welsh.) *Lladd,* to destroy.

LAHEY. Gaelic, *Leighiche,* a physician. *Lagh,* Gaelic, law, order; *Fear Lagha,* a lawyer.

LAING. Scottish dialect for long.

LAIRD. The same as Lord, from *L,* the, and *ord* or *aird,* Gaelic, supreme, high, eminence, highness; *Lerad,* Laird, from *radh,* Gaelic, saying, declaring, expressing, affirming an

8*

178   ETYMOLOGICAL DICTIONARY

adage or proverb; giving or uttering law, from the verb *abair*. (See Lord.)

LAKE. A servant. Latin, *lego*, to send.

LAM. (Danish.) Lame.

LAMB. The name was probably taken from the sign of a lamb at an inn, the young of the sheep kind; Welsh, *Llamer*, to skip; Gaelic, *Leum*. The primitive Celtic or Gaelic *Lam* signified armor, as a dart, a blade, or sword; hence, to *lam* signified to disable, injure, maim, from which we have lame and limp.

LAMBOURNE. Anciently written in the Cor. Br. *Lambron*, the inclosure of the round hill; *lan* being changed into *lam*, for the sake of the euphony or ease in speaking; from the Welsh *Llan*, an inclosure, and *bryn*, a hill.

LAMBERT. (Sax.) From *lamb*, and *beorht*, fair—fair lamb.

LAMMA. Welsh, *Llamu*, to skip, leap, jump; to maim or *lam*.

LAMPORT. (Cor. Br.) From *lam* or *lan*, a place, and *port*, a harbor, a place for ships.

LANCASTER. Local. A town and county of England, the castle or city on the *Loyne* or *Lan* river. The Britons called it *Caerwerydd*. (See Chester.)

LANDER. Welsh, *Llandir*. Glebe lands belonging to a parish church, or land containing mineral ore.

LANDON. (Cor. Br.) The inclosed hill or town, from *Lan*, an inclosure, and *dun*, a hill or town. *Landen*, a town of Belgium.

LANDSEER. (Dutch.) From *Landsheer*, a lord of the manor, from *land* and *heer*, a master or lord.

LANE. Old Gaelic, *Llane*, a plain; barren, sandy, level lands. Lane, a narrow way between hedges, a narrow street, an alley. "John of the Lane."

OF FAMILY NAMES.

179

LANGTON. Local. The long hill or town, so called from its oblong form.

LANHAM. A contraction of *Lavenham*, a town in Suffolk, England; whence the family originally came. Welsh, *Llyfn*, a smooth, level place.

LANMAN. A lance-man, spear-man.

LANPHEAR. "*Lann-feur*," Gaelic, grass-land; *Lann-fear*, a pike-man. *Lann*, an inclosure; a house; a church; land; a sword. *Feur*, grass; *fear*, a man.

LANSING. Local. (Dutch.) Low, flat lands; "*ing*," meadows; alluvial lands.

LANYON. (Cor. Br.) The furzy inclosure.

LAORAN. (Gaelic.) A person too fond of the fireside.

LARAWAY and **LARWAY.** (Fr.) A corruption of "*Le roi*," the king.

LARDNER. A swine-herd.

LARKINS. From *lark*, a sweet, shrill, musical bird, and *kin*, a child. *Learcean* or *Leargan*, a sloping, green, side of a hill, near the sea, from *Lear*, Gaelic, the sea.

LAROCHE and **LAROQUE.** (Fr.) The rock, a lonely mass of stone. *De La Roche*, "from the rock."

LARRY. Supposed to be an abbreviation of **Lawrence** (which see).

LLARY. (Welsh.) Mild, easy.

LATH. An old word for "barn," in Lincolnshire, England.

LATIMER. An interpreter. This name was first given to Wrenoc ap Merrick, a learned Welshman, interpreter between the Welsh and English. The name of his office descended to his posterity.

LATTON. From *Hlew*, A. S., and *ton;* the town on the eminence or side of a hill.

LAUD. From the same root as *loud*, widely celebrated, Latin, *laus. laudis*, praise; Welsh, *clod*; Gaelic or Irish, *cloth*; German, *laut*.

LAUDER. Local. A town in Berwickshire, Scotland.

LAUREL. The laurel or bayberry-tree, dedicated to Apollo, and used in making garlands for victors.

LAVENDER. A laundress; *Lavandière*, French, one who washes, from the Latin, *lavo*, to wash.

LAVEROCK. A Scotch word for a lark; also Dutch and Saxon.

LAW. (Scot.) A hill. *Laye*, old French, a hill.

LAWLESS. "*Lah-lios.*" Gaelic, *Lagh*, law, order, and *lios*, a court, a hall, a fortress, a place where law is administered. *Lau*, Cor. Br., praise, and *lis*, a court. *Lawless*, an outlaw.

LAWLEY. (Saxon.) A place in the hundred of Blackburn, Shropshire, from *Law*, low, and *ley*, a place, lea, or pasture.

LAWRENCE. Flourishing, spreading, from *Laurus*, the laurel-tree. Sir Robert Lawrence, of Ashton Hall, Lancashire, England, accompanied Richard I. to the Holy Land, 1191.

LAWRIE. Lawrence.

LAWSON. The son of Law, the familiar abbreviation of Lawrence.

LAYCOCK. Local. A village on the banks of the Avon, in Wiltshire, England. The name may be the same as *Lucock* that is, little Luke.

LEADBEATER. A name of trade, a worker in lead.

LEARNED. Local. (Gaelic.) The green, sheltered place near the sea, from *Lear*, the sea, and *nead*, a sheltered place. Or it may be a name given for scholarship, "John the Learned."

LEAVENWORTH. Local. (Welsh.) *Llyvngwerth*, the smooth, level farm, castle or court, or the worth or place on the river Leven.

OF FAMILY NAMES. 181

LEBY. Local. A town in Denmark.

LECHMERE. Local. This family originally came from the Low Countries. *Lech* is a branch of the Rhine, which parts from it at Wyke, and running westward, falls into the Maes, before Rotterdam; *mere*, a lake.

LEE, LEA, and **LEY.** A pasture, meadow, lands not plowed, a common, a sheltered place; *Lee*, a river, a stream, from *Lli*, Welsh, a stream.

LEECH. A physician.

LEFERRE. (Fr.) *Le Ferre*, the smith. Latin, *Faber*.

LEGARD. (Nor. Fr.) *Le Gard*, the guard or protector. Probably was first assumed from the possession of some trusty or confidential office.

LEGATT. *Legate*, an ambassador; *Leggett*, the son of Legge.

LEIGH or **LEGH.** Local. A town in England, a pasture or meadow, the same as Ley, or Lea. The frequency of this family name in Cheshire, England, led to the old proverb, "As many Leighs as fleas, Masseys as asses, and Davenports as dog's tails."

LEICESTER. From *Leicester*, a borough town in England. Saxon, *Leagceaster*, from *Leag* or *Ley*, a field or common, and *cester*, a camp or city, from the Latin *Castrum;* because, says Bailey, it was probably built hard by a *leag* or common; a camp of the Roman legion. (See Chester.)

LEIR or **LEAR.** Originally German, and derived from the town of Lear, on the Ems, in Westphalia.

LELAND. Local. *Laland*, an island in Denmark, the same as *Leylande*, the ancient manner of spelling the name, and denotes *Low lands*. In Welsh, *Lle* is a place, and *Lan* a church. *Lan* may signify any kind of inclosure, as *Gwinlan*, *Perlan*, an orchard, a word applied to gardens, houses, castles, or towns.

LEMON. (Fr.) A corruption of *Le Moin*, the monk.

182 ETYMOLOGICAL DICTIONARY

LENNON. (Gaelic.) *Leannon,* a lover, a sweetheart.

LENNOX. (Gaelic.) Local. From the County of Lennox, Scotland. The original name was *Leven-ach,* the field on the Leven, from the river Leven, which flows through the county, called in Latin *Levinia.* The river was so called from *Llyfn,* in the Welsh, which signifies a smooth, placid stream. *Leven-achs,* for a while spelt and written *Levenax,* and finally *Lennox.* Arkil, a Saxon, a baron of Northumbria, who took refuge from the vengeance of the Norman William under the protection of Malcom Canmore, appears to have been the founder of the Lennox family.

LENT. Some names were given from the festivals and seasons of the year in which they were born, as *Noel, Holiday, Pascal, Lent,* &c.

LEONARD. The disposition of a lion; lion-hearted; from *leon,* a lion, and *ard,* Teutonic, nature, disposition.

LEPPARD. A name probably taken from a coat of arms, a leopard.

LESLIE. This family, according to tradition, descended from Bartholomew de Leslyn, a noble Hungarian, who came to Scotland with Queen Margaret, about the year 1067. He was the son of Walter de Leslyn, who had assumed this surname from the castle of Leslyn, in Hungary, where he was born. Bartholomew being in great favor with Malcom Canmore, obtained from that prince grants of several lands in Aberdeenshire, which it is said he called *Leslyn,* after his own surname. Malcom de Leslyn, who succeeded him, was the progenitor of all the Leslies in Scotland.

Robert Verstegan, in his Antiquities, remarks on the word *ley* : " A combat having taken place in Scotland between a noble of the family of Leslie and a foreign knight, in which the Scot was victorious, the following lines in memory of the deed, and the place where it happened, are still extant :

"Between the *Less-Ley* and the Mair,
He slew the knight and left him there."

OF FAMILY NAMES. 183

The name may be derived from *Lesslo*, a maritime territory in Denmark.

LESTER, LEICESTER, and LEYCESTER. Local. A borough town in England; a camp of the Roman legion. (See Leicester.)

LEVEN. Local. A river in Lancashire, England, also a town, lake, and river in Lennox, Scotland, whence the county derives its name. (See Lennox.) From the Welsh *Llyfn*, smooth, placid—the smooth river. The Gaelic *Liomha-abhainn*, pronounced *Le-avon*, signifies the same thing.

LEVENWORTH. (Welsh.) Local. From *leven*, the open or bare place, and *worth*, a farm, castle, or mansion, or the worth on the river Leven.

LEVEQUE. (Fr.) A bishop.

LEVERET. A hare in the first year of its age.

LEVY. (Heb.) The same as *Levi*, joined, united, coupled; Jacob's third son.

LEWES. Local. An ancient town in Sussex, England, derived from the Welsh *Lluaws*, a multitude, a populous place. This town was formerly surrounded by walls, vestiges of which are still visible, and on the summit of a hill are the remains of its ancient castle.

LEWIS. In the Fr., *Louis*; Latin, *Ludovicus*; Teutonic, *Ludwig* or *Leodwig*, from the Saxon *Leod*, the people, and *wic*, a castle—the safeguard of the people. *Lluaws*, Welsh, signifies a multitude.

LEWKNOR. Local. A corruption of *Levechenora*, the denomination of one of the hundreds of Lincolnshire, England.

LEWTHWAITE or LOWTHWAITE. (Anglo-Saxon.) From *thwaite*, a piece of ground cleared of wood, and *lowe*, a hill, *law*, a hill or eminence; in Saxon, *Hlewe*.

LIGHTBODY. A writer, somewhere, derives this name from *Licht*, a dead body, a tomb, and *Bodee*, contracted from

184   ETYMOLOGICAL DICTIONARY

Boadicea,—meaning the tomb or grave of this British Queen ; a locality. The name, however, is more likely to have originated from bodily peculiarity.

LIGHTFOOT. A name given on account of swiftness in running, or expertness in dancing ; one who is nimble or active.

LILIENTHAL. (Ger.) Local. The vale of lilies, from *lilie,* a lily, and *thal,* a vale ; so *Blumenthal,* the vale of flowers. A town in Bremen, Hanover.

LILLY. A beautiful flower. *Llille,* in the Welsh, the place by the river or stream, from *Lli,* a stream, and *Lle,* a place. *Llu,* an army, a troop ; *Llellu,* the place of the army. In the Cornish-British *Lhy* is a troop, a company of horsemen, and *le* or *li,* a place.

LINCOLN. Local. From Lincoln in England. The name is derived from *Lin* in the Gaelic, Welsh, and Cor. Br., which signifies a pool, pond, or lake, and *coln,* the ridge or neck of a hill, so called from its situation, as it occupies the top and side of a steep hill on the river Witham, which here divides into three streams.

LIND. Local. (Swedish, Sax., Dan., and Dutch.) A place where the lime or linden-trees grow.

LINDALL. Local. From *Lin,* a brook, a lake, and *dal,* a dale.

LINDFIELD. Local. The field of linden or lime-trees.

LINDO. (Spanish.) Neat, spruce, fine.

LING. (Teutonic.) English, *long,* heath ; also, a species of long grass ; a long, slender fish.

LINDSAY or LINDSEY. Local. Sir William Dugdale says this surname is local, and was first assumed by the proprietors of the lands and manor of Lindsay, in the county of Essex, England. One of the Lindsays having contracted a friendship with Malcom Canmore, when in England, went with

OF FAMILY NAMES. **185**

him to Scotland, and was the progenitor of the Lindsays in that country.

The eastern part of Lincolnshire was originally called *Lindsey*, from the place abounding with linden-trees.

LINN or LINNE. Local. A pool, pond, or lake. Welsh, *llyn;* Cor. Br., *lyn;* Gaelic, *linne,* a pond.

LINNET. A singing bird.

LINTON. Local. From *Lin,* a lake or pool, and *ton,* a town. A parish in Roxburgshire, Scotland.

LIPPENCOT. Local. *Lippe,* a German principality and town on the river Lippe. *Cote,* side or coast. *Liban,* Saxon, *Leben,* German, to abide, to dwell, and *cot,* a cottage.

LISLE. (Fr.) Local. *L'isle,* an island.

LISMORE. Local. A parish in Argyleshire, Scotland. The name signifies the large gardens. *Lis* or *Lios,* Celtic, a garden, and *mor,* large.

LITCHFIELD. From the Saxon *lich,* a dead carcase, and *field,* because a great many suffered martyrdom there in the time of Diocletian. The name of a bishop's see in Staffordshire.

LITTLER. Derived from the town, village, or hundred of *Little Over,* corrupted to *Littler,* in the county of Cheshire, England, where the family resided in the time of Edward I.

LIVERMORE. (Welsh.) From *lleufer,* a light, and *mawr,* great—the great light. A name given to the first Christian king of Britain, hence called by the Romans *Lucius,* which has in the Latin the same signification.

LIVINGSTONE. Local. A barony in West Lothian, Scotland, so named from one *Livingus* living there in 1124; hence *Livingston.*

LIZARD. (Gaelic.) Local. The high fortress, from *lios,* a fort, an inclosure, or garden, and *ard,* high.

186   ETYMOLOGICAL DICTIONARY

LLARY. (Welsh.) Mild, easy.

LLOYD or LHUYD. (Welsh.) Gray or brown.

LOBDALE. (Gaelic.) Local. *Lub*, bending, curving, and *dail*, a narrow vale or meadow.

LOCKMAN. A Scottish word for the public executioner.

LOGAN. (Gaelic.) An inclosed plain or low-lying place. If the residence of a Briton was on a plain, it was called *Lann*, from *Lagen* or *Logen;* if on an eminence, it was termed *dun*.

LONSDALE. Local. Derived from the town of Lonsdale, in Westmoreland, England, so named from the river *Lon* on which it is situated, and *dale*—the dale on the Lon.

LOOMIS or LOMMIS. (Welsh.) Local. From *lom*, bare, naked, exposed, and *maes*, a field, a name of place—the place in the open field.

LOPPE. Local. An uneven or winding place, a bend.

LORD. A term of civil dignity, a master, ruler, the proprietor of a manor, derived from the Anglo-Saxon *ord*, which comes from *ored*, a governor, with the prefix of the letter *L, le*, denoting the person or place. Gaelic. *ard, ord*, high, lofty, the prime chief, superior. *Lord* has been derived from *Hlaford*, which is compounded of *Hlaf*, a loaf, and *ford*, to give,—a bread-giver.

LORIMER. A maker of bits or bridles.

LOSSIE. Local. A river of Scotland, in Elgin or Morayshire.

LOUDOUN. From the parish of Loudoun in Ayrshire, Scotland. The name is compounded of *Law* and *dun*,—a pleonasm, as both words signify a hill. The hill-hill.

LOUGHLIN. The ancient Britons or Welsh called the Baltic Sea *Lychlyn*, and the Scandinavian sea-pirates who infested the coasts of Britain received the same appellation. Norway is called *Llychlyn*.

LOUTH. (Br. and Welsh.) From *lowcth*, a garden.

OF FAMILY NAMES.

187

LOVE. (Danish.) A lion.

LOVEL. The original family name of Lovel was, in olden times, Percival, so called from a place in Normandy, until Asceline, its chief, who flourished in the early part of the twelfth century, acquired from his violent temper the soubriquet of *Lupus* (the Wolf). His son William, Earl of Yvery, was nicknamed *Lupellus*, the little wolf, which in after times was softened into *Lupel*, and at last to *Luvel* or Lovel.

LOWE. A hill.

LOWER. The same as *Burder*. *Louw* or *low* is a Scotch word for flame or fire.

"Low-bellers," according to Blount, "are men who go with a light and a bell; by the sight thereof birds sitting on the ground become somewhat stupefied, and so are covered with a net, and taken."

LOWRY or **LOURY.** Signifies in Scotch a crafty person, or one who lowers, that is, contracts his brow; hence a "*lowry day*"—cloudy.

LUCAS. The same as *Luke*, luminous. *Lucas*, arising to him.

LUDBROCK. (Dutch.) Leather or hairy breeches.

LUDLOW. Local. From the ancient town of Ludlow, in North Wales. *Llud*, in Welsh, signifies whatever connects or keeps together, the same as *caw*. *Llud*, a prince of the Britons, a commander; Welsh. *Llywydd*, and *lowe*.

LUMLEY. (Gaelic and Welsh.) The bare place, from *lom*, bare, and *lle*, a place.

LUSHER. (Dutch.) *Lauscher*, a hider, a skulker.

LUSK or **LOSCE.** (Welsh.) A burning or searing. Gaelic, *Loisg*, to burn.

LUTHER. The widely famed or celebrated, derived from the German *loth* or *laut*, loud, famed, fortunate, and *er*, honor— "*fortune and honor*." *Lauter*, Ger., bright, clear, pure.

188 ETYMOLOGICAL DICTIONARY

LYNCH. A strip of greenwood between the plowed lands in the common field; a small hanging wood.

MABAN. (Welsh.) A child, a bairn.

MACAULEY or MACAULA. (Celtic.) The son of the rock.

MACE. A staff borne as an ensign of office.

MACKLIN. The same as McLean (which see).

MACLAY. (Gaelic.) The son of Clay (which see).

MACONOCHIE. The son of Conochie or Duncan, a name borne by the chieftain of the Campbells.

MADDOCK. (Welsh.) The same as Madoc, a proper name common among the Welsh, from *mad*, good, and the termination *oc* or *og*, the same as the termination *y* or *ous* in English. The terminations *c* and *ac*, denote fixedness, force, plenitude. *Og*, in its simple form, signifies animation, activity; also, possessing that which precedes it; *oc*, greatness, grandeur; *ox*, quickness, promptitude.

MADISON. The son of Mathew or Matilda.

MAGOON. (Gaelic.) A corruption of *Macgowan*, which signifies the son of the smith, from *Mac*, son, and *gow*, a smith; or it may be the same as *McCoun*, from *Mac*, son, and *ceann*, a head or chief—the son of the chief.

MAGUIRE or M'GUIRE. (Gaelic.) The son of *Guaire*, which is the Gaelic for Godfrey. Guaire was son of Alpin, King of Scotland.

MAHOMET. (Turkish.) Glorified.

MAHON. (Celtic or Gaelic.) A bear.

MAIGNY. (Fr.) Local. An old province of France lying to the east of Bretagne, whence the name came.

OF FAMILY NAMES.

MAINARD or **MAYNARD**. (Ger.) Of a powerful disposition, stout-hearted. *Maynhard* was one of the barons who went into England with William the Conqueror, and whose name is in the roll of Battle Abbey.

MAIN or **MAYNE**. Local. From a French province of that name. *Magne*, great, large, rich, powerful, the same as *magnus* in Latin.

MAITLAND. Local. A tract of flat, meadow land.

MAJOR. An officer next in rank above a captain.

MALLARD. (Belgic.) A wild drake. *Meallard*, local, Gaelic, a high mound, a hill or eminence, from *meall*, a hill, and *ard*, high.

MALLERY. (Fr.) A corruption of the French *Mallieure;* in Latin, *Malus Leporarius*—a name given for ill hunting the hare, according to Camden.

MALLET or **MALET**. This name has been ascribed by some to a place so termed in Normandy, and by others to the courageous blows of the family in battle. *Malleus, Maule, Mall*, and *Mallet* was one of the offensive weapons of a well-armed warrior, being generally made of iron, and used to destroy by pounding or bruising the enemy through or under the armor, that could not be penetrated by edged or pointed weapons. Edward I. was called *Malleus Scotorum*. All the families of this name in England trace their descent from the renowned William Lord Mallet de Graville, one of the great barons who accompanied William the Conqueror.

MALMESBURY. From the town of Malmesbury in Wiltshire, England, said to be so called by *Malmutius*, a king of the Britons. It was anciently called *Maidulphesburgh*, from *Maidulph*, a Scottish saint and hermit who built an abbey there, and opened a school. Bede writes it *Adelmesbirig*, from *Adelm*, the scholar of Maidulph; others derive it from a part of the names both of the scholar and teacher.

MALONE. One of the descendants of the house of O'Connor, Kings of Connaught, being tonsured in honor of St. John, was called *Maol Eoin*—Bald John, from *Maol*, bald or tonsured, and *Eoin*, John, and this was corrupted into *Malone*.

MANDEVILLE. From the Latin *De Magna villa*, that is, of or from the great town.

MANN. (Ger.) Gentleman or master, the same as *Herr*. *Man*, in the Welsh, signifies freckled or spotted; also, a spot, a place.

MANNERING or **MANWARING.** A corruption of Mesnilwarin, Welsh, from *Mesnil* or *Maenol*, a farm.

MANNERS. (Fr.) From *Manoir*, and that from the Latin *Manere*, to stay or to abide. Lands granted to some military man or baron by the king, a custom brought in by the Normans.

Manners, first Earl of Rutland, soon after his creation, told Sir Thomas More that he was too much elated by his preferment, and really verified the old proverb, "Honores mutant *Mores*."

"Nay, my lord," retorted Sir Thomas, "the proverb does much better in English, 'Honors change *Manners*.'"

It is the opinion of Camden that this family received its name from the village of *Manor*, near Lanchester, in Durham, England.

MANNUS. A god celebrated among the Germans as one of their founders.

MANSER. (Dutch.) From *Mansoir*, a male issue, a boy. *Mansaer*, in the Welsh, is a stone-mason.

MANSFIELD. Local. From a town in Nottinghamshire, England, of the same name, so called from the Saxon *manrian*, to traffic, and *field*—a place of trade.

MANSLE. Local. A town of France in the province of Angoumois.

OF FAMILY NAMES. **191**

MAR. Local. From the district of Mar, in Aberdeenshire, Scotland. *Mar*, Welsh, activity; *Maor*, Gaelic, an officer of justice.

MARCH. A boundary, a limit; the boundary-lines between England, Scotland, and Wales, were called "The Marches." Lords Marches were noblemen who anciently inhabited, guarded, and secured these marches.

MARCHANT. Fr., *Marchand*, a merchant.

MARK. The same as *Marcus*, a field; polite, shining.

MARSHALL. A name of office—master of the horse, anciently, one who had command of all persons not above princes. Teut., *Marschalk;* French, *Mareschal.*

MARSH. (Teutonic.) *Maresche,* Morass, a fen, a tract of low, wet land.

MARSHMAN. One dwelling near a marsh.

MARTIN. This name may be derived from the Latin *martius,* warlike, from *Mars,* the God of War. In the Gaelic, *mor* is great, and *duin,* a man. *Morduin,* a chief, a warrior.

MARVEN. Gaelic, *Morven,* a ridge of very high hills.

MASENFER. German, *Messenfer,* a great fair or market for merchants.

MASSEY or MASSIE. Local. From the town and lordship of Massey, near Bayeux, in Normandy.

MASSENGER. A corruption of the French *messager,* a messenger or bearer of dispatches.

MASTEN or MOSTYN. (Welsh.) Local. A place or house inclosed, from *Maes,* a field, and *din,* inclosed, fortified. *Moestuin,* in the Teutonic and Dutch, signifies a garden, a place cultivated. The Gaelic *dun,* and the Welsh *din,* a fortified hill or fort, are synonymous. The Saxon *tun* signifies an inclosure, a garden, a village, a town, and *tun* or *tuin,* in Dutch, a garden, a protected place.

192   ETYMOLOGICAL DICTIONARY

Camden relates, that in the time of Henry VIII., an ancient worshipful gentleman of Wales being called at the panel of a jury by the name of Thomas-Ap-William-Ap-Thomas-Ap-Hoel-Ap-Euan Vaughn, etc., was advised by the judge to leave that old manner. Whereupon, he afterward called himself *Mostyn,* according to the name of his principal house, and left that surname to his posterity. *Mostyn,* a village in Flintshire, Wales. On Mostyn hill, in Flintshire, Wales, is a remarkable monument to the sun, a place of Druid worship.

MATHER. Welsh, *Madur,* a benevolent man. *Medwr,* a reaper. *Mathair,* in Gaelic, is a mother.

MATTHEW. (Heb.) The gift of the Lord.

MATTISON. The son of Matthew.

MAUER. (Ger.) A wall.

MAXWELL. One *Macchus,* in the eleventh century, obtained lands, on the Tweed, in Scotland, from Prince David, to which he gave the name of *Macchus-ville,* since corrupted to *Maxwell.* Maxwell is *Macsual,* in Gaelic, from *Mac,* son, and *sual,* small, little.

MAY. Probably given to a child born in that month. *May,* in the Saxon, is a daisy, a flower; the fifth month in the year, beginning with January. Gaelic, *mai* or *maith,* good, pleasant, fruitful; *Mad,* Welsh. From *Ma* we have *mai,* the earth, the producer; *ma,* mother, tender, kind.

MAYO. Local. The name of a county and town in Ireland, the plain near the water, from *Moi* or *Moy,* Gaelic, a plain, *Moy,* a river, and *ai,* a region or territory; the region or tract on the river Moy.

McALLISTER or **McCALLISTER.** The son of Alister, the Gaelic, for Alexander. *Callester,* in the Welsh, signifies a flint, figuratively, an invincible man. *Galluster,* in Cor. Br., expresses might, power.

McANDREW The son of Andrew.

OF FAMILY NAMES.

McARDLE or McCardle. (Gaelic.) From *Mac*, son, and *ardal*, literally, the son of the high-rock, figuratively, high prowess or valor.

McBAIN. The son of Bain. *Bean* or *Ban*, white, *Donald Bean*, Donald the white.

McBRIDE. The son of Bride (which see).

McCABE. The son of Cabe. *Caob*, Gaelic, a bough, branch, a clod, lump, a bit or piece of any thing. *Ceap*, the top of a hill, a sign set up in time of battle.

McCAMUS. The son of Camus (which see).

McCALLEN. The son or descendants of Callen or Colin. This name was given to the descendants of Sir Colin Campbell, or Colin the Great, who flourished toward the end of the thirteenth century, at Lochore, Scotland.

McCARTHY. The son of *Carrthach*, an Irish chieftain, who lived in the eleventh century.

McCLIS. From *Mac*, son, and *Clis*, active, quick, ingenious.

McCOUN. (Gaelic.) From *Mac*, son, and *Ceann*, head or chief; the son of the chief.

McCRACKIN or McCHARRAIGIN. The son of the rock, figuratively, the son of the brave.

McCREE. (Gaelic.) From *Mac*, son, and *Righ*, king,—the king's son; or from *cridhe*, the heart, figuratively, brave, bold, generous; also a term of endearment.

McCULLOUGH. The son of Cullough. *Cullach*, Gaelic, a boar, figuratively, a brave man.

McDHOIL or McDOWELL. (Gaelic.) The son of Dowell or Dougall, the dark stranger. From *dhu*, black, and *gall*, a native of the low country of Scotland; any one ignorant of the Gaelic language; a foreigner, a stranger. The same as McDougall.

McDERMOT. The son of Dermot (which see).

194   ETYMOLOGICAL DICTIONARY

McDONALD or McDONELL. This family was for many centuries reputed the most powerful of any in the Highlands of Scotland, being styled "King of the Isles," for many generations, during which they were successful in asserting their independence. . *Somerled,* Thane of Argyle, flourished about the year 1140, and was the ancestor of all the McDonalds. He married the daughter of Olans, Lord of the Western Isles, whereupon he assumed the title of *"King of the Isles."* He was slain, in 1164, by Walter, Lord High Steward of Scotland. Donald, from whom the clan derived their name, was his grandson.

McDONNOUGH. (Gaelic.) The son of Donnach, the same as Duncan, safe, able to defend.

McDOUGALL. The son of Dougall, that is, the black stranger, the foreigner, or native of the Lowlands.

McDUFF. (Gaelic.) The son of the captain, from *Mac,* son, and *Duff,* a captain.

McFADDEN. (Celtic.) The son of Faddan. *Fada,* Gaelic, tall; *Phaudeen,* Gaelic, "little Patrick," and *Mac,* son; Mac Phaudeen, the son of little Patrick.

McFARLAND. The son of *Pharlan,* or *Partholan,* the Gaelic for *Bartholomew.* Malcom McFarlane, descended from Alwyn, Earl of Lennox, founder of the clan McFarlane, lived about 1344, in the reign of Malcom IV., King of Scotland.

Tradition gives the following fabulous origin of the name. A nephew of one of the old Earls of Lennox, having killed, in a quarrel, his uncle's cook, was obliged to flee the country. Returning after many years, he built a castle upon an island above Inversnaid, in the Highlands, where he, and the island after him, received the appellation of *Farland.* Hence *McFarland,* the son of him who came from the Far-land.

McPHERSON. The same as McPherson.

McGINNIS. (Gaelic.) The son of *Ginnis, cine,* a race, *ois,* numerous. *gen* or *gin,* to beget, a numerous clan or race.

OF FAMILY NAMES.

195

McGOOKEN or McGUCKEN. (Gaelic and Celtic.) From *Mac*, a son, and *Gugan*, a bud or flower. This name is the same in the Welsh or Cor. Br.

McGOWAN. (Gaelic.) From *Gow*, a smith; the son of a smith, Smithson.

McGRATH and McGRAW. (Celtic or Gaelic.) From *Gradh*, love, fondness, virtue, prosperity. *Mac* and *rath*, the son of prosperity.

McGREGOR. The descendants of Gregor, who was the son of Alpin, King of Scotland. A family of great antiquity, and of distinguished ancestors. (See Gregor.)

McGUIRE. The son of *Guaire* or Godfrey. *Guaire* was a son of Alpin, King of Scotland.

McHARD or McHARG. (Welsh, Cor. Br., and Gaelic.) The son of the brave or the handsome. *Mac 'Arg*.

McILDOEY. From *Mac*, son, *gille*, a youth, and *dhu*, black; the son of the black youth.

McILDOUNEY. (Gaelic.) From *Mac*, son, *gille*, a youth, and *doinne*, brownishness;—the son of the brown-haired youth.

McILHENNY. (Gaelic.) The son of the old man.

McILROY. (Gaelic.) From *Mac*, *gille*, and *ruadh*, red-haired; —the son of the red-haired young man.

McINNIS. The son of Innis.

McINTOSH. The son of the *leader* or *first*. *Tosh*, and *Toshich*, signify the beginning or first part of any thing; so *Toshich* came to denote the general or leader of the van. The McIntoshes derive themselves from McDuff, who obtained his right from Malcom Canmore.

McINTYRE. (Gaelic.) The son of *Kintyre;*—a promontory, or headland, from *Cean*, head, and *tir*, land. Also the son of the carpenter.

McKAY. The same as McKie (which see).

196   ETYMOLOGICAL DICTIONARY

McKELLY. The son of Kelly (which see).

McKENSIE. (Gaelic.) The son of the chief, head, or first. Same as McKenneth; the son of Kenneth, signifying, chief, head, or first.

McKIBBEN. (Celtic.) From *Mac*, son, and *Ceobbinn*, the top of the hill.

McKIE. (Celtic or Gaelic.) The son of a dog; figuratively, the son of a champion. The Britons, Celts, and Gauls, applied the names of various animals to their heroes, indicative of strength, endurance, courage, or swiftness. This name is derived from *Mac*, son, and *cu, kei,* or *ki,* a wolf-dog. The common hound was called *Gayer*.

McKINNON. Originally McFingon, the son of Fingon, who was the youngest son of Alpin, King of Scotland.

McKIRNAN. The son of Kiernan. *Karnon*, Cor. Br., the high rock; *Cuirnin*, Celtic, a bush; *Cuirnean*, Gaelic, a small heap of stones.

McLAUGHLIN. The son of Laughlin, or the expert sailor. See Laughlin.

McLAURIN. The son of *Labhruinn*, or Lawrence.

McLEAN. MacGillean. From a Highland chieftain of the name of Gillean, who was the progenitor of this family.

This Gillean was a celebrated warrior, and was called Gillean-ni-Tuoidh, from his ordinary weapon, a battle-ax, which in the Gaelic is *Tuoidh*, which his descendants wear to this day in their crest, betwixt a laurel and a cypress branch. The posterity of this *Gillean* were therefore called *Mac Gillean*, in all ancient documents, and now of modern date *McLeans.* "*Magh Leamhna*," in the County of Antrim, the estate of the McLeans or Macklins.

McLEOD or McCLEOD. From *Mac*, son, and *Clode*, from Claudius, the second emperor who invaded Britain. Churchill says he was named *Claudius* because, through fear of death, he buried himself alive, being plucked by the heels out of a hole to be set upon the throne.

OF FAMILY NAMES.

McMAHON. (Gaelic.) The son of a bear; a hero.

McMANUS. The son of Manus or Magnus, the great, or renowned.

McMARTIN. The son of Martin, or the warlike.

McMASTER. The son of Master.

McMULLIN. The son of the miller.

McMURROUGH. The son of Murrough or Murrach; *Mor*, great, strong, and *ach*, battle. *Mur*, a wall, bulwark, and *ach*.

McMURTAIR. (Gaelic.) The son of a murderer.

McNAB. The son of *Nab*. *Nab*, the summit of a mountain or rock. The son of the *Abbot?* *Nab*, Persic, a chief, a prince.

McNAMARA. (Celtic.) From *Mac*, son, and *cu-marra* or or *con-marra*, "the hero of the sea." *Con-marra* was descended from *Cas*, King of Thomond, from whom came *McConmara*, or *Macnamara*. This family were anciently hereditary lords in the County of Clare.

McNEVIN. (Gaelic.) The son of Nevin. *Cnamhin, Naomh*, holy, sacred, consecrated; a saint.

McNIEL. The son of Niel (which see).

McNAUGHTON. McAn Achduinn. The son of the expert and potent, from *Mac*, Gaelic, son, *an*, of, and *achduinn*, tools and instruments of all kinds; able, expert, potent.

McPHERSON. The son of Pherson. Pherson is the son of *Pfarrer*, German, a parson, and that from *Pfarre*, a parish, a benefit, or living. *Pfarre* is derived from the Gaelic *Faire*, a watcher, to watch, an overseer, Episcopus.

McQUADE. *Quad*, Danish, a song, air, lay; a species of narrative poetry among the ancient minstrels. The *son* of the *Poet*.

McQUARIE or **McGUAIRE.** Son of Guaire or Godfrey. *Guaire* was son of Alpin, King of Scotland.

McQUEEN. That is, McOwen, the son of Owen. Originally McSweene.

198　　ETYMOLOGICAL DICTIONARY

McWILLIAM. The son of William. (See William.)

McWITHY. The son of the weaver, from the Gaelic *Mac*, a son, and *guithe*, Cor. Br., a weaver. In the Welsh, *gwehydd*, a weaver, *quethy*, Cor. Br., to weave.

MEAD. Local. A meadow, a tract of low land; the sense is, extended or flat, depressed land.

MEADOW. Local. Land appropriated to the culture of grass.

MECHANT. (French.) *Mechant*, bad, wicked.

MEDCAF. Local. The inclosed cell or church, from *midd*, Welsh, inclosed, and *caf*, a cell, a religious house.

MEEK. Mild of temper, soft, gentle. *Mac*, Gaelic, a son.

MEERS. Shallow water, or lake ;—a name of place.

MEHIN. (Welsh.) *Mochyn*, a pig; Gaelic, *Muc*, a wild boar.

MEIKLE. A lump or mass, much, big.

MEIKLEHAM. The large village ; the great house.

MEICKLEJOHN. (Scottish.) Large John, to distinguish him from *wee* John, or little John.

MELOR. (Welsh and Gaelic.) A soldier, from *melwr*, Welsh.

MELLIS. Sweet, from *Mel*, honey, or Gaelic, *milis*, sweet, or from *Milidh*, a soldier.

MELUN. Local. From the town of Melun, in France.

MENAI. Welsh. So called from *Menai*, a strait which divides the island of Anglesea from the coast of Wales. The *Mena* or *Mona*, worshiped by the Sequani, was the moon. The Gaels blessed the beams of this luminary that saved them from the danger of precipices, and Augustine says that the Gaelic peasants invoked Mena for the welfare of their women.

MENNO. Beardless; defective.

MENTETH or MONTEITH. Local. From a district in Scotland so called, through which the river Teth runs.

OF FAMILY NAMES.

199

MENZIES. Said to be originally *Maynoers, Meyners,* then *Menys* afterward *Meynes* or *Mengies,* and now *Menzies*—a branch of the family of *Manners,* in England, the name being originally the same. I think, rather, the name is derived from the parish of *Monzie,* in Perthshire, Scotland.

MERCER. One who deals in silks and woolen goods.

MEREDITH. This family is of British origin. Old chronicles relate that the first settlement of the family was situated on the Welsh shore, where the sea washed in with great impetuosity and noise, from whence it is added they took the name of *Meredyth,* or *Ameredith. Maredydd,* Welsh, the animated one.

MERLE or **MERRIL.** (Fr.) A blackbird. *Merel,* local, a town in Savoy.

MERTON. Local. From Merton, a town in Sussex, England, so called from *mere,* a lake or marsh, and *ton.*

MESHAW. (Fr.) *Mechant,* bad, wicked.

MESICK. (Dutch.) From *Maesyck,* a town on the river Maes, in the bishopric of Liege, Netherlands.

METCALF. In the Welsh, *medd* signifies a vale, a meadow, and *caf,* a cell, a chancel, a church, *i. e.,* the church in the vale.

The origin of the name, however, is given by tradition in this wise. In those days when bullfights were in vogue, in merry England, one of the enraged animals broke away from the combat, and was hotly pursued by horsemen. A certain John Strong happened to meet the bull on the top of a hill, and when attacked by the furious beast, he seized him in the nostrils with his left hand, and killed him. As he came to the foot of the hill, meeting several persons in the pursuit, he was inquired of whether he had met a bull; he replied he "*Met a calf,*" and from this circumstance was called afterward John *Metcalfe.*

METTERNICH. (Dutch.) From *Metter*, middle or in, and *naght*, night—middle of the night; born in the middle of the night. *Metternach*, local, the town next to the middle place, from *nach*, next, after, behind, at, or by.

MEYER. (Ger.) The magistrate of a city or town.

MEYEUL. Local. Came into England with William the Conqueror. The name is derived from a place in France.

MICHAEL. (Heb.) Who is like God?

MICKLE. From the Saxon Muchel; Scottish, Muckle, big.

MIDDLEDITCH. Local. The middle trench for draining wet land or guarding inclosures.

MIDDLETON. Local. From Middleton, a small town in Dorsetshire, England—the middle town.

MILBOURNE. Local. The mill brook, from *Miln*, a mill, and *borne* or *bourne*, a brook.

MILDMAY. Said to be derived from the Saxon *Mild*, soft or tender, and *dema*, a judge, and was given to one of the early ancestors of the family from his tempering the severity of the law with mercy.

MILFORD. Local. The ford by the mill.

MILLER. One who attends a grist-mill. *Meillear*, Gaelic, having large lips; *malair*, Gaelic, a merchant; *maillor*, Gaelic, from *maille*, armor, and *fear*, a man—a man in armor, having a coat of mail, a soldier.

MILLMAN. A man belonging to a mill.

MILLS. Local. Living near a mill. Gaelic, *Milidh*, a soldier, the *d* being silent.

MILNE. A mill. In Gaelic *Muileann* also signifies a mill; in Welsh, *Milain* implies firmness, fixedness of purpose.

MILNER. A miller.

OF FAMILY NAMES.

MILTHORPE. Local. From a village of that name in Westmoreland, England, so called from *mill*, and *thorpe*, a village —the mill-village.

MILTON. Local. From the town of Milton, in Kent, England. The mill-town, from the Saxon *miln*, a mill, and *ton;* or the middle town.

MINSTER. (Sax.) An abbey.

MINTURN. (Welsh.) Local. The round stones or circle of stones, from *min*, stones, and *turn*, a round, a circle; *trwn* and *tron*, Welsh, a circle.

MITCHELL. A corruption of Michael, or from the Saxon *Muchel*, big.

MIXE. Local. An ancient territory of France.

MOCHRIE. (Celtic.) My beloved, from *mo*, my, and *chree*, dear; a term of endearment, a sweetheart.

MOE. (Old English.) Large, tall, great.

MOEL. *Maol*, in the Gaelic, signifies bald.

MOELYN. (Welsh.) Bald-pate.

MOFFATT. Local. Derived from the town of Moffat, in Dumfriesshire, Scotland.

MOLEN. (Dutch.) A mill.

MOLLOY. (Cor. Br.) The dusty or hoary mill.

MOLYNEUX. (Fr.) Local. From Normandy, De Moulins, De Moulines, De Molineus. From *Moulins*, a town on the river Allier, in France, so called from the great number of water mills there. Fr., *Moulin*, a mill.

MONGER. Anciently an extensive merchant, now used to denote those who traffic in a single article.

MONK. Greek, μόνος; Welsh, *mon*, sole, separate, alone; Gaelic, *moanach*. A man who retires from the ordinary concerns of the world, and devotes himself to religion.

9

202 ETYMOLOGICAL DICTIONARY

MONROE. Local. Monadh Roe or Mont Roe, from the mount on the river Roe, in Ireland, whence the family came. Moine Roe, a mossy place on the Roe; M'unroe, from, of, or about the Roe. The river is sometimes written *Munree*.

MONSON. Derived, according to antiquarians, from the German word *Muntz*, but probably the son of Mon or Mun, a nickname for Edmund.

MONTAGUE. (Fr.) *De Mont aigue*—from the sharp or steep mountain.

MONTFORD. From the Latin *"De Monte Forte,"* that is, from the strong or fortified hill or mountain.

MONTGOMERY. A corruption of the Latin *"Mons Gomeris,"* Gomer's mount. *Gomer*, the son of Japhet, the hereditary name of the Gauls.

MONTMORICE. The mount of Morris; or from the Moorish mountains, perhaps natives of Morocco; some bearing this name went with William the Conqueror into England.

MOODY. A name given from the disposition. *Meudwy*, Welsh, an anchorite, a recluse, hermit, a monk.

MOERS. Derived from the town of *Moers*, in the Netherlands. *Moer* or *Moeras*, in Dutch, signifies a fen, marsh, or moor.

MOON. A corruption of *Mohun*, or it may be local, from the island Anglesey or *Mona*, so called, as some suppose, from *mwyn*, Welsh, mines, from its stone-quarries and mines; others derive it from *mon* or *mona*, alone, separated. *Mwyn*, Welsh, affable, pleasant.

MOONEY. *Meunier*, Fr., a miller.

MOORE or MORE. (Gaelic.) *Mor*, great, chief, tall, mighty, proud. *Moar*, a collector of manorial rents in the Isle of Man. *Moore*, from *moor*—John o' the Moor.

MORAN. A multitude. *Moran*, a contraction of Morgan, which signifies of or belonging to the sea.

OF FAMILY NAMES. 203

MORETON. (Gaelic.) Local. From *mor*, large, high, and *dun*, *ton*, a hill.

MORGAN. From *Mor*, the sea. and *gan*, born; the same as *Pelagius*—born on the sea, from the Greek πέλαγος, the sea. *Mor*, the sea, and *gan*, by or near—near the sea, a locality.

MORIARTY. (Gaelic.) Noble, illustrious, from *Mor*, great, and *artach*, exalted.

MORLEY. Local. From Morlaix, in Brittany, France, and derived from the Welsh or British word *mor*, the sea, and *ley*, a valley. It is situated near the sea, on a river of the same name.

MORSE. Probably a contraction of Morris. *Mors*, the name of a large island in Denmark, a marsh.

MORREL. Having yellow hair.

MORRIS. (Welsh.) From *Mawr* and *rys*, a hero, a warrior, a brave man. *Marth*, the great, the warlike, same as *Mavors*.

MORTON. (Gaelic.) Local. From the parish of Morton, in Nithsdale, Dumfriesshire, Scotland. *Mor*, big, great, and *dun*, *ton*, a hill.

MOSELEY. Local. *Moss-ley*, Sax., *Moose*, *Moyes*, or *Moss*, a mossy field or pasture.

MOTT. (Fr.) A round artificial hill.

MOULTON. Local. A small town in Devonshire, England.

MOUNTAIN. A name of place. This name once gave occasion to a pun which would have been excellent, had the allusion been made to any other book than the Holy Scriptures.

Dr. Mountain, chaplain to Charles II., was asked one day by that monarch to whom he should present a certain bishopric just then vacant. "If you had but faith, sire," replied he, "I could tell you to whom." "How so," said Charles, "if I had

204 ETYMOLOGICAL DICTIONARY

but faith." "Why, yes," said the witty cleric, "your majesty might then say to this *Mountain, be thou removed into that sea.*" The chaplain succeeded.

MOUNTJOY. A name adopted probably by one of the crusaders, from a place near Jerusalem, which, according to Sir John Mandeville, "men clepen Mount-Joye, for it gevethe joye to pilgrymes hertes, be cause that there men seen first Jerusalem * * * a full fair place, and a delicyous." Lower says, "Some religious houses in England had their *Mountjoys*, a name given to eminences where the first view of the sacred edifice was to be obtained. This name is still retained in a division of the hundred of Battel, not far from the remains of the majestic pile reared by William the Conqueror. Boyer defines '*Mont-joie*' as a heap of stones made by a French army, as a monument of victory."

MOXON. The son of *Moggie* or Margaret.

MOXLEY. Local. Probably *Mugasley*, from the Saxon *muga*, much, great, large, and *ley*, a field.

MULLIGAN. (Gaelic.) Local. *Mullechean*, the top or summit, a height.

MULLINS. (Fr.) A miller. "*De Moulin*," from the mill.

MUMFORD. The same as Montfort (which see).

MUNDY. Local. Derived from the Abbey of *Mondaye*, in the dukedom of Normandy.

MUNGEY. A corruption of *Mountjoy* (which see).

MUNN. A familiar abbreviation of Edmund.

MUNSEL. Local. From *Monsall*, a dale of Derbyshire, or a person originally from *Mansle*, in France.

MURRAY, MORAY. *De Moravia.* Some deduce this family from a warlike people called the *Moravii*, who came from Germany into Scotland, and affixed their own nomenclature to that district now called the *shire of Moray*. The root of the name is the same whether Moravian or Gaelic, and signifies the great water, from *mor*, great, and *an* or *av*, water.

OF FAMILY NAMES.

MURRELL. (Fr.) A sea wall or bank, to keep off the water; a name of place.

MUSGRAVE. King's falconer, from *Meus*, Sax., the place where the hawks were kept. and *grave*, keeper.

MYERS. The same as Meyer, the magistrate of a city or town; a very common name in Germany.

NAB. In the Persic, signifies a chief, a prince. *Nab*, English, the summit of a mountain, the top.

NAFFIS or **NEFIS.** (Fr.) From *Nefils*, that is, born son, from *Ne* and *fils*. *Nwyfus*, in the Welsh, signifies brisk, sprightly, active.

NAIRNE. Local. The name of a shire, river, and town in Scotland, whence the surname is derived. The name was taken from the river, which was called in Gaelic *uisge-n'fhearn*, from *uisge*, water, and *n'fhearn* (pronounced *nearn*, the "fh" having no sound), "the alders"—"the water of the alders," from the great number of alder-trees which grew on its banks.

NANCE. Local. From Nance or Nancy, a city of France, capital of the department of Meurthe, and signifies a valley; *nans* or *nantz*, in the Cornish British, is a plain, a dale, a level.

NAPIER. It is said that Donald, a son of the Earl of Lennox, for his bravery in battle, had his name changed by the king to *Napier*. After the battle, as the manner is, every one advancing and setting forth his own acts, the king said unto them, "Ye have all done valiantly, but there is one among you who hath 'Na Pier,'" and the king gave him lands in Fife and Goffurd. The name came, however, from taking charge of the king's napery or linen at the coronation of English kings, an office held by William De Hastings, in the time of Henry I.

NASH. Supposed to be a corruption of "*Atten-Ash*,"—at the ash. *Naish*, a place near Bristol, England. *Naisg*, Gaelic, made fast, bound, protected. Probably an old fortress or watch-tower.

ETYMOLOGICAL DICTIONARY

NAYLOR. A maker of nails.

NEANDER. Newman, Greek, νέος-ἀνὴρ, the new man.

NEEDHAM. Local. From *Needham*, a market-town in Suffolk, England—the village of cattle; Sax., *neat*, Danish, *nod*, a herd, and *ham*, a village. In another sense it may denote the clean, fair town.

NEAL. The same as Neil (which see). *Neal* may be sometimes a contraction of *Nigel*.

NEFF. French, *Naif*, artless, candid. *Nef*, a water-mill; the nave of a church.

NEFIS. Welsh, *Nwyfus*, sprightly. *Nefils*, French, a son born, descendant from.

NEIL and NEL. In the Cor. Br. signifies power, might, that is, the powerful or mighty. *Neul* or *Nial*, in the Gaelic, signifies a cloud or hue; figuratively, a dark complexion.

NELSON or NEILSON. The son of Neil or Nel.

NELTHROPE. From *Nehwl*, Gothic for near or nigh, and *thorpe*, a village; given to an individual living at such a spot near the village. [PLAYFAIR.]

NEQUAM. (Latin.) Dishonest, lazy. Alexander Nequam. of St. Albans, wishing to devote himself to a monastic life, in the abbey of his native town, applied to the ruler of that establishment for admission. The abbot's reply was thus laconically expressed:

"Si bonus sis, venias, si *Nequam*, nequaquam." If good, you may come; if wicked, by no means.

It is said he changed his name to *Neckham*, and was admitted into the fraternity.

NESS. A cape or promontory.

NETHERWOOD. Local. The lower wood.

NEVEU. (Fr.) A nephew.

NEVILLE. (Fr.) "*De Neuve ville*," of the new town. Neuville, a town in Poitou, France.

OF FAMILY NAMES. 207

NEVIN. (Gaelic.) *Naomh*, holy, sacred, consecrated. Welsh, *Nef*, heaven; *Nefanedig*, heaven-born; *Nefddawn*, heaven-gifted.

NEWBURY. (Sax.) New-town. A place in Berkshire raised out of the ruins of an old town called Spingham.

NEWTH. *Nuadh*, in the Gaelic, signifies new, fresh, recent.

NEWTON. Local. The name of several small towns in England—the new town.

NISBETT. Local. From the lands of Nisbett, in the shire of Berwick, Scotland.

NOAKES or **NOKES.** A corruption of *Atten Oak*, "at the oak;" *en* was added to *at* when the following word began with a vowel, as "John Atten Ash"—John Nash, that is, John at the Ash. Mr. John Nokes is a celebrated personage in legal matters, as well as his constant antagonist Mr. John Styles (John at the Style). The names are so common, that "Jack Noakes and Tom Styles" designate the rabble.

NOBLE. Great, elevated, dignified.

NOEL. (Fr.) Christmas; a name given probably to a child born at that time.

NOGENT. Local. From the town of Nogent, in the province of Champagne, France. The Nugents went from England into Ireland in the time of Henry II.

NORBURY. Local. The north town or village.

NORCUTT or **NORTHCOTE.** Local. The north-cot; so Eastcott and Westcott.

NORFOLK. Local. A county of England. *Nord-folk*, the north people, so called with regard to *Suffolk*, or the south people.

NORMAN. A native of Normandy, a northman. The inhabitants of Sweden, Denmark, and Norway were anciently so called.

208 ETYMOLOGICAL DICTIONARY

NORRIS. *Norroy*, or north-king; a title given, in England, to the third king-at-arms. *Norrie*, French, a foster-child.

NORTHAM. Local. The north house or village—*North-ham*.

NORTHOP. Local. A place in England; the north *thorp* or village.

NORTHUMBERLAND. Local. A county of England. *North-Humber-land*, the land on the north side of the river Humber.

NORTON. Local. From Norton, a town in Yorkshire, England. The north-town.

NORWICH. Local. From the city and seaport of Norwich, in Norfolk, England. The north-harbor, from *north*, and *wick*, a harbor or port.

NOTT. *Hnott*, Saxon, smooth, round, a nut. *Notted*, an old word for shorn, polled. The name may have come from wearing the hair short and smooth.

> "A *nott hed* had he, with a brown visage."—CHAUCER.

The following, it is said, was penned by the first wife of the Rev. Dr. Nott, on his asking her hand in marriage :

> "Why urge, dear sir, a bashful maid,
>   To change her single lot,
> When well you know, I've often said
>   In truth, I love you, *Nott*.
> For all your pain I do, *Nott*, care,
>   And trust me on my life,
> Though you had thousands,—I declare,
>   I would, *Nott*, be your wife."

NOTTINGHAM. Local. From the borough town of Nottingham, in England. Bailey says the name is corrupted from *Snottingham*, from the Saxon *Snottenga*, caves, and *ham*, a village, from the many caves and places of security found in that county.

NOWELL. The same as Noel (which see).

OF FAMILY NAMES.

NOX. Local. *Cnoc*, in the Gaelic, is a little hill, a hillock.

NOYES. *Noy* is an abbreviation for Noah. "In England, in the seventeenth century, Attorney-General Noy was succeeded by Sir John Banks, and Chief-justice Heath being found guilty of bribery, Sir John Finch obtained the office; hence it was said:

> "*Noy's* flood is gone,
> The *Banks* appear,
> *Heath* is shorn down,
> And *Finch* sings here."—LOWER.

In the Cornish British, *Noi* is a nephew, and *Noys* night.

NUGENT. (See Nogent.)

NYE. The familiar abbreviation of Isaac, among the Dutch. *Noie*, Danish, exact, precise, nice. *Ny*, Danish, new, recently produced. Lower gives the name from *Atten-Eye*, at the island.

OAKES. Local. From a dwelling near the oak-trees.

OAKHAM. Local. From the town of Oakham, in Rutlandshire, England, so called from *Oak*, and *ham*, the village by the oaks.

OAKLEY. Local. The fields or pasture abounding in oaks.

O'BIERNE. The same as O'Byrne. *O*, or *Ui*, signifies grandson, descendant. The descendants of Byrne. In the Welsh, *Bryn* is a hill; *Brenin*, a chief, a king.

O'BRIEN. The descendant of *Brien*, *i. e.*, exalted, noble.

O'BYRNE. Originally *O'Bran*, the descendants of *Bran*, an ancient king of Leinster; which signifies a *raven;* he was usually called *Bran Duv*, the black raven, from the color of his hair, and his thirst of prey.

O'CALLAGHAN. (Celtic or Gaelic.) The descendants or tribe of Callaghan, from *Ciallach*, prudent, judicious, discreet.

210 ETYMOLOGICAL DICTIONARY

OCHIERN or **OIGTHIERNA.** (Gaelic.) A term applied to the heir apparent to a lordship, from *Oig*, young, and *tierna*, a lord.

OCKHAM. Local. From *ock* or *ac*, an oak, and *ham*, a village, a town in Surrey, England, so called from the abundance of oaks growing there.

OCKLEY. (Sax.) From *ock* or *ac*, an oak, and *leag*, a field. The oak field.

O'CONOR or **O'CONNOR.** The descendants of Conor or Concovar, an Irish chieftain, who died in the year 971. (See Conor.)

O'DEVLIN. The descendant of Develin (which see)

O'DONNELL. The descendants of Donal, an ancient Irish family, who trace their descent through Donal to *Niallus Magnus*, the ancestor of the O'Neills, known as *Nial Niagallach*, Nial of the nine hostages. The O'Donnells ruled the territory of Tirconnell, for thirteen generations. (See Donald.)

O'DONOGHUE. The descendants of *Donogh* (which see).

O'DONOVAN. The descendants of Donovan, which is derived from *Dondubhan*, the brown-haired chief. This name was given to a celebrated Irish chieftain of the tenth century, who was killed by the famous Brian Boru.

O'DORCY. The descendant of Dorcy. Dorcy is a corruption of De Orsay, from *Orsay*, a town in Cleeve, Germany.

O'DOUGHERTY. The chief of the oak habitation, from O, high or chief, *doire* or *darach*, the place of oaks, and *tigh*, a habitation.

O'DUGAN. The descendant of Dugan (which see).

O'FLAHERTY. The descendant of Flaherty (which see).

OGDEN. Local. (Sax.) From *ock*, oak-tree, and *den*, a valley; the oak vale, or shady valley. *Ogduine*, in the Gaelic,

OF FAMILY NAMES.

211

signifies a young man, from *Og*, young, and *duine*, a man; *Ogdyn*, in the Welsh, has the same signification.

OGILVIE. Local. From the lands of *Ogilvie*, in Scotland. It may come from the Welsh *Ochil*, a high place.

O'GOWAN. The descendant of Gowan (which see).

O'HARA. The descendant of "*Hara*," Chaldee form of *ara*, a mountain. In Gaelic, *arra* signifies a pledge, treachery; *arr*, a stag, a hind; *arradh*, an armament; *ara*, plural of *ar*, slaughter, battle. *Hara*, Saxon, a hare.

O'KEEFE. The descendant of Kief. *Kief*, in the Danish, signifies brave, stout, courageous.

OLIFANT. An elephant.

O'LEARY. The descendant of Lary; *Llary*, Welsh, gentle, easy.

OLIVER. So named from the olive-tree, an emblem of peace.

OLLENDORFF. Local. From Oldendórf in Germany, so called from *Olden*, old, and *dorf*, a village.

OLMSTEAD. Local. A place or town by the green oaks, from *Holm*, an oak, and *stead*, a place. *Holme*, low lands on a river, an island.

O'MAHONY. The descendant of *Mahon*, which signifies a bear.

O'MALLEY. The descendant of Malley; *Mala*, Gaelic, the brow of a hill; *Maille*, smooth, placid, gentle.

ONDERDONK. (Dutch.) Under grace or pardon, from *onder*, under, and *dank*, thankfulness, gratitude.

O'NEIL. The descendants of *Neil*, that is, the powerful or mighty.

ONSLOW. Local. From the manor of Onslow, in Shropshire, England. *Aunslow* signifies a place on a river or stream.

O'QUIN. Anciently O'Con. The descendants of Con Ceadcaha, one of the early monarchs of Ireland.

ORCHARD. Local. An inclosure of fruit-trees. *Orcheard*, Gaelic, a goldsmith.

ORME. (French.) Local. An elm-tree.

ORMISTON. Local. The town or village of elms.

ORMSBY. From *orme*, an elm, and *by*, a town; a name of a place surrounded by elms.

ORR. Local. Derived from the river and town of Orr, in Scotland. *Or*, in Welsh and Gaelic, signifies a border, a boundary.

ORTON. Local. From the town of Orton, in Westmoreland, England. Gaelic, *Ord*, a hill of a round form and steep, and *ton*, a town a fortress.

ORVIS. *Urfhas*, in the Gaelic, signifies fair offspring. *Arvos*, Cor. Br., local, a place on or near an entrenchment, from *Ar* and *foss*.

OSBORN. (Sax.) From *hus*, a house, and *bearn*, a child—a family-child, an adopted child.

OSMUND. (Sax.) From *hus*, a house, and *mund*, peace.

OSTERHOUDT. (Dutch.) The east wood, from *oost* or *oster*, east, and *houdt*, a wood.

OSTHEIM. (Ger.) From *Ost*, east, and *heim*, a home, habitation or village.—From the east habitation or village.

OSTRANDER. (Dutch.) The lord of the east shore, from *oste*, east, *strand*, the shore, and *heer*, lord or master; he that must have his due of a stranded ship.

OSWALD. (Sax.) From *hus*, a house, and *wald*, a ruler—a house-ruler or steward; a king of Northumberland.

OTIS. (Greek.) From ὠτὸς, the genitive singular of οὖς, the ear, a name given from quick hearing.

O'TOOLE. Originally O'Tuathal—the descendants of *Tuathal*, which signifies " the lordly."

OF FAMILY NAMES.

OTTER. Local. *Oitir*, Gaelic, a low promontory jutting into the sea, a shoal.

OUDEKIRK. (Dutch.) Local. From a town of the same name in Holland, and signifies the old church, from *oude*, old, and *kerk*, a church.

OUSELEY. Local. From the river Ouse, in England, and *ley*, a field or place—a place on the river Ouse. The name *Ouse* is derived from the Gaelic *uisge*, water.

OUTHOUDT. (Dutch.) Local. The old wood.

OWEN. (Celtic.) The good offspring. *Oen*, Welsh, and Gaelic, *uan*, a lamb.

OXFORD. Local. From Oxford, in England, on the Isis, the seat of the celebrated university founded in 806; from *Ox*, Anglo-Saxon, water, corrupted by the Angles or Danes from the Gaelic *uisge* or *isk*, and *ford*, a pass or way—the ford across the Isis.

Bailey derives it from *Oxen-ford*, "the ford of the oxen," like the Greek *Bosphorus*, or from the river *Ouse*, and *ford*. The name of the river *Ouse* is derived from *uisge*, water.

PADDOCK. (Old English.) A meadow, croft or field; an inclosure in a park.

PAGE, Child, and Varlet, were names given to youths between seven and fourteen years of age while receiving their education for knighthood.

'AINE. *Paon*, Fr., a peacock. *Payne*, a pagan, unbaptized; a rustic.

'AISLEY. (Welsh.) Local. From *Plas*, a pass, and *lli*, a stream—the place of crossing the river.

'ALMER. A pilgrim, so called from the palm-branch, which he constantly carried as a pledge of his having been in the Holy Land.

> " Here is a holy *Palmer* come,
> From Salem first, and last from Rome."
> SCOTT'S MARMION.

214 ETYMOLOGICAL DICTIONARY

PANCOST. A corruption of *Pentecost*, the fifteenth day after Easter, a name probably given to a child born on that day.

PANGBOURN. Local. A town in Berkshire, England; *bourn*, a brook, a river.

PARDIE. A name given to one who was in the habit of swearing *Par-dieu*. Lower says, it is not a little curious that the French oath, "*Par Dieu*" has become naturalized among us, under the various modifications of *Pardew, Pardoe, Pardow*, and *Pardee*. So also we have the Norman name *Bigot*, from the habit of swearing "*Bi-God*."

PARSALL. Local. *Park-hall*, the same as Parshall. *Parcell* may be from *par-ciel*, "by heaven," a name given for the same reason as the preceding one.

PARIS. Local. The metropolis of France, on the Seine, anciently called "*Lutetia Parisiorum*," *Lutum*, mud, from its situation in a marshy place. A place where the *Pars* or *Peers* met in Congress. *Paro*, to make civil or military arrangements; *Paries*, a wall, a walled town; *Peri*, an island.

PARKE. A piece of ground inclosed, and stored with deer and other beasts of chase.

PARKER. The keeper of a park.

PARKMAN. The same as Parker.

PARNELL. The same as Pernell, from *Petronilla*, Italian, pretty stone. A wanton, immodest girl.

PARRET or **PERROT.** Local. From *Peraidd*, Welsh, the sweet or delicious river, now the *Dee*.

PARRY. (Welsh.) Probably a contraction of *Ap Harry*, the son of Harry. In the Welsh it also signifies ready, prepared, equal, like; *Para*, endurance, one capable of enduring. The name may be local, from *Parys*, a mountain in Wales, so called from *parhous*, inexhaustible (mines); or *Pres*, brass, copper, ore.

OF FAMILY NAMES.

215

PARSHALL. Local. *Park-hall*, the hall, or mansion in the Park.

PARSON. We suppose that its first founder was a clerical character or parson. From the Latin *Persona*, that is, the *person* who takes care of the souls of his parishioners.

PATRICK. From the Latin *Patricius*, noble, a senator; the name of the tutelary saint of Ireland.

PATTERSON or PATTISON. Patrick's son, the son of Patrick.

PAUL. Signifies little, small. Latin, *Paulus*, Greek, παῦλος.

PAXTON. Local. From the town of Paxton, in Berwickshire, Scotland.

PAYNE. Local. From a place called Payne, in Normandy.

PEABODY. There is an ancient tradition (we give it for what it is worth), that this name was derived from one *Boadie*, a kinsman of Queen Boadicea, who assisted her in her revolt against the Romans. After the Britons were subdued by the Romans, Queen Boadicea dispatched herself by poison, and Boadie, with a remnant of the Britons, escaped to the mountains of Wales. *Boadie*, among the Cambri or Britons, signified a man or a great man, and *Pea* signified a large hill, a mountain, from which Boadie came to be called Peabodie, or *the Mountain man*, which became the name of the tribe.

PEACOCK. Taken from the name of the well-known fowl; *pea*, contracted from the Latin, *pavo*, Saxon, *pawa*, French, *paon*,—a name given from a fondness of display.

PEARSON or PIERSON. *Pierre-son*, the son of Pierre or Peter.

PEDIN. Local. *Pedn*, Cor. Br., is a hill; the head of any thing.

PEEBLES. Local. From the town and shire of Peebles, in Scotland. *Pobl*, Welsh, people, and *lle*, a place; *Pobull*, Gaelic, people, and *eis*, many; the place of many people.

216 ETYMOLOGICAL DICTIONARY

PEELE. Local. A tower, a castle, a spire, a steeple, as *Carne-pele*, the spire rock. *Pele*, Fr., a bald-pated man.

PELHAM. Local. From the lordship of Pelham, in Hertford-shire, England, either from *peele*, a tower, castle, or from *pool*, a small lake, and *ham*, a village.

PELL, according to Bailey, is a house; in the Welsh it signi-fies, far off, at a distance.

PELLETIER. (Fr.) A furrier, or skinner.

PELLYN, now **PILLINGS.** (Cor. Br.) The distant pool. *Pyling*, an old word denoting a superstructure.

PENDLETON. Local. The summit of the hill, Gaelic, from *pendle*, the summit, and *dun*, a hill. *Pen-dal-ton*, the town at the head of the valley.

PENGILLY. (Cor. Br.) The head of the grove.

PENN. (Cor. Br.) The top of a hill; the head.

PENNANT. (Cor. Br.) From *Pen*, a head, and *nant*, a vale, or dingle; the head of the dingle; the principal mansion of the family, Bychton, in Wales, being situated at the head of a considerable dingle on the old family estate.

PENNINGTON. Local. Derived from the manor of Pen-nington, in Lancashire, England, anciently Penitone, written in the Doomsday-Book, *Pennegetum.*

PENEY. Local. A town in Savoy; the head of the water, from *pen* and *eau;* also a pinnacle.

PENNY or **PINNY.** The top of a mountain or hill. A mountain in Spain is called by the inhabitants " La *Penna* de los Enamorados," or the Lover's Rock. The word has the same meaning as the English *pinnacle.*

PENNYMAN or **PENNYMON.** (Welsh.) Local. *Pen-y-mon*, the top of the mountain.

OF FAMILY NAMES. 217

PERCY, PIERCY, PERCEY. Local. The renowned family of *Percy*, of Northumberland, England, derived their name from Percy Forest, in the Province of Maen, Normandy, whence they came, which signifies a stony place, from *pierre*. It may signify a hunting place, from *pirsen*, Teutonic, to hunt; *percer*, French, to penetrate, to force one's way.

PERKINS. From *Peir* or *Peter*, and the patronymic or diminutive termination *ins*,—little Peter, or the son of Peter.

PERRIGO. Local. From *Perigeux*, a town of France.

PERRY. If not synonymous with Parry, it is local, from *Pierre* (Fr.), a stone, signifying a stony place, abounding in rocks.

PEVENSEY. Local. A village in Sussex, England, the landing place of William the Conqueror, in 1066, derived from *Pau*, Welsh, a tract of pasture land, and *aven(s)*, a river, and *aig*, the sea, standing at the mouth of a river, near the sea. The name is also Gaelic, and has the same meaning. *Biadhabhainisg*, or *Pababhainisg*.

PEYTON. Assumed by the proprietors of Peyton, a small town near Boxford, in Suffolk, England. They were descendants of William Mallet, one of the favorites of William the Conqueror.

PHELPS. Supposed to be the same as Phillips (which see). The name may come from the Danish, *Hvalp*; Swedish, *Valp*, a whelp.

PHILIP. (Greek.) A lover of horses, from φίλος, and ἵππος.

PHIPPEN. A corruption of *Fitz Penn*, from the Norman, *Fitz*, a son, and *Penn*. The son of *Penn*.

PHYSICK. The art of healing diseases. A name given to a physician.

PICKERING. Local. A market town of north Yorkshire, England, with the remains of a castle.

PICKERSGILL. Local. The stream inhabited by pike or pickerel.

10

218   ETYMOLOGICAL DICTIONARY

PIERCE. The same as Piercy or Percy (which see).

PIERPONT. (Fr.) *De Pierre Pont,* from the stone bridge;
in Latin, *De Petra Ponte.*

PIGGOT and PICKETT. Pitted with the small-pox, spotted
in the face, from the French *Picoté.*

PIGMAN. A dealer in pigs. A man by the name of Johnson, in Staffordshire, England, who followed this occupation,
was generally called Pigman, and he willingly recognized
this cognomen.

PILCHER. A maker of *pilches,* a kind of great coat or upper
garment, in use in the fourteenth century.

> " After gret heat cometh cold,
> No man cast his *pylch* away."—CHAUCER.

PILLINGS. Same as *Pellyn* (which see).

PITTMAN, PUTMAN. A man living near a well or spring;
Saxon, *pit;* Danish, *put,* a well or spring.

PLAYFAIR. Local. The play ground, a place where fairs
were held, and holidays kept.

PLAYSTED. The place appropriated to amusement, or any
exercise intended for pleasure.

PLEASANTS. Local. From a suburb of the city of Edinburgh, called " The Pleasants," where anciently was a priory
of nuns, which was dedicated to St. Mary of *Placentia,* of
which the name " Pleasants" is a corruption.

PLYMPTON. Local. (Cor. Br.) From *Plym,* a river, and
ton, a town. The town situated on the river Plym, in Devonshire, England.

POLK. An abbreviation of Pollock (which see). Mr. Polk, the
late President, is third in descent from a Mr. Pollock.

POLLARD. A tree having its top cut off; a fish; *Poularde,*
French, a fat chicken; *Pol,* Dutch, a loose or lewd man,
and *ard,* disposition. *Poule-ard,* chicken-hearted.

OF FAMILY NAMES.

219

POLLEY. Local. From Poilley, in the province of Orleans, France, whence the family originally came.

POLLOCK. Local. Derived from the parish of *Pollock*, in Renfrewshire, Scotland. The name is from the Gaelic *Pollag*, "a little, pool, pit, or pond," a diminutive of *pol*, a pool. It is vulgarly pronounced Pock or Polk.

POMEROY. (Fr.) *Pomme-roi*, a kind of apple, the royal apple, king's apple, or king of apples; a name probably given to a gardener for his skill in raising them, or a name of place where such apples were raised.

POINDEXTER. (Fr.) The same as *Hotspur*, or spur the steed; *poin* being derived from *pungo*, to pierce, to prick, and *dexter*, right, as opposed to left; a word expressive of readiness of limbs, adroitness, expertness, and skill.

POITEVIN. A name given to a native of Poitou, France.

POOLE. Local. A small collection of water in a hollow place, supplied by a spring; a small lake. "John at the Pool," became "John Pool." A town in Dorsetshire, England.

POPE. Greek and Latin, *Papa*, father.

PORCHER. This name originated with *Simon Le Porcher*, hereditary grand huntsman to Louis Capel, King of France, from whose official duty of slaying the *boar*, the name is derived.

PORSON. The same as Parson, or a corruption of Power-son, the son of Power.

POWERS. (Welsh.) From *Powyr*, a descendant of Leod, who was the father of *Mandebrog* or *Mandubratius*.

POWELL. A contraction of the Welsh *Ap Howell*, the son of Howell. It may also be deduced from *Paul*, of which it was a former orthography:

> "After the text of Crist, and *Powel*, and Jon."
> WRIGHT'S CHAUCER, 7229.

POTTER. One who makes earthen vessels.

POTTINGER. An apothecary is so called in Scotland.

220 ETYMOLOGICAL DICTIONARY

POULTON. Local. From the town of Poulton, in Lancashire, England, also a place near Marlborough, in Wiltshire, so called from *Pool*, a small lake, and *ton*. a town.

POYNDER. A bailiff, one who distrains.

PRATT. From the Latin *Pratum*, a meadow. *Prat*, in the Dutch, signifies proud, arrogant, cunning.

PRESCOT. (Welsh.) Local. From Prescot, a small town in England, so called from *Prys*, a coppice, and *cwt*, a cottage.

PRESSLEY. Local. A coppice, from the Welsh *Prys*, shrubs, brushwood; Gaelic, *preas*, bushes, shrubs, and *lle*, a place, meadow or pasture lands.

PRESTON. Local. A town in Lancashire, England. The town in the coppice, or the bushy hill, from *Prys* and *ton*; also, *Preston*, the town where brass is found or manufactured, from *Pres*, brass, Welsh.

PRICE. (Welsh.) A corruption of *Ap Rice*, the son of Rice.

PRICHARD. (Welsh.) A contraction of *Ap Richard*, the son of Richard.

PRIDEAUX. (Fr.) From *Presd'eaux*, near the water.

PRINDLE. A croft or small field.

PRINGLE. Local. *Prencyll*, a hazel-wood, from *pren*, Welsh, a wood, and *cyll* or *coll*, hazel. *Pringle*, an obsolete Scottish coin.

PRODGERS, PROGERS, or PROGER. A contraction of *Ap Roger*, the son of Roger.

PROVOOST or PROOST. A name of office, a president of a college; the chief magistrate of a city.

PUGH or PYE. A contraction of *Ap Hugh*, the son of Hugh, "u" having in Welsh the sound of "y."

PUTNAM. (Dutch.) From *Put* or *Putten*, a well, and *ham*, a house or town. Welltown, or the house by the well.

PUTZKAMMER. (Ger.) A dressing-chamber, a room for dress and ornaments; a chamberlain.

OF FAMILY NAMES. 221

PYE. A contraction of *Ap Hugh* (see Pugh); also, a bird; there was an old sign of a pye over an inn in London called *Pye Corner*.

QUACKENBOSS. (Dutch.) *Quickenbosch*, a thicket, a grove of roan-tree, mountain-ash, a species of service-tree.

QUENTIN or **QUINTIN.** From the Latin *Quintus*, "the fifth," a name given to the fifth son. *Quentin*, a town in Cotes du Nord, France, so called from St. Quentin, who died there.

QUIGLY. Gaelic, *Cuigealach*, of or belonging to a distaff or hand rock; perhaps a thrifty person, or from resembling a distaff in bodily peculiarity.

QUIN. Local. From *Quin*, a village in Clare county, Ireland.

RADCLIFF. Local. A place in Lancashire, England, so called from a cliff of red rock.

RADFORD. (Cor. Br.) The fern way.

RADLAND. (Cor. Br.) The fern land.

RADNOR. (Cor. Br.) The enclosure of ferns.

RAFFLES. (Danish.) From *Raefel*, long-lubber, lath-back, inactive, sluggish.

RAINSFORD. Local. A corruption of *Ravensford*.

RALEIGH. *Rhawlaw*, in the Welsh, signifies a lieutenant, a vicar; and *Rheoli*, to govern, to rule. It may be local, from *Ral*, Raoul or Ralph, and *leigh*, or *ley*, a field or place.

RALPH. (Sax.) From *Rad*, counsel, and *ulph*, help, French, *Raoul*, Latin, *Rodolphus*, a helper, a counselor.

RALSTON. Local. Ralph, one of the descendants of Mac Duff, Thane of Fife, obtained a grant of land in Renfrewshire, and, as was common in those days, called the place after himself, *Ralphstown*, which was softened into *Ralston*.

RAMAGE. Branches of trees; a coppice where birds sing.

222 ETYMOLOGICAL DICTIONARY

RAMSEY. Local. From *Ea,* Saxon, water, or an isle, and *Ram,* Ram's Isle, a place in Huntingdonshire, England; where the family originated, and afterward settled in Scotland. *Ramus,* Latin. branches, young trees—the isle of underbrush, branches, or young trees; a place where cattle browse. *Reomasey,* Saxon, from *Reoma,* the rim, edge, extremity, a border, and *ey,* an island.

RAMSDEN. (Sax.) Local. The winding valley, or the extremity of the valley.

RAN. (Sax.) Pure, clear.

RAND. (Dutch.) The border, a borderer.

RANDAL, RANDOLPH, or RANDULPH. (Sax.) These names have the same signification. *Fair-help,* from *Ran,* fair, and *ulph,* help.

RANDER. Local. (Gaelic and Welsh.) A tract of land on a point or promontory. *Rand,* Danish, the rim, border, edge.

RANKIN. This name may be derived from the Danish *Rank,* right, upright, erect. If the name is Gaelic, it would come from *Roinn,* a promontory, share, or division, and *Ceann,* head; the head of the promontory, a name of place. *Ranken,* in the Dutch, signifies pranks, tricks.

RANNEY. Local. *Renaix, Reinow,* or *Renais,* a town of Switzerland. *René* (Latin, *renatus*), renewed, born again, regenerated.

RANSOM, RANSOME. The price paid for redemption from captivity or punishment.

RATHBONE. (Sax.) An early gift.

RAPP. *Rap,* in Danish, is swift, nimble. *Rap,* Dutch, nimble, quick; "*rap gasten,*" a nimble fellow.

RAWDON. Local. From the lands of Royden, near Leeds, in Yorkshire, England.

OF FAMILY NAMES.

223

RAWLEY. (Welsh.) *Rhawlaw*, a vicar. (Evans.)

RAWLINGS. From *Raoul*, French for Ralph, and the patronymic termination *ings ;—*Ralph's son.

RAWLINSON, The son of Rawlings.

RAWSON. A corruption of Ravenson, or it may be Ralph's son.

RAY. This name may have several origins. *Ruadh* and *Reagh*, Gaelic, swarthy, red, sandy complexioned. *Re*, the moon. *Ray*, a beam of light, luster. *Re*, from *ruo*, to rush, applied to a stream, rapids, whence the river *Reay*, in Caithness, Scotland. *Rea*, Cor. Br., wonderful, strange. *Rhe*, Welsh, a run, *Rhedu*, to run. *Rhae*, Welsh, a battle, the place of a battle ; a chain.

RAYMER. (Dutch.) *Roemur*, one who extols, praises, boasts. *Raumer*, German, a person employed in clearing or cleaning.

RAYMOND. (Teut.) From *Rein*, pure, and *mund*, mouth; pure mouth, one who abstains from wanton discourses. *Raymund*, German, quiet peace.

RAYNER. (Danish.) Raner, a leader of the Danes, who invaded Britain ; a pirate, a robber, a term given to a warrior.

RECORD. The same as *Rikerd*, or *Richard*, of which it is a corruption, liberal-hearted, rich in disposition.

REDDEN or RODDEN. Local. (Cor. Br.) A place of ferns. *Rodon*, a town in Bretagne, France.

REDDENHURST. Local. *Reddon*, Cor. Br., fern, and *hurst*, Saxon, a wood or grove.

REED and READ. (Sax.) From *Rede*, advice, counsel, help, or from the fenny plant, a reed.

REESE, RHEESE. (Cor. Br.) Pushing, violent ; a strong or powerful man. *Riese*, in German, signifies a giant. Welsh, *Rhys*, a rushing. *Rees*, a town of Germany, on the Rhine.

224 ETYMOLOGICAL DICTIONARY

REEVES. From *Reeve*, a bailiff, provost, or steward, *Shire-reeve, Wood-reeve*, (Sheriff, Woodruff.)

REINARD and REYNARD. (Teut. or Sax.) From *Rein*, pure, and *ard*, nature, disposition; honest, incorrupt.

REINHART. (Dutch.) A pure heart, from *rein*, pure.

RENARD. (Fr.) A fox, cunning.

RETZ. Local. A town in Moravia.

REYNOLDS. (Sax.) Sincere or pure love from, *Rhein*, pure, and *hold*, the old English for love. It also may signify strong or firm hold.

REYNOLDSON. The son of Reynolds.

RHEFELDT. The deer-field, from the Dutch *rhee*, a roe, and *feldt*, a field.

RHODES. Local. From the island of Rhodes, in the Mediterranean Sea. *Rhodes*, a town in Guienne, France.

RIAN. Gaelic, *Ria*, a provincial chief. *Rian*, manner, order, arrangement, sobriety, good disposition.

RICE. Another form of *Rys*, Welsh, to rush, a rushing; figuratively, a hero, a brave, impetuous man. The same as Rees.

RICH. Wealthy, opulent; anciently, great, noble, powerful.

RICHARD or RICARD. (Sax.) Of a powerful, rich, or generous disposition, from *ric*, rich, and *ard*, nature or disposition.

RICHARDSON. The son of Richard.

RICHMOND. (Sax.) From *ric*, rich, and *mund*, mouth— rich-mouth; figuratively, eloquent.

RICKETTS. A corruption of *Ricards*, from *Richard* (which see).

RIDDELL. Local. From lands in the county of Yorkshire, formerly called the *Ryedales*.

OF FAMILY NAMES. 225

RIDDER and **RITTER.** The same as *Ruyter*, a knight, a chevalier.

RIGGS. From the Danish *rig*, wealthy, rich; or the name may be local, and denoting a steep elevation, a range of hills, or the upper part of such a range.

RING. (Dutch.) Local. A Canton; a district of an ecclesiastical congregation.

RINGE. (Danish.) Mean, low, small, little; a ring, circle. Local, a round place.

RINGGOLD. (Welsh.) Local. *Rhingol*, a cleft, cliff, or steep bank.

RIPLEY. Local. A market-town in west Yorkshire, England, from the Saxon *rypan*, to divide or separate, and *ley*, uncultivated lands, a pasture.

ROBERTS. (Sax.) From *Rod*, counsel, and *bert* or *bericht*, bright or famous—famous in counsel.

ROBY. (Danish.) From *Ro*, rest, repose, and *by*, a town— the peaceful town.

ROCHESTER. Local. From a city in Kent, England, so called from *Roche*, French, a rock, and *chester*, from the Latin *castrum*, a city or castle; an uneven, rough, and stony place. *Reoh*, Saxon, and *Rauh*, German, signify rough, rugged, uneven. (See Chester.)

ROCHFORT. Local. A town of France—"the strong rock."

ROE. (Gaelic.) Red-haired. Nor. Fr., *Rou*, Rufus.

ROEMER. (Dutch.) From *Roem*, glory, renown; a praiser, a boaster.

ROGER. (Teutonic.) *Rhu*, rest, quiet, peace, and *gard*, a keeper; or *Rhu-geren*, one desirous of rest; *Rodgarus*, all counsel or strong counsel.

ROLAND, ROLLIN, and **RODLAND.** (Sax.) Counsel for the land.

20*

226　　ETYMOLOGICAL DICTIONARY

ROMAINE. The same as Roman, from Rome; also, strong.

ROMANNO. Local. From lands in the county of Peebles, Scotland. so called from a Roman military way, leading from the famous Roman camp at Line to the Lothians, which passed through the middle of those lands, from which they were called *Romanno*.

ROOF. Probably the same as Reeve, an officer or steward. *Ruf,* German, reputation, famous, renowned.

ROORBACK. (Dutch.) Noisy brook. A town in Bavaria, Germany.

ROOT. Local. A place lying low, the base, foot, or bottom of a mountain, the lower part of land.

ROSENCRANS. (Danish.) *Rosenkrands,* a garland of roses; in Dutch, the place of rose-trees.

ROSEVELDT. (Dutch.) The field of roses.

ROSS. (Gaelic.) Local. A shire of Scotland. *Ros,* a peninsula, an isthmus, a promontory. *Rhos,* in Welsh, is a moor, a bog. *Ros,* in Cor. Br., is a mountain, a meadow, a common. *Rose* and *Rosh* signify a valley or dale between hills.

ROSWELL. *Rosveldt,* the rose-field; *Rosville,* the town on the heath or promontory.

ROTH. (German.) Red color.

ROTHSCHILD or ROSCHILD. From a town in Denmark, which is said to take its name from a river with which it is watered that drives several mills. *Roe,* in the ancient Danish language, signifies a king, and *kille,* a stream of water or brook, *i. e.,* the king's brook. Some have given the signification " Red-shield" to the name, from *Roth,* red.

ROUSE. (Fr.) Red, red-haired, same as Rufus.

ROUSSEAU. (Fr.) One having reddish hair, carrot color. *Ruisseau,* local, a brook.

OF FAMILY NAMES. 227

ROWE. Local. A river that overflows its banks. Rowe, *Rue*, Fr., a street; *Roe*, Gaelic, red-haired.

ROWEL. Local. From the river *Rouel*, in the Netherlands.

ROWEN. Local. A town in Bohemia; *Rouen*, a town in France; *Rowan*, a tree, the mountain-ash.

ROWLE. (Cor. Br.) Rule, order, law; *Rheol*, Welsh, rule, law.

ROWLEY. (Sax.) Local. From *Row*, sweet or pleasant, and *ley*, a field.

ROWNTREE. *Rowan-tree*, the mountain-ash, so named from that kind of tree growing near the premises.

ROY. (Gaelic.) *Ruadh, Roe, Roy*, red-haired; also *Roye*, a town in England. *Roi*, French, king, whence Le Roy.

RUFUS. (Fr.) Red, from the color of the hair.

RUE. Local. From *Reaux*, in Hainault, Netherlands. Fr., *Rue*, a street.

RUGGLES. Local. A town of France, on the Eure.

RUNDELL. A contraction of Arundle (which see). *Rundle* also signifies a sparrow.

RUNNION or RUNON. (Gaelic.) A small hill.

RUSBRIDGE. Local. From the town of Rousbrugge, in Germany.

RUSS. A Russian, so called in Holland.

RUSSELL. (Fr.) Red-haired, somewhat reddish; carrot-color.

RUSSEY. Local. A town in Doubs, France.

RUTGERS. (Dutch.) *Rudgert*, the same as Roger, quiet, tranquil; one desirous of rest, a keeper of rest; *Rodgarus*, strong counsel.

228 ETYMOLOGICAL DICTIONARY

RUTHERFORD. Local. From the lands of Rutherford on the river Tweed, in the parish of Maxton, Roxburgshire, Scotland. The name is derived from the Welsh *Ruthr*, rushing, swift, and *fford*, a ford or way.

RUTHVEN. From the lands and barony of Ruthven, in Perthshire, Scotland; a river of the same name; " *Ruithabhainn*," i. e., the rushing or swift stream.

RUYTER. A knight or chevalier, in the Dutch or German, and sometimes written *Ritter*, having the same signification as the English Rider.

RYDER. A forest officer, being mounted, and having the supervision of a large district. In the ballad of William of Cloudesly, the king, rewarding the dexterity of the archer who shot the apple from his child's head, says:

> "I give thee eightene pence a day,
> And my bowe thou shalt bere;
> And over all the north countre
> I make thee chyfe *rydere*."

RYE. (French.) Local. From *Rive*, a coast, a shore, a bank, border.

RYNDERS. Local. A town in North Jutland; the same as Rander.

SACKVILLE. A corruption of the Latin *De Sicca villa*, that is, from the dry town.

SAFFORD. Local. A corruption of Seaford, a town of Sussex, England.

SALES. *Sahl*, or *saal*, in German, signifies a hall or court. French, *salle*. The name may be local, and derived from the river Sale, in France, or Saal, a river in Bavaria.

SALISBURY or SARISBURY. (Sax.) Local. A city and capital of Wiltshire, England. The town of health; the dry

OF FAMILY NAMES. 229

town. The old town of Salisbury anciently stood upon a hill where there was no water, but it is now situated in a valley, and a little brook runs through the streets. The name was sometimes written *Salusbury*, that is, the healthy hill or town.

SALTER. A name of trade, one who sells salt.

SANDFORD. Local. From Sandford, a place in Westmoreland, England—the sand-ford.

SANDS. (Danish.) Sense, wit; or it may be from *Sand*, *Sandy*, a Scottish abbreviation of Alexander.

SANGSTER. (Scottish.) A song-maker or singer.

SANXAY. (Fr.) Local. From the town of Sanxay, in Poitou, France.

SATERLEE. Local. A place in England where *Saturn* was worshiped by the pagan Saxons.

SAXE. A Saxon, so called in Holland. In Athelstan's song of victory, given in the Saxon Chronicles, A.D. 938, *secce* signifies a fight; *secga*, a warrior; *seax* or *secce*, a sword, any sharp instrument. Latin, *sica*, a dagger.

SAXTON. An under officer of the church, the same as Sexton. Local, *Sax-town*, a town of the Saxons.

SCARBOROUGH. (Sax.) Local. From the seaport and borough of Scarborough, in Yorkshire, England, from *scear*, a sharp rock or hill, and *burgh*, a town or fort; literally, a hill, from *bergh*. The town or fort on or by the sharp-peaked rocks.

SCARRET. Local. *Scear*, a rocky cliff. *Scarard*, the high cliff; *Leskerret*, a market-town in Cornwall, England. The old part of the town stands upon rocky heights.

SCARDSDALE. A valley in Devonshire, England, so called from the Saxon *scearres*, indented or sharp disjointed rocks called *scars*, and *dale*, a valley.

230　ETYMOLOGICAL DICTIONARY

SCHAFFER. (Dutch.) He that dishes up or provides victuals. *Shaffer*, German, a shepherd, a pastor, a swain.

SCHELL. (Old English.) A spring.

SCHELLDEN. (Old English.) The spring in the valley, from *schell*, a spring, and *dene*, a valley. *Skell* is also a well, in the old northern English.

SCHENCK. (Ger.) From *schenke*, an inn or public house; a name of place.

SCHERMERHORN. (Dutch.) From *Shermer*, a fencer, and *hoorn*, a horn, which emblematically expresses strength or power.

SCHOONHOVEN. (Dutch.) From the name of a town in South Holland, and signifies fine gardens or courts, from *schoon*, beautiful, and *hof*, plural, *hoven*, gardens or courts.

SCHOONMAKER. (Dutch.) From *Schoenmaker*, a shoemaker.

SCHUYLER. (Dutch.) *Van Schuyler*, from the place of shelter. *Schuiler*, a hider; *Schuil*, a shelter, a hiding-place. *Schuler*, German, a scholar.

SCOTT. A native of Scotland. Nennius uses both *Scythæ* and *Scotti* indifferently. Strabo considers *Scythæ* and *Nomades* synonymous terms. The original word in Ossian is *Scuta*, which literally signifies "restless wanderer," hence the propriety of the name *Scuite* or Scot.

SCRANTON. (Dutch.) From *schrantsen*, to tear, seize, or break, so named, perhaps, from his warlike propensities.

SCROGGS. Local. From *Scrog*, a stunted shrub, bush, or branch, given probably from the location of the dwelling.

SEAFORD. Local. From a seaport town of that name in Sussex, England.

SEAFORTH. Local. The name of a projection of the sea on the east coast of Lewis, on the Long Island, Scotland—" the forth or frith of the sea."

OF FAMILY NAMES. 231

SEAVER. (Gaelic.) *Saibher*, rich; *Sever*, local, a town in France.

SEAMAN. A sailor, one who follows the sea.

SEARS. (Cor. Br.) From *sair*, a carpenter or sawyer; Welsh, *saer ;* Gaelic, *saor*, a carpenter.

SEATON. Local. That is, *sea-town*, a parish in Perthshire, formerly called Errol. (See Seton.)

SEBRIGHT. From *Se*, Saxon, used the same as the article *the*, and *bright*. The illustrious, the renowned.

SEDGWICK. The town or harbor abounding with sedge, *wick*, a town or harbor.

SEGUR. (Ger.) Powerful, victorious, from *sieg*, victory. Dutch, *zege*.

SEIX. Local. A town in Arriege, France.

SELBY. Local. A market-town in west Yorkshire, England, on the Ouse. Danish, *Seile*, to sail, to navigate, and *by*, a town. *Seil*, a sail. A place of boats or sails.

SELKIRK. Local. A borough town of Scotland. *Cellkirk*, a religious house. A *cell* was anciently that part of a temple within the walls. *Sel-carrik*, Cor. Br., the high rock; *Sel*, a view, a prospect, Welsh, *syllu*, to look, and *carrik* or *craig*, a rock.

SELLENGER. A corruption of St. Leger, and that from St. Leodeger.

SELLICK. (Cor. Br.) Local. A name of place, and signifies in open view, remarkable, conspicuous. *Crugsellick*, in Verian, the barrow in open view, from *sel*, a view.

SEMARD. A corruption of St. Medard.

SEMPLE or **SIMPLE.** A corruption of St. Paul.

232   ETYMOLOGICAL DICTIONARY

SETON. Local. From lands of that name in Haddingtonshire, Scotland, which were so called because the town thereof was situated close upon the sea, and which gave name to the family of Seton, so renowned in Scottish annals.

SEVERN. Local. A river rising in the mountain Plynlimmon, in Wales.

SEVERINS. Local. Mountains in Languedoc, France.

SEWARD. High admiral, who kept the sea against pirates, from *sea*, and *ward*, a keeper.

SEWALL and SEWELL. Probably from *sea* and *wall*, a structure of stone or other materials intended for a defense or security against the sea. This name, though seemingly local, may have various significations; *suil*, in the Gaelic, is a willow; *suail*, small, inconsiderable. *Su*, south, and *wold*, *wald*, *wild*, *well*, an uncultivated place, a wood, a plain, a lawn, hills without wood: *Suwold, Suwall, Suwell.*

SEYMOUR. A corruption of St. Maurus.

SHADDOCK or SCHADECK. Local. The name of a lordship in Germany.

SHAN. (Celtic.) Old; *shanty*, an old house.

SHANACH. (Gaelic.) *Sionnach*, a fox.

SHANE. The Celtic for John.

SHANNON. (Gaelic.) From the Shannon, a river of Ireland. The tranquil, gentle river, from *sen*, gentle, and *abhain*, a river. *Shan-eon*, the tranquil river. *S* before a vowel, in the Gaelic, has the sound of *sh*. The river *Seine*, in France, has the same signification. *Shanon*—the ancient river, from *sean*, old, and *oun* or *obhain*, a river.

SHAW. (Scotch.) A lawn, a plain surrounded by trees, or an open space between woods.

OF FAMILY NAMES. 233

SHELDON. (Cor. Br.) Local. The spring in the valley, from *schell*, a spring, and *dene*, a small valley.

SHELLEY. Local. Derived from Shelley, in Essex, Suffolk, and Yorkshire, England, from *Schell*, a spring, and *ley*, a field.

SHEPPY. Local. From an island in the county of Kent, so called from the Saxon *Sceap-Ea*, or *Sceap-Ige*, that is, the Sheep's Isle, because sheep abundantly multiplied there; called also *Ovini*, from the Latin *ovis*, a sheep.

SHERARD. Said to be derived from one *Scirrard*, who came with William the Conqueror, and obtained lands in Chester and Lancaster, England. As a local name, it may signify in Anglo Saxon, a high cliff; rocky heights, from *Scearard*.

SHERLOCK. (Gaelic.) From *Saor*, pronounced as with "*h*" after the "*S*," signifying *clear*, and *loch*, a lake, the clear lake.

SHERMAN. A shearman, one who used to shear cloth.

"Villain, thy father was a plasterer, and thou thyself a *shearman*."
Stafford to Jack Cade. Shaks. Henry VI.

SHERWOOD. From the Saxon *sher* (*scir*), clear, and *wood*, *a clearing in the wood*, or the *cleared woods*; or as Bailey gives the word, "*Sheer-wood*, in Nottinghamshire." It may be derived from *shire*, (Sax.) *scire*, (Ger.) *schier*, to divide, a portion or division of land; of which divisions there are forty in England, twelve in Wales, and twenty-four in Scotland.

SHIEL. Local. A river and loch or lake, in the south-west of Inverness-shire, Scotland. *Shiels* were shepherd's huts, a term used by the Northumbrian Saxons, to denote the temporary shelters of shepherds.

SHOLTIS. (Ger.) *Schultheiss*, a mayor, magistrate.

SHORT. Alluding to stature, not tall.

234   ETYMOLOGICAL DICTIONARY

SHREWSBURY. Local. A town in Shropshire, England, from the Saxon *Scrube*, a shrub, a small tree, and *burgh*, a town.

SHRIEVES. A sheriff, from *scir* and *reeve*, the bailiff of a *shire* or division. The shire-reeve.

SHUCK. (Dutch.) Signifies twelve or a dozen, and is applied to sheaves in a harvest field.

SHUCKBURGH. Local. A place in Warwickshire, England. From Saxon, *soc*, an immunity, privilege, baronial or royal court, and *burgh*, a town or city—a privileged place, or place possessing a particular court or jurisdiction.

SHURTLIFF. Local. The "short cliff;" separated, cut off, from the Saxon, *sceort*, short, and *cliff*.

SHUTE. Local. From the castle of Shute, in Normandy, France.

SIDDONS. (Welsh.) From *syddyn*, a farm—a farmer.

SIGURD. The same as *Segur*, powerful.

SIKES. Local. A small spring well.

SIMEON. (Heb.) Hearing.

SIMMONS. A corruption of Simeon or Simon.

SIMS. A contraction of Simeon or Simon, the son of *Sim*.

SINCLAIR. A corruption of St. Clair, and that from St. Clara, from the Latin *clarus*, pure, renowned, illustrious.

SINGEN and SINDEN. A corruption of St. John, which is generally pronounced *Singen*.

SISSON. Local. Derived from *Sissonne*, a town in France.

SKEFFINGTON. (Sax.) Local. From *sceap*, a sheep, and *ton*, a town. The sheep-town. The name of a small village in England.

SKELTON. (Sax.) Local. The hill of separation or boundary.

OF FAMILY NAMES. 235

SKENE. Some derive their names, as well as their arms, from some considerable action, and thus, it is said, a second son of one Struan Robertson, for killing a wolf in Stocket Forest, Athol, Scotland, with a *dirk*, in the king's presence, got the name of *Skene*, which signifies a dirk, Gaelic, *Sgian*, and three dirk-points in pale for his arms. *Skians*, Cor. Brit., implies witty, skillful, knowing.

SKIDMORE or **SCUDMORE.** (Cor. Br.) From *scoudh*, or *scuth*, the shoulders, and *mor*, big, large.—Broad shoulders. *Scheidmuur*, Dutch, a partition or division wall.

SLACK. Local. A valley, or small shallow dell.

SLADE. Local. A long flat piece or slip of ground between hills.

SLAVEN. (Celtic.) From *sliabh*, a mountain, a mountaineer.

SLEEPER. (Dutch.) A cartman, or one who carries goods on a sledge.

SMITH. The most common of all surnames, and might of itself furnish matter enough for a volume. The word is derived from the Anglo-Saxon *Smitan*, to smite or strike.

> "From whence comes *Smith*, all be he knight or squire,
> But from the *Smith* that *forgeth* at the fire?"
>
> VERSTEGAN.

Among the Highland clans, the smith ranked third in dignity to the chief, from his skill in fabricating military weapons, and his dexterity in teaching the use of them.

In Wales there were three sciences which a villain (tenant) could not teach his son without the consent of his lord, *Scholarship, Bardism,* and *Smithcraft.* This was one of the liberal sciences, and the term had a more comprehensive sense than we give to it at this time. The smith must have united in this profession, different branches of knowledge which are now practiced separately, such as raising the ore, converting it into metal, etc.

236   ETYMOLOGICAL DICTIONARY

The term was originally applied to artificers in wood as well as metal, in fact, to all mechanical workmen, which accounts for the great frequency of the name.

The New York City Directory for 1856 (in which the names of the heads of families only, are given,) contains the names of more than eighteen hundred Smiths, of whom seventy-four are plain James Smiths, and one hundred and seventeen, John Smiths!

We see in the papers, that *John Smith* dies, is married, hanged, drowned, and brutally murdered, daily! *John Smith* doesn't identify anybody, and is therefore *no name at all.*

This numerous family is the subject of many laughable anecdotes and witty sallies. A wag, on a certain occasion, coming late to the theater, and wishing to get a seat, shouted at the top of his voice, "Mr. Smith's house is on fire!" The house was thinned five per cent., and the man of humor found a snug seat.

In many neighborhoods the name is so frequent that it is necessary to append some *soubriquet* to identify the person.

"Can you tell me where Mr. Smith lives, mister?" "Smith—Smith—what Smith? there are a good many of that name in these parts—my name is Smith." "Why, I don't know his t'other name, but he's a sour, crabbed sort of fellow, and they call him 'Crab Smith.'" "Oh, the deuce! s'pose I'm the man."

But the best piece of humor relating to the name is the following which we take from Lower, which appeared some years since in the newspapers, under the title of

"THE SMITHS.

"Some very learned disquisitions are just now going on in the journals touching the origin and extraordinary extension of the family of ' *the Smiths.*'

"Industrious explorers after derivatives and nominal roots, they say, would find in the name of *John Smith* a world of mystery; and a philologist in the *Providence Journal*, after

OF FAMILY NAMES.

having written some thirty columns for the enlightenment of the public thereanent, has thrown down his pen, and declared the subject exhaustless.

"From what has hitherto been discovered, it appears that the great and formidable family of the Smiths are the veritable descendants, in a direct line, from Shem, the son of Noah, the father of the Shemitish tribe, or the tribe of Shem; and it is thus derived—Shem, Shemit, Shmit, Smith. Another learned pundit, in the *Philadelphia Gazette*, contends for the universality of the name John Smith, not only in Great Britain and America, but among all kindred and nations on the face of the earth. Beginning with the 'Hebrew, he says, the Hebrews had no *Christian* names, consequently they had no Johns, and in Hebrew the name stood simply Shem· or Shemit; but in the other nations John Smith is found at full, one and indivisible. Thus, Latin, Johannes Smithius; Italian, Giovanni Smithi; Spanish, Juan Smithas; Dutch, Hans Schmidt; French, Jean Smeets; Greek, 'Ιον Σκμίτον; Russian, Jonloff Skmittowski; Polish, Ivan Schmittiwciski; Chinese, Jahon Shimmit; Icelandic, Jahne Smithson; Welsh, Iihon Schmidd; Tuscarora, Ton Qa Smittia; Mexican, Jontli F'Smitti.

"And then, to prove the antiquity of the name, the same *savant* observes, that 'among the cartouches deciphered by Rosselini, on the temple of Osiris in Egypt, was found the name of Pharaoh Smithosis, being the ninth in the eighteenth dynasty of Theban kings. He was the founder of the celebrated temple of Smithopolis Magna.' We heartily congratulate the respectable multitude of the Smiths on these profound researches—researches which bid fair to explode the generally received opinion that the *great* family of the *Smiths* were the descendants of mere horse-shoers and hammer-men!"

SNELL. (Dutch.) *Snel,* agile, swift. nimble.

SNODGRASS. Local. Grass trimmed and smooth; short grass.

238   ETYMOLOGICAL DICTIONARY

SNOW.   (Dutch.)   From *Snoo*, cunning, subtle, crafty, sly.

SNYDER.   (Ger.)   From *schneider*, a tailor.

SOLDEN.   Local.   A town in Westphalia, Germany.

SOMER.   Alluvial land.   Gaelic and Welsh, *so* for *swl* or *sal*, soil, and *mer*, a lake, water, the sea.

SOMERVILLE.   The village near a marsh or lake; *So mer*, a marshy soil, near water or the sea. *So*, for *swl*, *sal*, the earth, soil, land. *Samhradh*, Gaelic, summer, from *Samh*, the sun. *Somerset* may have been so called because the primitive inhabitants had an altar to the sun, *samh*, or because the country lay to the south.

SOMMER.   (Fr.)   From *sommer*, to sum or cast up; one who directs or commands. *Summere*, Dan., to sum up.

SOULÈ.   Local.   A small territory in France, between Bearn and the Lower Navarre.

SOUTHCOTE.   The south cot; so *East-cott* and *West-cott*.

SOUTHWELL.   Local.   A town in Nottinghamshire, England.   The south well or plain.

SPALDING.   Local.   From the town of Spalding, in Lincolnshire, England. *Spalding*, a ravine, from the German *spalte*, a ravine.

SPARK.   To disperse, to scatter, to sparkle.

SPAAREN.   Local.   A river in North Holland.

SPELMAN.   (Danish.)   From *Spillemand*, a fiddler. *Spille*, to game, to play.

SPENCE.   An abbreviation of Spencer.

SPENCER.   (Nor. Fr.)   *Le Despenser*, a steward.   The ancestor of the family assumed the name *Le Despenser* (Latin, *dispensator*), from being steward to the household of William the Conqueror.

SPICER.   A name of trade, a grocer.

OF FAMILY NAMES. 239

SPIEGEL. (Dutch.) A looking-glass.

SPIER. *Spere*, to ask, to inquire; a word used formerly in Scotland and the north of Ireland. The name may be from *spear*, a long-pointed weapon used in war, and given for some exploit in battle, or taken from a sign over an inn. "John at the Spear."

SPINK. A bird, a finch.

SPOOR. (Dutch.) A spur; that which excites; a locality, as the spur of a mountain; whatever projects; the track or foot-prints of beasts.

SPOTTEN. (Ger.) To mock, deride, ridicule.

SPRAGUE. From *Spraak*, Dutch, speech, language,—figuratively, eloquent.

ST. ALBANS. Local. A town in Hertfordshire, England, so named from a Pagan deity, *Alban*, which name signifies a high hill, the *Verulam* of the Romans. Offa dedicated a church to Alban, the proto-martyr of Britain, in the time of Diocletian.

STAATS. *Staats* is the nick-name in Dutch for *Eustace*, or Eustatius, which is derived from the Greek εὐ, and ιστημι, well-established, firm, unyielding.

STACY. A seeming form of the Latin *Statius*, from *Sto*, to stand, stationed, standing still, fixed.

STAINES. An old word for stones; a market town in Middlesex, England.

STAIR. Local. (Gaelic.) Stepping stones in a river; a path made over a bog.

STAIRN. (Gaelic.) Din, noise. *Styrn*, Saxon, stubborn, severe.

STALKER. A fowler who goes warily and softly in pursuit of his game; one who walks on stilts over ditches in pursuit of moor-fowl.

240   ETYMOLOGICAL DICTIONARY

> "The fowler is employed his limed twigs to set,
> One underneath his horse to get a shoot doth *stalk*,
> Another over dykes upon his stilts doth walk."—DRAYTON.

STANHOPE. Local. From the town of Stanhope, in the bishopric of Durham, England. From *stan*, stone, and *hope*, the side of a hill, or low ground amid hills.

STANLEY. Local. A market-town in Gloucestershire, England. The place of a tin mine, *stan*, tin, Welsh, *ystaen*, and *ley ;* or from the Saxon, *stan*, a stone, and *ley*—the stony place.

STANTON. From *stan*, a stone, and *ton*, a hill or town.

STANWOOD. (Saxon.) From *stan*, a stone, and *wood*—the stony wood.

STAPLETON. (Saxon.) From *stapel, stapol, stapula*, a staple, fastening, stake, and *ton*,—a town inclosed or fenced round with stakes.

STARK. Anglo Saxon, *Starc*, German *Starck*, strong, firm, confirmed to the utmost degree.

STARKEY. Strong of body, from *Stark*.

STARR. (Ger.) Stiff, rigid, inflexible.

STEAD. A place enclosed, a station or standing place. *Stad*, and *stede*, in Dutch, signifies a town.

STEANE or STEEN. (Danish and Dutch.) A stone.

STEARNS or STERN. Severe in look, harsh, bold. *Stierne*, Danish, a star.

STEBBINS or STUBBINS. Local. From a town of the same name called Stebbings, originally *Stubing*, in Essex, England. So called from *stub*, Saxon, *styobe*, Latin *stipes*, the stump of a tree, and *ing*, a field or meadow.

STEELE. A name given, in all probability, to a person who was inflexible, hard, firm, or enduring.

OF FAMILY NAMES. 241

STEIN. Local. A town in the isle of Sky, Scotland. *Stein,* German and Danish, a stone.

STELL. (Ger.) A place, station, office.

STEMME. (Dan.) Voice, vote, suffrage; also to tune, to agree, to accord.

STENNETT. (Dan.) Local. From *stenet,* stony, rocky.

STETSON. *Stedson,* in Danish, is a *stepson.*

STEVENS. From Stephen, from the Greek Στέφανος, a crown.

STEWART. Walter, the son of Fleance, and grand-son of Banquo, was created, by Malcom III. Lord High Steward of Scotland, from which office his family afterward took and retained the name of Stewart, and from them descended the royal family of *Stuart.*

STILL. Quiet, calm, silent. A vessel used in the distillation of liquors. " John at the *Still.*"

STIMANDS. (Dan.) From *Stimand,* a robber, highwayman.

STIRLING. Local. From the city of Stirling, the Gaelic name of which is *Strila,* by some supposed to signify " the place of strife," from *Stri-thralla.*

A Mr. Stirling, who was minister of the barony church of Glasgow, during the war maintained against the insatiable ambition of Louis XIV., in that part of his prayer which related to public affairs, used to beseech the Lord that he would take the haughty tyrant of France, and shake him over the mouth of hell, " *but good Lord,*" added the worthy man, " *dinna let him fa' in.*" This curious prayer having been mentioned to Louis, he laughed heartily at this new and ingenious method of punishing ambition, and frequently afterward gave as a toast, " The good Scotch parson."

STOCKER. One who stocks, stores, or supplies. *Stalker,* one who *stalks,* a *fowler* who goes warily and softly in pursuit of his game.

11

242 ETYMOLOGICAL DICTIONARY

STOCKING. Local. From *Stoc*, Saxon, a place, and *ing*, low land, a meadow.

STOCKTON. Local. A town in Durham, on the Tees, England, from *stoke*, a place, a settlement, and *ton*, a town.

STODDARD. Concerning the origin of this name there is a tradition, that the first of the family came over with William the Conqueror, as standard-bearer to Viscompte De Pulesdon, a noble Norman, and that the name is derived from the office of a standard-bearer, and was anciently written *De La Standard*, corrupted to *Stodard* or *Stodart*.

STOKES. Local. A parish in Buckinghamshire; also, towns in Suffolk and Gloucestershire, England. The name signifies a place, a settlement. *Stuge*, Danish, a ravine.

STOKESBY or **STUKEBY.** Local. *Stugeby*, the village in the ravine.

STONE. Local. A town in England. The name was probably given to an individual who resided near or by some remarkable stone, or at a place called Stone. "Will at the Stone."

STORR. (Dan.) From *storre*, greater, larger, stout, strong.

STOUGHTON. Local. This family derive its name from *Stoche* or *Stoke*, a place in Surrey, England, and *tun*, a word signifying an inclosure.

STOVER. (Dan.) A fleet hound, a name given for swiftness or love of hunting.

STOWE. A fixed place or mansion; a town, a garrison.

STRACHAN. (Gaelic.) Local. From the parish of Strachan in Kincardineshire, Scotland, formerly *Strathaen*. The name may come from *stra* or *strath*, a vale, from the root *strath*, a valley, through which a river runs, and *chan* or *ceann*, the head, meaning "the head of the valley," or "a little valley," from *Strathan*.

OF FAMILY NAMES.

243

STRAIN. Local. A town in the north of Scotland, written *Strane*. It may be a contraction of Strachan, a little *strath* or valley.

STRATTON, STRETTON. (Cor. Br.) Local. The hill full of fresh springs.

STRICKLAND. This name came from *Strick-land* or *Stirk-land*, that is, "the pasture ground of young cattle," called *stirks* or *steers*, in the parish of Moreland, Westmoreland Co., England, where the family once had considerable possessions.

STRINGER. One who made or fitted the strings to the bows in the time of archery.

"In war if a string break, the man is lost and is no man, and his weapon is gone, and although he have two strings put on at once, yet he shall have small leisure and less room to bend his bow, therefore, God send us good *stringers* both for war and peace."—ASCHAM.

STRYKER. (Dan.) From *strige*, to strike, to roam, to travel, hence a worker at a trade, a traveler.

STUKLEY or **STUKLY.** (Gaelic.) Local. From *stuc*, a little hill jutting out from a greater, a cliff, and *ley*, a place. *Stugley*, Danish, a ravine, a place near a cliff.

STYLES. A very common name "At the Style"—John Atte Style—John Styles. (See Noakes.)

SULLIVAN. (Celtic.) From *suil*, eye, and *ban*, fair—the fair-eyed.

SULLY. (Fr.) Local. From the town of Sully, in the province of Orleans, France.

SULT. (Gaelic.) *Suilt* or *Sult*, comeliness, beauty, fat.

SUMMER. So called, probably, from the season summer. The word is derived from the Saxon *Sumer ;* Celtic or Gaelic, *samh*, the sun. *Summer*, one who casts up an account. The name may be a corruption of *Sumner*.

244   ETYMOLOGICAL DICTIONARY

SUMNER, SOMNER, SOMPNOURE. One whose duty consisted in citing delinquents to the ecclesiastical courts; an apparitor; literally, a *summoner*.

> "Sim *Somnor*, in hast, wend thou thi way,
> Byd Joseph and his wyff, be name,
> *At the coort to apper* this day,
> Hem to pourge of her defame."
> CROWN MYSTERIES.

Chaucer gives us a description of the Sompnour in his Canterbury Tales.

SUMPTER. A teamster or groom who drives beasts of burden. A "*sumpter-horse*," a horse which carries necessaries for a journey.

SUNDERLAND. Local. A seaport town in the county of Durham, England. Land separated, divided, parted.

SURTEES. Local. From *Sur-Tees*, that is, on the river Tees or Tay, in the county of Durham, England, where the first of the family settled.

SUTPHEN. (Dutch.) Originally Van Zutphen, that is, from the city of Zutphen, in Germany.

SWARTWOUT. (Dutch.) The same as the English *Blackwood*, from *Zwart*, black, and *woud*, a wood.

SUTER, SUTTER, and SHUTER. A shoemaker, one who sews or stitches.

SUTTON. Local. A town in Devonshire, England—the south town.

SWAIM. Local. From *Schwaim*, a town in Lower Bavaria.

SWANE. (Dan.) A swan. *Swain*, a youth, a servant, a herdsman.

SWEET. *Swede*, a native of Sweden. *Swit*, of Switzerland.

OF FAMILY NAMES. 245

SWETTENHAM. A name of place, from *sweete*, pleasant or agreeable, and *ham*, a village.

SWEYNE Gaelic, *Sean;* Cornish, *Swoen;* Welsh, *Swyn*, a charm.

SWIFT. Local. A name given for swiftness in moving. It may be local, from *Swift*, a river of England.

SWINBURN. Local. *Sweyne's burn* or boundary, from *bourn*, a boundary.

SWITS. A native of Switzerland, so called in Holland.

SWITZER. A Swiss, a native of Switzerland.

SYLVESTER. Belonging to the forest, a woodman, from *Sylva*, Latin, a wood.

SYMES. Supposed to be a variation of *Sims*, from *Simon* or *Simeon*.

SYMINGTON. Local. From a parish by that name in the north-west of Kyle, Ayrshire, Scotland; originally *Symonstown*, so called from Simon Lockard or Lockart, who held the lands under Walter, the first Stewart.

TABOR. Local. *Tabur* or *Tobar*, Gaelic, a spring-well, water, a river. *Tabor*, a city in Bohemia, which the Hussites fortified and made the seat of their war for twenty years; on this account they were called *Taborites*. The family may probably derive their name from this city.

TAGGART. *Tycwrdd*, Welsh, a meeting-house. *Tagair*, Gaelic, to plead a cause, claim as a right, to reason, to debate.

TAITE or TATE. (Gaelic.) Pleasure, delight. *Tate*, learned. *Tad*, in Welsh, is a father, and *Taid*, a grandfather.

TALBOT. A mastiff.

246   ETYMOLOGICAL DICTIONARY

TAPPAN. (Welsh.) Local. The top of the hanging rock, from *tap*, a hanging rock, and *pen*, top or head.

TASKER. A thrasher.

TATTERSALL. Local. From the town of Tattersall, in Lincolnshire, England.

TAYLOR. A name of trade. We find this name modified to Tay*leure*, the orthography having been changed by the bearers to hide what they thought the lowness of its origin. So Smith is changed to *Smyth*, Turner to *Turnour*, etc.— as Camden says, "Mollified ridiculously lest their bearers should seem villified by them."
A Mr. Taylor, who, from this false pride, had changed his name to Tay*leure*, once haughtily demanding of a farmer the name of his dog, the man replied, "Why, sir, his proper name is Jowler, but since he's a consequential kind of puppy, we calls him *Jouleure!*"

TEDDINGTON. Local. A place on the Thames, so called from the tide ending there, before the building of London bridge—"tide-ending town," corrupted to Teddington.

TEFFT or TEFT. Local. A piece of ground where there has been a house.

TELFAIR. (Italian.) *Tagliaferro*, pronounced Tollifer. Fr., *tailler*, to cut, and *fer*, iron. It is said that the first of the name was so called from having cut a bar of iron in two with his sword. A smith.

TELFORD. Local. The narrow or straightened pass or way, from the Welsh *tel*, tight, and *ford*, a way. Anglo-Saxon, *Tillford*, at the ford or shallow place in a river. "At-illford," corrupted to Tilford.

TEMES. Local. *Thamesis*, the Thames, so called from the meeting together of the rivers *Tame* and *Isis*, the chief river of Britain.

OF FAMILY NAMES.

247

TEMPLE. From the manor of Temple, in Wellesborough, Leicestershire, which name was given by the old Earl of Leicester, one of the Knights Templars, who usually gave the name of Temple to their lands.

TENBROOK. (Dutch.) *Ten*, at, and *broek*, a brook, a stream, or marsh—the house or place at the brook.

TENEYCK. (Dutch.) Ten oaks, or at the oaks.

TENNANT. *Tenant*, a person holding lands under another, from *Teneo*, Latin, to hold. Local, *Tyn*, Welsh, a stretch, and *nant*, a ravine.

TENNISON and TENNYSON. From *Tenesone*, a place in Gottespunt or Cazdee, in Switzerland. If the name be not local, it is probably a corruption of *Dennison*.

TERRIL, TIRREL. Local. The little tower.

TERWILLIGER. Dutch, "*Der Willikeur*," a by-law, a statute. "*Der willige-waar*," serviceable ware, or ware that sells well.

TEW. (Welsh.) Fat, a corpulent person.

THEOBALD. God's power; but in the Saxon *Theobald* signifies powerful or bold over the people. In the Saxon *Psalter theod* is the same as *gentes*, and the English nation is often called Engla-Theod. See Tibbits.

THOMAS. (Heb.) A twin.

THOMLIN, and THOMLINSON. From Thom or Thomas, and *ing* or *ling*, a child or descendant—the son of Thomas.

THOMS. An abbreviation of Thomas; *Tom*, local, Gaelic and Welsh, a round hillock or knoll, a rising ground, an eminence, any round heap, a tumulus.

THOMSON. The son of Thomas.

THORN. Local. A town in England; a tree or bush armed with spines or sharp shoots. "Will at the Thorn."

THORPE. A village. Dutch, *Dorp*.

THRASHER. One who thrashes grain.

THROCKMORTON. A corruption of *At Rock-moor-town,* "a town on a rock in a moor," in the vale of Evesham, Fladbury, Warwickshire, England, whence the name was derived.

THURSTON. Local. The hill or town where the Saxon god *Thor* was worshiped by the Anglo-Saxons.

THWAITE and THWAYTES. Local. A piece of ground cleared of wood, from the Anglo-Saxon *thweotan*, to cut. In some places in England the word signifies a rivulet; marshy ground; also, a meadow.

TIBBITS. Has the same signification as Theobald, of which it is a corruption. *Theobald* is in the French *Theobaud*, pronounced *Tibbo*, whence *Tibbauds* or Tibbitts. *Theobald* is derived by Camden from *Theod*, the people, and *bald*, brave or bold, that is, powerful or bold over the people. B. Rhenanus derives it from *Theos*, God, and *bald*—God's power.

TICE. (Dutch.) A familiar abbreviation of *Matthias*.

TICHBOURNE. Anciently *At Itchen-bourne*, that is, a person settled at the head of a fountain of the river Itchen. The river Itchen is in Southampton county, England. At the head of the river, near Alresford, the first ancestor of this family resided, long before the Conquest.

TICHENOR. Local. Probably a corruption of *At Itchenor*, '*T Itchenor*, from the river Itchen; the name of a village in Sussex, England.

TIERNAY. (Gaelic.) *Tighearna*, a lord, a judge, a landed proprietor. (See Tournay.)

TIFFANY. A maker or vender of silk. Tiffany was a sort of light silk used by painters to trace the outlines of a picture through.

TILMAN. One who works a farm.

OF FAMILY NAMES.

249

TILL. Local. The name of a river in England.

TILLINGHAST. Local. A place where auctions are held; buying, selling, dividing, paying over. German, *theilen;* Dutch, *deelen,* to separate, divide, pay over. *A dealing house.*

TILLY. Local. A town of France.

TILMONT. Local. A town in Brabant, Netherlands.

TILTON. Local. Derived from Tilton, a village in England, probably an ancient place of tilting, or tents. *Tilt,* Saxon, a tent.

TING. Local. Among the ancient Gaels or Celts the place where courts were held, and justice administered, was called *Ting, i. e.,* to surround; the circle, the temple, or round hill. The Tings at first were only judicial, but, in process of time they became legislative. The most remarkable object of this kind is the Tynwald, in the Isle of Man. *Thing,* Saxon, a cause, meeting, a council; German, *ding,* a court. Dutch, *Dinger,* a pleader.

TEESDALE. Local. The dale on the Tees, a river of England, that separates the counties of Durham and York, and enters the German ocean below Stockton.

TOBY. The Welsh for Thomas.

TODD. *Tod,* a Scotch word for a fox.

TOLLMACHE. (Nor. Fr.) Tolling of the bell.

TOLMAN. A collector of toll. In Dutch, *Taalman* is an interpreter, from *Taal,* language, tongue. "*Constantine Tolmaen,*" in Cornwall, is an ancient place of Druid worship. *Tolmaen* is usually applied to a stone that is perforated, from *tol.* a hole, and *maen,* a stone; *twll mwn,* Welsh, a mine, shaft, or pit.

TORRY. Local. *Torr,* Gaelic, a conical hill or mountain, a mound, a grave, a tower; piled up, formed into heaps; to heap up, to bury.

11*

250 ETYMOLOGICAL DICTIONARY

TOUCEY. Local. From the town of Toucey in the province of Champagne, France.

TOURNAY. Local. From Tournay, a town in Artois, France, and may signify the tower or castle near the water. *Tierna*, in Gaelic, written *Tighearna*, means a landlord, a lord, or judge, and was applied to all great men, and is derived, according to Dr. MacPherson, from *te* or *ti*, an old word for *one*, and *eren*, land, as implying a landed gentleman; I think the root of the name is *Tir*, land, and *earr* or *earran*, a division, share, or portion.

TOWERS, Peels, and Castles, were places of defense. Tower is derived from *tor*, Gaelic and Saxon, French *tour*, Welsh, *twr*, a heap or pile, applied to conical hills, and to round buildings erected for strength or security.

TOWNER. A dweller in a town.

TOWNSEND. Local. One who lived at the end of the town.

TRACY or **TRACEY.** Local. A village in the Department of Oise, France. E. Tracy came with William the Conqueror into England. Sir William Tracy was most active among the four knights that killed Thomas à Becket, on which account tradition reports, it is imposed on the Tracys for miraculous penance, that whether they go by land or water, the wind is always in their faces, hence an old saying,

"The Tracys have always the wind in their faces."

"If this were so," says Dr. Fuller, "it were a favor in a hot summer to the females of that family, and would spare them the use of a fan." The word may signify a rampart, a terrace.

TRAILLE. (Gaelic.) A servant, sloven, slave.

TRAIN. (Gaelic.) *Treun*, brave, valiant, bold.

TRAINEUR. (Fr.) A straggler.

OF FAMILY NAMES. 251

TRELAWNEY. Local. (Cor. Br.) The open town near the water; from *Tre*, a town, *lawn*, open, and *ey*, water.

TREMAINE. Local. (Cor. Br.) The town on the shore or sea-coast, from *Tre*, a town, and *mayne*—the stone town, the river or passage town.

TRENOR, TRAINOR, TRAINER. (Gaelic.) *Treunmhor*, very brave; *Treun*, Gaelic, brave, valiant; *er* or *or*, the termination of *fear*, a man.

TREVELYAN. Local. (Cor. Br.) *Trevellyan*, the town of the mill. Welsh, *Tremelin*, or *Trevelin*.

TREVOR. Local. (Cor. Br.) From *Trevear*, the great town.

TRIPP. According to tradition, this name was given to Lord Howard's fifth son, at the siege of Boulogne. King Henry V. being there, asked how they took the town and castle. Howard answered, "*I tripp'd up the walls.*" Saith his majesty, "*Tripp* shall be thy name, and no longer Howard," and honored him with a scaling-ladder for his coat of arms.

This tradition, as well as many others I have given, is not very probable, but I give them insertion because they are curious and amusing, and some of them may be founded on actual occurrences.

TROTTER. (Fr.) *Trotteur*, a person always on the trot; a rambler.

TROUBLEFIELD. Local. A corruption of the Norman name *Tuberville*.

TROWBRIDGE. Local. A town in England. The name signifies "through the bridge;" perhaps given for some feat of daring, or bodily courage.

TRUAX. (Cor. Br.) The place on the waters, from *Tre*, a town, and *aux*, waters; or, if from the French, "*the three waters.*"

TRUE. Local. From Trieu, a river in Bretagne, France. *Tre* signifies a town.

252   ETYMOLOGICAL DICTIONARY

TRULAN. (Gaelic.) *Truaillean*, a pitiful person, a sneak.

TRULL. A slut, a vile wench, a strumpet; a name derived from the mother.

TUDOR. The Welsh for *Theodore*, or in old English, pious, as *Tudor Belin*, the pious king.

TUPMAN. A breeder of rams, which are called, in some places in England, *Tups*.

TUPPER. According to the celebrated poet by this name, Martin Farquhar Tupper, it is a corruption of part of the motto of the family, "*Tout perdie.*"

TURCOTTE. (Welsh.) *Turcwt*, a craggy, abrupt pinnacle, or tower, from *Tur*, a tower, and *cwt*, abrupt, cut off, implying defense. *Tor*, or *Tur*, a Saxon deity, and *cot*, a house, *Thorcot*.

TURNBULL. This name had its origin in some feat of personal strength or courage. There is the following tradition of its origin: A strong man of the name of *Ruel*, having turned a wild bull by the head, which violently ran against King Robert Bruce in Stirling Park, received from the king the lands of Bedrule, and the name of Turnbull.

TURNOUR. There is a tradition that this family derive their name from their ancient place of settlement in Normandy, which being a black castle, was called *Le tour noir*, whence the lords thereof were called *Les Sires de Tournoir*, and by contraction *Tournor*. One of the family went with William the Conqueror into England. It is probably the same as *Turner*, a name of trade, the orthography being changed.

TURTON. From Turton, in the hundred of Shelfold, in Lancashire, probably so called from Saxon, *Tur* or *Tor*, a tower, or *Thur*, or *Thor*, one of the Saxon deities, and *ton*—either a town having a tower, or sacred to Thor.

TUTHILL or **TUTTLE.** Local. A town in Caernarvon, Wales, near the coast.

OF FAMILY NAMES. 253

TWICKENHAM. Local. A village of Middlesex, England. *Tweywicken*, the "*two wickens*," or wares on the river, and *ham*, a village.

TWING. (Danish.) From *Twinge*, to force, master, subdue; or a name perhaps given from his dexterity in archery. *At Wing*, may be abbreviated to Twing.

TWOPENNY. From the Flemish *Tupigny*, from *Tup*, a ram, and *ign* or *ine*, quality, disposition, the same as *ignus*, in Latin.

TYNG. (See Ting.)

TYNTE. Tradition gives the following derivation: In the year 1192, at the celebrated battle of Ascalon, a young knight of the noble house of Arundel, clad all in white, with his horse's housing of the same color, so gallantly distinguished himself on the field, that Richard Cœur de Lion remarked publicly after the victory, that the maiden knight had borne himself a lion, and done deeds equal to those of six croises (or crusaders). Whereupon he conferred upon him for arms, a lion on a field, between six crosslets, and for his motto,

"*Tinctus* crurore Saraceno." "Stained with Saracen blood."

Whence his descendants assumed the name of Tynte, and settled in Somersetshire, England.

TYSON. The son of *Tys*, an abbreviation, among the Dutch, of Matthias.

UDINE. Local. A town in the north-east of Italy.

UHLAN or ULINE. May come from *Ulen* or *Ulens*, a place now called Flensburgh, in Denmark; a name given from the sound made by the ebbing and flowing of the sea.

ULMAN. (Ger.) All man.

ULMER. *Allmer*, all famous, renowned. *Ollmor*, Welsh, the whole sea.

254 ETYMOLOGICAL DICTIONARY

UNDERHILL. Local. Under the hill.

UNDERWOOD. Local. Under the wood.

UNWIN. (Dan.) Invincible.

UPHAM. Local. The house or town on a height.

UPTON. Local. The high hill, or the town on the height.

URRAN. (Cor. Br.) From *urrian*, the border, boundary, or limit of a country.

USHER. An officer of a court who introduces strangers; the under-master of a school.

USTICK. Studious, affectionate, learned.

VACHER. (Fr.) A cow-herd; a keeper of cows.

VALE. Local. Low land between hills, a valley.

VALENTINE. From the Latin *Valentinus*, a name derived from *valens*, able, puissant, brave.

VALK. (Dutch.) A hawk, a falcon.

VAN ALSTYNE. Local. From the old or high stone, Dutch.

VAN AMEE, VAN NAMEN, and VAN NAME. Local. From the city of Namen or Namur, in the Netherlands.

VAN ANTWERP. (Dutch.) Local. From the city of Antwerp, which signifies the *wharf*, or the place of *wharfing*, casting anchor, or tying up the ships.

VAN ARDEN, VAN AERDEN, and VAN ORDEN. Local. From *Aerden*, a town in Holland.

VAN ARNHEM, VAN ARNUM, VAN ORNUM. Local. From *Arnheim*, a city in Guilderland, Holland.

VAN BUREN. (Dutch.) Local. From the town of Buren, in Holland.

OF FAMILY NAMES. 255

VAN BUSKIRK. From the church in the wood, from *Bos*, a wood, and *kerk*, a church.

VAN CLEVE or **VAN KLEEF.** From the city of Cleve or Cleves, in Westphalia, Germany.

VAN CORTLANDT. (Dutch.) From the short land; *kort*, short, and *landt*, land.

VAN CUREN or **VAN KEUREN.** (Dutch.) Local. From the territory of an elector in Germany. *Keur*, German, an elector.

VAN DAM. Local. From the town of *Dam*, in Holland, which signifies a mole or bank to prevent inundations, and where towns were frequently built, as Amsterdam (Amstel-dam), Rotterdam.

VANDENBURGH. (Dutch.) From the hill.

VANDENHOFF. (Dutch.) From the garden; *hof* also signifies a *court* as well as a *garden*, so that it may be, from the court.

VANDERBILT. (Dutch.) *Byl*, in Dutch, signifies a hatchet or bill. *Byltye*, a little hatchet or bill. *Die Byltye* was a nickname given to ship-carpenters at Amsterdam, hence *Van de Bylt*.

VANDERBOGART. (Dutch.) From the orchard.

VANDERHEYDEN. So named from Heyden, an ancient town in Holstein, Denmark.

VANDERLINDEN. Corrupted to Van O Linda—from the linden-trees or grove of linden.

VANDERLIPPE. Local. From the town of Lippe, in Germany.

VANDERMARK. (Dutch.) From the *Mark*. *Mark* was the denomination of a kind of county which made the bound or limit of a country — like the British *marches*. Hence *mark-graaf*, marquis, the keeper of the marks or marches.

ETYMOLOGICAL DICTIONARY

VANDERPOEL. From the marsh or lake.

VANDERSPEIGLE. (Dutch.) From the looking-glass; figuratively, neat, fine, spruce.

VANDERVEER. (Dutch.) From the ferry; *Veer* signifying a ferry. *Veere*, or *Ter Veere*, is the name of a town in Holland, whence probably the name originated.

VANDERWERKEN. (Dutch.) From the *workers ; werken*, plural of *werk ; werker*, a worker.

VANDERZEE. (Dutch.) From the sea; a child being born at sea during a violent storm, his parents gave him the name of *Storm Vanderzee.*

VAN DOUSEN and **VAN DUZEN.** (Dutch.) From the town of *Doesen*, in Lower Saxony.

VAN DYCK. (Dutch.) From the dyke; a bank or mound thrown up to prevent inundations from the river or sea.

VAN EPS. Local. From the town of Eep, in Holland.

VAN HOOVEN. Local. From Hoeven, a town in Holland.

VAN HORN and **VAN HOORN.** Local. From the town of Horn or Hoorn, in Holland.

VAN HUISEN, VAN HOOSEN, and VAN HUSEN. Local. From Huizen, a town on the Zuyder Zee, in Holland.

VAN INGEN. Local. From Ingen, a town in Holland, near the river Lech.

VAN LOON. Local. From Loon, a town on the river Maes, in Holland.

VAN NESS. Local. *Naze*, a cape or promontory. Van Naze or Van Ness, from the Cape.

VAN NORDEN. Local. From Naarden, a town in Holland.

VAN NOSTRAND. Properly *Van Ostrand* (which see).

VAN OSTRAND. From the east shore; *oost*, east, and *strand*, shore or coast.

OF FAMILY NAMES. 257

VAN PATTEN. Local. From Putten, a town in Holland.

VAN RENSSELAER. Local. *Van rand Soleure, i. e.,* from the border of Soleure, a canton of Switzerland; *Van,* from, *rand,* border, margin.

VAN STANTVOORDT. Local. From Zandvoort, a town in North Holland.

VAN SCHAACK, VAN SCHAICK, VAN SCHEYK. Local. From the town of *Scheyk,* in Holland.

VAN SCHOONHOVEN. (Dutch.) Local. From the town of Schoonhoven, in South Holland, which signifies " fine gardens;" from *schoon,* fine, and *hof,* a garden or court, plural *hoven.*

VAN SLYCK. Local. From the channel called *Het Slaeck,* in the Netherlands, which makes *Tolen* an island. *Slyk,* Dutch, signifies dirt, mire. *Van Slyk,* "from the dirt."

VAN STEINBURGH. (Dutch.) From the stone-hill.

VAN TESSEL or VAN TASSEL. (Dutch.) From *Tessel* or *Texel,* an island in North Holland.

VAN TIEL. Local. From the town of Tiel, in Holland.

VAN VECHTEN. (Dutch.) From Vechten, on the river Vecht, in Holland.

VAN VLECK. (Dutch.) From the town of Vleck, in Holland, which signifies a little open town.

VAN VOLKENBURG. Local. From Valkenburgh, a town on the river Geuse, Netherlands.

VAN VORST or VAN VOORST. Local. From the town of Vorst, in Holland. *Vorst,* in Dutch, signifies a prince; *Forst,* German, a forest.

VAN VRANKEN. (Dutch.) From *Frankenburgh,* an old town of the *Franki,* or free men.

VAN WINKLE. Local. From the town of Winkel, in Holland.

VAN WOERT and **VAN WORT.** Local. From Woert, a town in Holland.

VAN WORDEN. Local. From Woerden, a town in Holland.

VAN WYCK. Local. From Wyck, a town on the river Lech, in Holland.

VAN ZANDT. (Dutch.) From the sand; or from Zante, an island in the Mediterranean.

VASSER. (Fr.) A corruption of *Vavasour*, one who holds an estate next to a lord.

VAUGHAN. (Welsh.) The same as *Bychan* or *Vychan*, little, small in stature.

VEDDER or **VEEDER.** (Dutch.) Father, or literally begetter, feeder.

VENTON. (Cor. Br.) A spring well.

VERBECK. (Dutch.) From *ver*, far, distant, and *beek* or *beck*, brook. The distant brook.

VERNON. Local. From Vernon, a place in Normandy.

VESEY. Local. Wet or fenny land, near the water, subject to inundation; the same as *Fossey*. Cor. Br., *Vosey*, the ditch or fort near the water.

VIBBARD. (Dutch and Danish.) From *vi*, or *wi*, holy, sacred, and *bard*, a poèt.

VICKERS. Vicar, the incumbent of a benefice; one who performs the functions of another. *Vicar*, Cor. Br., a sovereign lord.

VIELLE or **VELAY.** Local. A town of France, in Languedoc, the ancient *Velannia*.

VILLIERS. Local. From a place so called, in France.

VINE. Local. Taken from the plant that bears the grape; a vineyard. "Will at the vine." "Will Vine."

OF FAMILY NAMES. 259

VIPONT. *De Veteri Ponte*, from the old bridge.

VIRGO. (Latin.) A maid, a damsel. *Virago*, a stout woman. *Virgo*, local, Latin, a Roman aqueduct.

VIVIAN. (Welsh.) *Vyvian*, the small water.

VOGEL. (Dutch.) A bird, a duck; figuratively, a cunning fellow, a fine young blade.

VOORHEES or **VOORES.** (Dutch.) From *voorhuis*, the fore-room of a house below, a hall.

VROOMAN. (Dutch.) From *vroom*, honest, valiant, religious, and *man*—an honest or valiant man.

WADE. (Dutch.) From *weide*, a meadow or pasture.

WADSWORTH. The same as *Woodsworth*, the farm or place in the wood.

WAITE. Local. The same as *Thwaite*, a piece of ground cleared of wood, a meadow.

WAKEFIELD. Local. A market-town in west Yorkshire, England—the watch-field.

WAKEMAN. A title given to the chief magistrate of Rippon, in Yorkshire, England; a watchman.

WALDGRAVE. (Sax.) From *wald*, a forest, and *grave*, a ruler or lord.

WALDEN. (Sax. and Ger.) A wood, a woody place.

WALDRON. *Wald*, Saxon, a wood.

WALES, WALLIS, WALSH. A native of Wales, a name given by the Anglo-Saxons to the Britons who originally came from Gaul, which the Saxons pronounced *Wealas*, *Wales*, *Welsh*, and *Wallia*. A principality of Great Britain, on the west of England, one hundred and twenty miles long, and eighty broad.

ETYMOLOGICAL DICTIONARY

WALKER. In the north of England and south of Scotland a fulling-mill is still called a walk-mill. This name may signify either a fuller or an officer whose duty consisted in walking or inspecting a certain space of forest ground.

WALL. "John at the Wall"—John Wall.

WALLACE or WALLIS. The same as *Wales* or *Welch*, and formed thus—*Gaulish, Wallish, Wallis*, and also *Welsh* or *Welch*, a name given to the Britons by their Danish and Angles invaders, because they originally came from Gaul.

WALLER. A *Gauler* or *Waller*, a foreigner, from the Anglo-Saxon "*waller-went*," foreign men, strangers.

WALLOCK. In Gaelic, *Guala* is a mountain projection, and *loch*, a lake. *Wallock*, a highland dance. *Guallak*, Cor. Br., a brag, a boaster.

WALLOP. Local. From the town of *Wallop*, in Hampshire, England.

WALPOLE. Local. From *Walpole*, a town in Norfolk, England.

WALSH. A Gaul, which the Germans pronounce with a "*w*," as Wallic for Gaulic. *Wallis, Wallish, Walsh*. The Welsh were originally from Gaul. (See Wales and Wallace.)

WANDS. Local. A place where *Woden* was worshiped by the Anglo-Saxons, from which we have Wodensday or Wednesday. *Wand*, Danish, water; *wansted*, Danish, a watering-place.

WALTER. A wood-master or keeper of the wood.

WALTON. Local. The name of several villages in England, from *wald*, a wood, and *ton*.

WAMPLE or WEMPLE. Local. A river of England, from *wem* or *uiam*, a cleft, a cave, a low place, Gaelic; and *poll*, a small lake, a pond, and the same in Welsh.

OF FAMILY NAMES.

261

WARBURTON. Local From a township in Cheshire, England, spelled in the Doomsday Book *Werburghtune,* so called from a monastery there situated dedicated to St. Werbergh.

WARE. Local. A town in Hertfordshire, England, so named from the *wear* in the river Lee, at that place.

WARD. A keeper, one who guards or defends.

WARDLAW. Local. The parish of Kirkhill, in Moray, Scotland, was formerly called *Wardlaws,* because the garrison of Lovat were accustomed to keep watch or *ward* on the *law* or hill.

WARNE. An alder-tree, a ship's mast.

WARREN. From *Guarenna* or *Varenna,* in the county of Calais, in Normandy, whence they came into England with William the Conqueror. The primary sense of the word is to stop, hold, or repel, to guard, keep off.

WARRENDER. From *Warren,* and *der,* from the old British *dour,* water, probably given to a Warren who lived near some water or river.

WARWICK. Local. The county town of Warwickshire, England. Camden derives it from *guarth,* Cor. Br., a safeguard, a garrison, and *wick,* Saxon, a port or city. Somner says it was formerly called "*wearing-wick,*" from *wear* and *wick,* a harbor.

WASHINGTON. Local. Originally *Wessyngton* or *De Wessyngton.* The name was taken from the place in England where the family originated; from *weis,* a wash, a creek setting in from the sea, the shallow part of a river, *ing,* a meadow or low ground, and *ton,* for *dun,* a hill or town— the town on the wash or salt river or creek.

WASSEN. Local. From *Wessen,* a town in Switzerland. *Wassen,* in Dutch, signifies to grow, increase.

WATCOCK. The son of Wat or Walter, *cock* signifying, little.

262 ETYMOLOGICAL DICTIONARY

WATERS. Local. A name given to one who navigated the waters, or resided near them.

WATKINS. From *Wat*, and the patronymic termination *kins;* the son of Wat or Walter.

WATKINSON. The son of Watkins.

WATSON and **WATTS.** The son of Walter.

WAY. Local. A road or passage of any kind; a name given to one who resided there. " Will o' the Way."

WAYLAND, WEYLAND. Local. From the Dutch, "*Weiland*," pasture-ground, meadow-land.

WEBSTER. A maker of webs, a weaver.

WEEDEN. Local. So named from *Weedon*, a town in Northamptonshire, on the river Nen. *Gwid-ton*, the woody hill.

WEIDMAN. (Dutch.) From *Weid*, a pasture or meadow, and *man*,—a herdsman.

WELBY. Local. From *Weald-by*, which signifies a habitation in a wood or grove.

WELD. A wood, sometimes written *Weald*, the woody part of a country.

WELDEN. Local. From *Weald*, woody, a wood, and *den*, a valley.

WELLER. (Ang. Saxon.) *Wellere*, a hollow or gulf. Probably the same as Waller (which see).

WELLS. Local. A name given to a person who resided there. "John, at the Wells"—John Wells. A bishop's see in Somersetshire, so called from the wells or springs there.

WEMPEL. Wampull, a river in England. Wimpole, a place in London, a flag-staff. *Wem*, a town in England, also in Scotland, and signifies a hollow place, a cave; *Wempool*, the pool in the hollow or low place.

WEMYSS. Local. First assumed by the proprietors of the lands anciently called Wemyss-shire, in Fife-shire, Scot-

OF FAMILY NAMES.

263

land, which contained all that tract of ground lying between the lower part of the waters of Ore, and the sea. These lands received their name from the great number of caves that are there, all along the sea-coast. A cave in the old Gaelic or Celtic, was called *vumhs* or *uamh ;* from that these lands received the name of Vumhs-shire— *Wemys-shire.* The family of Wemyss derive their origin from the family of Macduff, Maormor of Fife, in the reign of Malcom Canmore. The lands now forming the parish of Wemyss, are said to have been part of the estate of Macduff, Shakespeare's well-known Thane of Fife.

WENDELL. (Dutch.) *Wandelaar*, a walker, hence a traveler. The name may be local, and derived from *Wandle*, a river in Surrey, England.

WENTWORTH. Local. The *Worth*, farm, or place, on the river *Went*, in Northumberland, England.

WERDEN. (Ger.) Local. From *Wehr*, a fortification, and *den*, a hill; a town in the Netherlands called Woerden.

WESTALL. Local. The *West-Hall.*

WESTCOTT. The west cot; so Eastcott, and Southcote. *Westmacott*, Saxon, a banker, a money lender.

WESTMORELAND. Local. A county of England; the " West-moor-land."

WESTERVELDT. (Dutch.) The west field, from *Wester*, west, and *veldt*, a field.

WESTON. The west town. Derived from a small village in England.

WETHERBY. Local. A town in west Yorkshire, England; the wide or extended village ; *Weider*, Dutch, a herdsman, *Weideri*, the place of fattening cattle, and *by*, a village.

WETHERSPOON, WITHERSPOON, WODDERSPOON. Local. A grazing-place in the spur of a mountain or hill; *Weider*, Dutch or Saxon, and *span*, to unite, bend, extend.

264   ETYMOLOGICAL DICTIONARY

WETHERWAX. (Dutch.) *Weiderwacht,* from *weider,* a herdsman, and *wacht,* a watch, a guard ; *weide,* a pasture, a meadow ; *weideri,* a pasture for fattening cattle.

WETSEL. Local. From *Wezel,* a town on the lower Rhine.

WHALLEY. Having greenish white eyes; wall-eyed. This name is also local, and is the name of a village in Lancashire, England.

WHEADEN and WHEDEN. An old English west country term for a silly fellow. Also the name of a small village in England, whence the name may be derived.

WHEALDON or WHIELDON. Local. (Cor. Br.) A place where mines are worked. *Wheal* is frequently applied to signify a mine, and *dun* or *din,* a hill.

WHEATON. Local. So called from a place of the same name on the river Nen, Northamptonshire, England. *Whitton,* Saxon, the white hill. *Whiddon,* Cor. Br., white.

WHEELER. A name of trade.

WHEELOCK. From a village in Cheshire, England, of the same name.

WHITBY. That is "White-town," or bay; a town in Yorkshire, England.

WHITE. A name given from the color of the hair, or complexion. The name may be also local, derived from the Isle of *Wight,* on the coast of Hampshire, so called from the Welsh, *Gwydd,* wood, from its primitive forest.

WHITING. (Sax.) The white or fair offspring. The Saxon termination *ing,* denoted offspring or child, as *Cuthing,* the child of Cuth, *Dun-ning,* the brown offspring, &c.

WHITLOCK. (Sax.) Fair hair.

WHITFIELD. Local. The white field.

WHITFORD. Local. The white ford.

OF FAMILY NAMES.
265

WHITMAN. From *wight*, in old English, lively, quick, and *man*, or from the Dutch, *wight*, weighty, ponderous, *Wightman*, a stout man, or it may be, after all, simply *White-man*.

WHITNEY. (Sax.) From *Hwit*, white, and *ea*, water, or *ige*, an island; a town in Oxfordshire, England.

WHITTAKER. Local. The north part of a graveyard allotted to the poor was called *whittaker*, from *wite*, a penalty, and *acre*,—a place of burial for criminals. A culprit who could not discharge the penalty or *wite* became a "*witetheow*," and was buried in the *wite-acre*. Bailey defines Whittaker "the north-east part of a flat or shoal—the middle ground."

WICKER. A man of the creek or bay, from *Wick*, a creek, bay; a village. *Uakker*, Danish, valiant, brave.

WICKHAM. (Sax.) From *wic*, the winding of a river or port, and *comb*, a valley. A town in Buckinghamshire, England—the sheltered, place, house, or town.

WICKLIFF. (Sax.) From *Hwic*, white, and *klif*, a rock or cliff; or rather from *wic*, a Saxon word for borough or village, the town on the cliff; a village six miles from Richmond, in Yorkshire, England, from which the family derive their name, and of which they were possessed from the time of the Conquest by William the Conqueror till the year 1606. Wycliffe translated the Bible in 1338, and one half of the nation before his death are said to have embraced, in a greater or less degree, his opinions, which spread with rapidity over Europe.

WIGAN and **WIGGIN.** Local. From *Wigan*, a town on the river Douglass, Lancashire, England.

WILBERFORCE. Local. That is, Wild-boar-foss, a dike, a ditch. *Wil-burgh-foss.*

WILBRAHAM. For *Wilburgham* or *Wild-burgh-ham.* Local. A town in Kent, England.

WILBUR or **WILBOR.** A contraction of Wildboar.

12

WILCOX. From Will, and *cock*, which signifies, little. Will's son, Williamson. "A willcock," one rather obstinate.

WILDER. A traveler, foreigner, or pilgrim, the same as *Waller*, from the Saxon *wealh*, a traveler, or one who inhabits the forest or grounds uncultivated.

WILKINS. From *Wil*, and the patronymic termination *kins*, the son of William.

WILKINSON. The son of Wilkins.

WILLARD. One who has a determined disposition, from *will*, choice, command, and *ard*, the Teutonic of *art*, strength, nature, disposition.

WILLET. Little William, or the son of William.

WILLIAM. From the Belgic *Guild-helm*, harnessed with a gilded helmet; or, as others say, from *Welhelm*, the shield or defense of many.

WILLIAMSON. The son of William.

WILLIS. Willy's, the son of Willy, the "s" being added for *son*.

WILLOUGHBY. Local. From the lordship of Willoughby, in Lincolnshire, England, given to a Norman knight by William the Conqueror.—The town or habitation by the willows.

WILMOT. May be a corruption of *Guillemot*, a name frequent in France in early times, derived from *Guillaume*, William.

WILSON. The son of William or Will.

WILTON. Local. From a town in Wiltshire, England, so called from the river *Willey*, and *ton*, a town.

WILTSHIRE. Local. A county in England; Welsh, *gwyllt*, a wild, forest, a desert, and *shire*, a division, a county.

WIMPLE. (Dutch.) A streamer, pendant.

WINCH. Local. A place in the county of Norfolk, England. *Ynys*, Welsh, an island.

OF FAMILY NAMES. 267

WINCHCOMBE. (Sax.) Local. From *wincel*, a corner, and *comb*, a valley—a valley encompassed on each side with hills.

WINCHEL. (Dutch.) From *Winschaal*, a wine-bowl, a wine-shop; German, *Weinsall*, a wine-hall or shop.

WINCHESTER. Local. A city of Hampshire, England, called *Caerwynt* by the Britons, from *Caer*, a city, town, or fortified place, and *gwint*, wind, from its being a *windy place*. The Welsh *gwin* signifies wine, as if called the "*Wine City*." So Howel, in his Londonopolis, quotes from old Robert of Glo'cester:

> "In the country of Canterbury most plenty of fish is;
> And most chase of beasts about Salisbury I wis,
> And London ships most, and *wine at Winchester*,
> Soap about Coventry, and iron at Glo'cester;
> Metal, lead, and tin in the county of Exceter,
> Euorwick of fairest wood, Lincoln of fairest men,
> Cambridge and Huntingdon most plenty of deep venne,
> Ely of fairest place, of fairest sight, Rochester."

Bailey defines it the "White City," from the Welsh "*Caer guenif*," because it is built upon a chalky soil.

WINDHAM. Local. A town in the county of Norfolk, England, said to be a corruption of *Wimund-han*, "the home or village of Wimund."

WINDSOR. Local. A town in Berkshire, England. The name is a corruption of *Wind-shore*, from the winding shore of the Thames in that place.

WINEGAR. (Dutch.) From *Wyngaard*, a vine.

WINEKOOP. (Dutch.) Something to drink upon the bargain.

WING. Local. A village in the county of Buckingham, England.

268   ETYMOLOGICAL DICTIONARY

WINGFIELD. Local. From the manor of Wingfield, in Suffolk, England.

WINNE. (Welsh.) The same as *Gwynne*, white.

WINSHIP. Probably the same as Wineshop. Saxon, *Win*, German *Wein*, and *Sceapian*, Saxon, to make, furnish; a maker or vender of wine.

WINSLOW. Local. From the town of Winslow, in Buckinghamshire, England.

WINTERTON. Local. From the village of Winterton, in the county of Norfolk, England, so called from its cold situation.

WINTHROP. Local. A corruption of Winthorp, or *Winethorpe*, the wine village, from *win*, wine, and *thorp*, a village.

WIRE, WEIR, WARE. Local. A market town of Hertfordshire, England. Saxon *Waer*, to defend, to hold, protect. *Wear*, a fence of stakes or rods set in a stream for catching fish; a dam.

WISE, and WISEMAN. A name given for the quality of wisdom.

WISHART. Some ancient writers say, that Robert, son of David, Earl of Huntingdon, took on him the cross, and distinguished himself in the Holy Land, where, from his gallant exploits against the Saracens, he received the name of *Guishart*, that is, *Wise-heart*, now *Wishart*.

WISWALL. Local. From *Weisweil*, a town in Baden, on the Rhine, Germany.

WITHERINGTON. A contraction of *Wooderington*. From Saxon *wyderian*, to wither, and *dun*, a hill. The withered or dry hill. A place in Northumberland, England. *Weiderington*, the place of pasturing cattle, Dutch, *Weide*, a pasture, *weider*, one who takes care of cattle, a herdsman.

WITTER. (Dutch.) A whitener, a fuller, bleacher.

OF FAMILY NAMES.

WOLSEY or WOOLSEY. Local. That is, the *Wolds-ley*, from *wold*, a wood, a lawn, and sometimes a plain, and *lle*, or *ley*, a place.

WOOD. A surname very ancient in Scotland, first called *De Bosco*. The family bore trees in their coat of arms.

WOODRUFF. *Woodroof*, from *Wood-reeve*, the governor or keeper of a wood, a forester.

WOODWARD. Wood-ward, a forest-keeper or officer, who walked with a forest-bill, and took cognizance of all offenses committed.

WOODWORTH. Local. The farm or place in the wood..

WOOL. One having short, thick hair. It may be a corruption of *Wolf*, or *Will*.

WOOLLEY. Local. *Wold-ley*, uncultivated lands, hills without wood.

WOOSTER. A corruption of *Worcester* (which see).

WORCESTER. Local. A county and city of England, which Bailey derives from Sax. *Were*, a forest, and *Cester*, a camp or city. I prefer deriving it from *Warcester*, the city or castle of strife, from the Saxon *Woer*, war, strife, with which the ancient British name agrees, called *Caerwrangon*, the castle or fort of strife and contention. It was a boundary for many years between the Britons and Saxons. (See Chester.)

WORTH. (Sax.) Local. A court, farm, possession, place, field or way ; the place valued, sold, or granted.

WYLIE. A form of *Willie* or William ; or wily, artful, sly.

WYMAN. (Dutch.) From *Weiman*, a huntsman, a hunter; one who shoots the game.

YAGER. (German and Danish.) *Jager*, a huntsman. *Yogere*, also signifies a sweet-heart.

270 DICTIONARY OF FAMILY NAMES.

YALE. Local. From a lordship of the same name in Wales.

YARE. (Sax.) Ready, dexterous, eager.

YARROW. A plant; the millfoil, or plant of a thousand leaves.

YATES. An old word for *Gate*. The same as Gates.

YEOMAN. A man free-born, a freeholder; one next in order to the gentry.

YETT. A gate, a way, a passage, the same as Yates.

YORK. Local. A city in England next in esteem to London. Verstegan derives its name from *Eure-ric* or *Eouer-ric*, of *Euere*, a wild boar, and *ryc*, a refuge; a retreat from the wild boars which were in the forest of Gautries. The Romans called the city *Eboracum;* it is memorable for the death of two emperors, Severus and Constantius Chlorus, and for the nativity of Constantine the Great.

YOUNGHUSBAND. A surname borrowed from the social relations.

YOUNGLOVE. Given on account of his age, and tender affection.

YULE. (Sax.) Christmas, borrowed from this festival, or the time of nativity. Ὑλε, Greek, a wood, a forest.

CHRISTIAN NAMES.

CHRISTIAN NAMES.

NAMES OF MEN.

AARON. (Heb.) Signifies a *mountaineer*, a mount of strength.

ABDALLAH. (Turkish.) The servant of God.

ABEL. (Heb.) Signifies vanity, breath.

ABIATHAR. (Heb.) Excellent father.

ABIEZER. (Heb.) My father's help.

ABIJAH. (Heb.) The will of the Lord, or the Lord is my father.

ABISHUR. (Heb.) My father's attention.

ABNER. (Heb.) The lamp or son of the father.

ABRAHAM. (Heb.) The father of a great multitude.

ABSALOM. (Heb.) A father of peace.

ADAM. (Heb.) Taken out of red earth.

ADIEL. (Heb.) The witness of the Lord.

ADOLPHUS or ADOLPH. (Sax.) From *Ead*, happiness, and *ulph*, help—happy help.

ADRIAN. (Latin.) Local. From the city of Hadria. Gesner derives it from the Greek άδρος, great or wealthy.

ÆNEAS. (Lat.) Laudable.

12*

AGRIPPA. (Lat.) *Æger-partus*, one that causeth pain at his birth, who is born with his feet foremost.

ALAN. Is thought by Julius Scaliger to signify a hound in the Sclavonian, and Chaucer uses *Aland* in the same sense.

ALBERT. (Ger.) All bright or famous.

ALEXANDER. (Greek.) An aider or benefactor of men, a powerful auxiliary, from ἀλέξω, to aid, assist, and ἀνήρ, a man.

ALFRED. (Sax.) All peace.

ALMOND. *Allemand*,—a German.

ALPHONSO. (Gothic.) Our help, from *Helpuns*.

ALWIN. (Sax.) From *alle*, all, and *win*, a victor—all victorious.

AMASA. A forgiving people.

AMBROSE. (Greek.) From Ἀμβρόσιος, immortal.

AMOS. Loading, weighty.

ANDREW. (Greek.) A brave man. Ἀνδρεία, courage, bravery, manhood, from Ἀνήρ, a man.

ANTHONY. (Greek.) From Ἄνθος, a flower, flourishing, beautiful, graceful.

APOLLOS. One that destroys or lays waste.

ARCHIBALD. (Ger.) A powerful, bold, and speedy learner or observer.

ARIEL. (Heb.) Light or Zion of God.

ARNOLD. (Ger.) According to Camden, signifies honest, but the Germans write it *Ernold*. *Probus* in Latin.

ARTEMAS. Holy, agreeable.

ARTHUR. (Br.) A strong man. (See fuller derivation in Dictionary of Surnames.)

OF CHRISTIAN NAMES. **275**

ASA. Physician or cure.

ASAHEL. The work or creature of God.

ASENATH. (Heb.) Peril or misfortune.

ASHER. (Heb.) Happy, blessed.

AUGUSTUS. (Lat.) Noble, royal, imperial.

AUGUSTINE and AUSTIN. (Latin.) A contraction of Augustine, from *Augustinus*, imperial, royal, great, or renowned.

AZARIAH. Assistance.

BALDWIN. (Ger.) The speedy conqueror or victor, from *bald*, quick or speedy, and *win*, an old word signifying victor or conqueror.

BAPTISTE. (Greek.) Βαπτιστὴς, a baptizer, the title of St. John.

BARDULPH. (Ger.) The same as *Bertulph*, fair help.

BARNABY and BARNABAS. (Heb.) Son of consolation.

BARNABAS. Son of the prophet, or consolation.

BARTIMEUS. (Heb.) The son of Timeus. Timeus signifies perfect, honorable, admirable.

BARTHOLOMEW. (Heb.) The son of him who maketh the waters to mount.

BARZILLAI. (Heb.) Made of iron, or the son of contempt.

BASIL. (Greek.) From Βασιλεὺς, a king; royal, kingly.

BENEDICT. (Latin.) From *Benedictus*, blessed, well spoken of, or a person wishing all good.

BENJAMIN. (Heb.) The son of the right hand.

BENNET. A contraction or rather a corruption of Benedict, from the Latin, *Benedictus*, blessed.

276 ETYMOLOGICAL DICTIONARY

BENONI. (Heb.) Son of my grief, sorrow.

BERIAH. (Heb.) In fellowship.

BERNARD. (Teutonic.) Of a child-like disposition.

BERTRAM. (Sax.) Fair and pure.

BEULAH. (Heb.) Married.

BOAZ. (Heb.) In strength, a pillar.

BONIFACE. (Lat.) Well-doer.

BOTOLPH. (Sax.) Help-ship or sailor. Sailors in that age were called *Botescarles*.

BRIAN and BRIANT. (Fr.) Shrill-voiced.

CÆSAR. (Latin.) From *cædo*, to cut,—a name said to have been given to one who was cut from his mother's womb. *Cæsaries*, a head of hair.

CAIUS. Parents' joy.

CALEB. A dog, cow, or basket.

CALISTHENES. (Greek.) Beautiful and strong.

CARADOC. (Br.) Dearly beloved.

CARLOS. The same as Charles.

CHARLES. (Ger.) From *carl*, strong, stout, courageous, valiant.

CHESTER. A surname, now used as a Christian name. From the city of Chester, so called from the Latin *castrum*, a fortified place, a camp. Chester was the principal encampment of the Romans in Britain.

CHRISTIAN. The derivation of this name is evident.

CHRISTOPHER. (Greek.) From Χριστός, Christ, literally, *anointed*, and φέρω, to bear; Christ's carrier.

CLARENCE. (Lat.) From *Clarus*, clear, bright.

OF CHRISTIAN NAMES.

CLAUDIUS. (Lat.) From *Clauda*, the name of an island near Crete. A name given to a native of that island. It signifies a broken or a weeping voice.

CLEMENT. (Lat.) *Clemens*, meek, gentle, kind.

CONRAD. (Ger.) Able counsel.

CONSTANTINE. (Lat.) *Constantinus*, fast, firm, unyielding.

CORNELIUS. (Latin and Greek.) From *cornu*, a horn, and ἥλιος, the sun.

CRISPIN. (Lat.) *Crispinus*, from *crispus*, having curled hair.

CUTHBERT. (Sax.) Famous, bright, of clear skill or knowledge.

CYPRIAN. (Greek.) From the isle of Cyprus.

CYRUS. An heir, or miserable.

DANIEL. (Heb.) Judgment of God.

DAVID. (Heb.) Beloved, dear.

DEMETRIUS. (Greek.) Belonging to Ceres.

DENIS, or DENNIS. A contraction of Dionysius (which see).

DERRICK, DERICK, and DIRK. (Dutch.) An abbreviation of Theodorick (which see).

DIODORUS. (Greek.) From Διὸς, Jove or Jupiter, and δῶρος, a gift—the gift of Jove.

DYONYSIUS. (Greek.) A name of Bacchus, the god of wine.

DIOTREPHES. (Greek.) Nourished by Jupiter, from Διὸς, genitive of Ζεὺς, Jupiter, and τρέφο, to feed, to nourish.

DOMINICK. (Lat.) From *Dominica*, the Lord's day; Sunday, from *Dominus*, the Lord. A name given to a child born on Sunday.

278   ETYMOLOGICAL DICTIONARY

DUNSTAN. (Sax.) From *dun*, a hill, and *stan*, a stone—a name of place.

EBENEZER. (Heb.) The stone of help.

EDMUND. (Sax.) From *Ead*, blessed, and *mund*, peace—blessed peace.

EDWARD. (Sax.) From *Ead*, blessed, and *ard*, nature or disposition.

EDWIN. (Sax.) From *Ead*, blessed or happy, and *win*, a conqueror.

ELDAD. (Heb.) Loved or favored of God.

ELEAZER. (Heb.) The help or court of God.

ELI. (Heb.) The offering or lifting up.

ELIAB. (Heb.) God, my father.

ELIAS. (Heb.) God the Lord, or the strong Lord.

ELIHU. (Heb.) He is my God himself.

ELIJAH. (Heb.) The same as Elias (which see).

ELIPHALET. (Heb.) The God of deliverance.

ELISHA. (Heb.) Salutation of God.

ELIU. (Heb.) The same as Elihu.

ELIZUR. (Heb.) God is my rock, or strength.

ELON. (Heb.) Oak, or grove, or strong.

ELYMAS. In Arabic signifies a magician.

EMMANUEL. (Heb.) God with us.

ENEAS. (Greek.) Laudable, from αἰνέω, I praise, prudent, discreet, in Gaelic, *Aongaos*.

ENOCH. (Heb.) Dedicated, disciplined, well-regulated.

ENOS. (Heb.) Fallen man.

OF CHRISTIAN NAMES. 279

EPAPHRAS. (Heb.) Covered with foam.

EPHRAIM. (Heb.) That brings fruit, or that grows.

ERASMUS. (Greek.) Ἐράσιμος, amiable, lovely, same as Erastus.

ERASTUS. (Greek.) From Ἐραστὸς, lovely or amiable.

ERNEST. (Sax.) *Eornest*, earnest.

ESEK. (Heb.) Contention, violence, or force.

ETHELARD. (Sax.) Noble disposition.

ETHELBERT. (Sax.) Noble-bright, or nobly renowned.

ETHELSTAN. (Sax.) Noble-jewel, precious stone, or most noble.

ETHELWARD. (Sax.) Noble keeper.

ETHELWOLD. (Sax.) Noble governor.

ETHELWOLF. (Sax.) Noble helper.

ETHAN. Strength.

EUGENE. (Greek.) From Εὐγενὴς, nobly born.

EUSTACE. (Greek.) From Εὐστάθὴς, standing firm, resolute.

EVERARD. (Sax.) Always honored.

EZEKIEL. God is my strength.

EZRA. A helper.

FABIAN. (Lat.) From *Fabius*, a kind of bean.

FELIX. (Lat.) Happy.

FERDINAND. (Ger.) From *Fred*, peace, and *rand*, pure, that is, pure peace.

FRANCIS. From *Franc*, free, not servile, or bond.

FRANKLIN. A freeholder. (See Dictionary of Surnames.)

FREDERICK. (Ger.) Rich peace, or peaceable reign.

280 ETYMOLOGICAL DICTIONARY

FULLBERT. (Sax.) Full-bright.

FULKE. (Sax.) Some derive it from the German *Vollg*, noble and gallant, but Camden from *Folc*, the English-Saxon word for people, folk; like the Roman *Publius*, beloved of the people and commons.

GABRIEL. (Heb.) A man of God, or God is my strength.

GAIUS. (Greek.) Earthly. From Γαῖος, corruptible, mortal.

GALLIO. Milky.

GAMALIEL. (Heb.) Recompense of God.

GARRET. A corruption of Gerard (which see).

GEDEON. (Heb.) He that bruises and breaks.

GEFFREY. (Ger.) From *Gau*, joyful, and *fred*, peace; joyful peace.

GEOFFREY. (Sax.) From *Gau*, glad, and *fred*, peace.

GEORGE. (Greek.) A husbandman, from Γεωργὸς.

GERARD. (Sax.) From *Gar*, all, and *ard*, nature.

GERMAIN. (Ger.) All victorious.

GERVAS. (Ger.) All sure, firm, or fast.

GIFFORD. (Ger.) Liberal disposition.

GILBERT. (Ger.) Bright pledge, from *Gisle*, a pledge; **or** gold-like bright, from the Saxon, *Geele*, yellow.

GILES. *Ægidius*, Latin of Αἰγὶς, Greek, a goat's skin; so the old writers derive it, but it is more probably from the German *Gisel*, or *Gesel*, a companion.

GODARD. (Sax.) From *God*, God or good, and *ard*, nature —endowed with a divine disposition.

GODFREY. (Ger.) God's peace, godly.

GODWIN. (Sax.) Converted, or victorious in God.

OF CHRISTIAN NAMES.

281

GRACCHUS. (Lat.) Thin.

GREGORY. From the Greek Γρεγορέω, to watch, watchful, a shepherd.

GRIFFITH. (Br.) Strong faith.

GUILBERT. The same as Gilbert.

GUY. A guide, leader, or director.

HADRIAN, and ADRIAN. (Lat.) From the city Hadria, whence Hadrian the Emperor had his origin. Gesner derives it from the Greek Ἀδρος, wealthy.

HAMON. (Heb.) Faithful.

HANNIBAL. Gracious lord.

HAROLD. (Sax.) Leader of the army, or love of the army.

HAZEL. (Heb.) One that sees God.

HEBER. One that passes, anger, wrath.

HECTOR. (Greek.) Defender.

HEMAN. (Heb.) Their trouble, tumult, in great numbers.

HENGIST. (Sax.) Horseman.

HENRY. (Sax.) From *Einrich*, ever rich, or from *Honoricus*, honorable.

HERBERT. (Sax.) From *Here*, an army, and *beorht*, bright, —the glory of the army. Verstegan derives it from *Here*, an army, and the Teutonic *bericht*, instructed,—an expert soldier.

HERMON and HARMON. (Ger.) General of an army.

HERCULES. (Greek.) Glory or illumination of the air.

HEZEKIAH. (Heb.) Strong in the Lord.

HIEL. (Heb.) God lives, or the life of God.

HILDEBERT. (Ger.) Bright or famous lord.

HIRAM. (Heb.) Exaltation of life.

HOMER. (Greek.) Ὅμηρος. A hostage, a pledge or security.

282 ETYMOLOGICAL DICTIONARY

HORACE. From Latin, *Horatius.* (See below.)

HORATIO. (Lat.) *Horatius,* from the Greek, ὀρᾱτὸς, or ὀρατῖκὸς, of good eyesight.

HOSEA. (Heb.) Salvation.

HUBERT. (Sax.) Of clear, bright color.

HUGH. High, or exalted.

HUMPHREY. (Sax.) From *Hum-fred,* house-peace.

ICHABOD. (Heb.) Where is the glory.

IRA. (Heb.) City watch, or heap of vision.

ISAAC. (Heb.) Laughter.

ISAIAH. (Heb.) Salvation of the Lord.

ISRAEL. (Heb.) A prince of the strong God.

IVAN. The same as John in Gaelic and Welsh.

JACOB. (Heb.) He that supplants, a supplanter.

JAEL. (Heb.) A kid, ascending.

JAMES. (Heb.) The same as Jacob.

JARED. (Heb.) One that rules or descends.

JASPER. (Greek.) From Ἰασπις, a precious stone of a green color, transparent, with red veins.

JASON. (Greek.) Ἰᾶσων. He that cures, from Ἰάομαι, to heal.

JEDEDIAH. (Heb.) Beloved of the Lord.

JEREMIAH. (Heb.) Exaltation or grandeur of the Lord.

JEREMY. (Heb.) High of the Lord.

JESSE. (Heb.) My present, or who is to be.

JOAB. (Heb.) Paternity.

OF CHRISTIAN NAMES.

283

JOB. (Heb.) He that weeps.

JOEL. (Heb.) One that wills or commands.

JOHN. (Heb.) Signifies the grace or gift of the Lord.

JONADAB. (Heb.) Liberal, one who acts as a prince.

JONAH and JONAS. (Heb.) A dove.

JONATHAN. (Heb.) The gift of the Lord.

JOSCELIN. A diminutive from *Jost* or *Justus*, just.

JOSEPH. (Heb.) Increase, addition.

JOSHUA. (Heb.) The Lord, the Saviour.

JOSIAH. (Heb.) The fire of the Lord.

JUDAS. (Heb.) Same as Judah, praise of the Lord.

JULIUS. (Greek.) Soft haired, or mossy-bearded.

JUSTIN. (Lat.) From *Justus*, just, virtuous.

KENARD. (Sax.) Kind disposition.

KENHELM. (Sax.) Defense of his kindred.

KENNETH. (Gaelic.) From *Ceann*, the head—a chieftain.

LAMBERT. (Sax.) Fair lamb.

LAWRENCE. (Lat.) Flourishing.

LAZARUS. (Heb.) Lord's help.

LEGER. (Ger.) *Leodegar*, gatherer of peoples.

LEMUEL. (Heb.) God is with them.

LEO. (Lat.) A lion.

LEOFSTAN. (Sax.) Most beloved.

LEOFWIN. (Sax.) Win love, or to be loved.

284 ETYMOLOGICAL DICTIONARY

LEONARD. (Sax.) Lion-like disposition.

LEOPOLD. (Ger.) Defender of the people.

LEVI. (Heb.) One who is held and associated.

LEWIS. A contraction of *Ludovicus*, Latin for the Teutonic *Ludwig*, from *Leod* or *Lud*, the people, and *wick*, a castle—the safeguard of the people.

LINUS. Nets.

LIONEL. (Lat.) *Lionellus*, little lion.

LOUIS. (Fr.) Contraction of Ludovicus or Ludwig. (See Lewis.)

LUCIUS. (Lat.) From *lux*, light. A name first given to children born at the dawning of the day.

LUKE and LUCAS. (Greek.) Luminous.

MADOC. (Br.) Good.

MALICHI. (Heb.) My messenger or angel.

MANOAH. (Heb.) Rest, or a gift.

MARCELLUS. (Lat.) From *Mars*, the god of war—martial, warlike.

MARCUS and MARK. (Lat.) A name first given to children born in the month of March. Marcus also means polite, shining.

MARMADUKE. (Ger.) From *Mermachtig*, which in old Saxon signified more mighty.

MARTIN. (Lat.) From *Martius*, Mars, the god of war.

MATTHEW. (Heb.) The gift of God.

MATTHIAS. (Heb.) The gift of the Lord.

MAXIMILIAN. A name devised by the Emperor Frederic the Third, who composed it for his son and heir from the

OF CHRISTIAN NAMES.

285

names of the two Romans whom he most admired, *Q. Fabius Maximus*, and *Scipio Æmilianus*, with the hope that his son would imitate their virtues.

MICHAEL. (Heb.) Who is like God? One of the names of Christ.

MILES. (Lat.) *Milo*, from *Milium*, a kind of grain called millet. Some think it to be a contraction of *Michael.*

MORDECAI. (Heb.) Bitter contrition.

MORGAN. (Br.) A seaman, from *mor*, the sea; like the Latin, *Pelagius, Marius.*

MORICE. From the Latin, *Mauritius*, and that from *Maurus*, a moor.

MOSES. (Heb.) Drawn forth.

NAOMI. (Heb.) Beautiful, comely.

NATHAN. (Heb.) Given.

NATHANIEL. (Heb.) The gift of God.

NEAL. (Fr.) From the Latin *nigellus* or *nigel*, black or swarthy.

NERO. (Lat.) Strong.

NICHOLAS. (Greek.) Victorious, from $\nu\iota\chi\acute{\alpha}\omega$, to conquer.

NIGEL. From the Latin *Nigellus*, black, swarthy.

NOAH. (Heb.) A ceasing or rest.

NOEL. (Fr.) The same as the Latin *natalis*, given first in honor of the feast of Christ's birth to such as were born on Christmas day.

NORMAN. From Normandy, so called from the Northmen who settled there from the north of Europe.

ETYMOLOGICAL DICTIONARY

OBADIAH. (Heb.) Servant of the Lord.

OLIVER. From the Latin *Oliva*, an olive-tree, an emblem of peace.

OSBERN. (Sax.) House-child.

OSBERT. (Sax.) Domestic brightness.

OSMUND. (Sax.) House-peace.

OSWOLD. (Sax.) House-ruler or steward.

OTHO. A faithful reconciler, according to Petrus Blesensis.

OWEN. (Celtic.) The good offspring.

PASCAL. From *Pascha*, the passover.

PATRICK. (Latin.) From *Patricius*, a peer, a noble, a name given first to senators' sons.

PAUL. (Lat.) From *paulus*, little, humble, small in stature.

PAYNE. From the Latin *Paganus*, now out of use, meaning a man exempt from military service.

PELATIAH. (Heb.) Deliverance or flight of the Lord.

PERCIVAL. (Nor.) From *Percheval*, a place in Normandy.

PEREGRINE. (Lat.) A stranger, a foreigner.

PETER. (Greek.) From πέτρος, a stone or rock.

PHILEBERT. (Ger.) Much bright fame, very famous.

PHILEMON. (Greek.) Φιλήμων. A kiss or loving.

PHILIP. (Greek.) From φίλος, a lover or friend, and ἵππος, a horse—a lover of horses.

PHILETUS. (Greek.) Φιλητὸς. Beloved or amiable.

PHINEAS. (Heb.) Face of trust or protection.

PIUS. (Lat.) Pious.

POMPEY. (Lat.) *Pomposus*, full of pomp.

OF CHRISTIAN NAMES.

287

QUINTIN. (Lat.) From *quintus*, the fifth, a name given to he fifth born.

RALPH. (Sax.) Contracted from Rodolph or Rodolphus, from *Rode*, counsel, and *ulph*, help.

RANDAL. (Sax.) Corrupted from Randulph, from *rein*, pure, and *ulph*, help.

RANDOLPH. The same as Ranulf or Randal.

RAPHAEL. (Heb.) The healing of God.

REUBEN. (Heb.) The son of vision.

REUEL. (Heb.) Shepherd or friend of God.

REYNOLD. (Sax.) Sincere or pure love, from *rein*, pure, and *hold*, love.

RICHARD. (Sax.) From *ric*, rich, and *ard*, nature or disposition—of a liberal disposition.

ROBERT. (Sax.) Famous in counsel, from *Rode*, counsel, and *beorht*, bright.

ROBIN. Same as Robert.

RODERICK. (Sax.) Rich in counsel, from *Rode*, counsel, and *ric*, rich.

ROGER. (Ger.) Quiet, desirous of rest.

ROLAND. (Ger.) Counsel for the land.

RUFUS. (Nor. Fr.) Red.

RUPERT. Probably the same as Robert.

SALATHIEL. (Heb.) I besought God.

SALMON. (Heb.) Peaceable.

SAMSON. (Heb.) His sun or his ministry.

SAMUEL. (Heb.) Heard of God, a prophet.

SAUL. (Heb.) Asked or lent of the Lord; also a grave.

SEBASTIAN. (Greek.) From Σεβαστὸς, reverend or majestical, the same as the Latin Augustus.

288 ETYMOLOGICAL DICTIONARY

SETH. (Heb.) Set as a foundation.

SIGISMUND. (Sax.) From *sige*, victory, and *mund*, peace, one who procures peace yet so as by victory. Verstegan and Junius derive it from the Teutonic *Siege*, victory, and *mund*, mouth, one who conquers by good words: so *Sighelm*, victorious defense; *Sigebert*, victorious fame.

SIMEON. (Heb.) Hearing, obeying.

SIMON. Same as Simeon.

SOLOMON. (Heb.) Peaceable, perfect, or that recompenses.

STEPHEN. (Greek.) From Στέφανος, a crown or garland; honor, distinction.

SWITHIN. (Sax.) From the old English *switheahn*, very high, like the Latin *Celsus*.

SYLVANUS. (Lat.) Wood-man, or rather wood-God.

SYLVESTER. (Lat.) Woodman.

TERENCE. Lat., *Terentius*, tender.

TERTULLUS. A liar or impostor.

THEOBALD. (Sax.) From *theod*, the people, and *bald*, bold, —bold over the people; sometimes corrupted to Tibald or Thibald.

THEODORE. (Greek.) From Θεὸς, God, and δῶρον, a gift—the gift of God.

THEODORIC. (Sax.) From *Theod*, the people, and *ric*, rich —powerful or rich in people; contracted to *Terry* with the French, and *Derick* and *Dirck* with the Dutch.

THEOPHILUS. (Greek.) From Θεὸς, God, and φίλος, a lover or friend—a lover of God.

THOMAS. (Heb.) A twin, double, called in Greek Δίδυμος, of two hearts, because of his doubting.

OF CHRISTIAN NAMES. 289

TIMEUS. (Gr.) From τίμιος, perfect, honorable, admirable.

TIMON. (Gr.) Honorable, worthy, from Τίμων.

TIMOTHEUS. (Greek.) An honorer of God, from Τίμων, one who honors, and Θεὸς, God.

TIMOTHY. (Greek.) Same as Timotheus, an honorer of God.

TITUS. (Lat.) Honorable.

TOBIAS and TOBIAH. (Heb.) The goodness of God.

TOBY. A corruption of Tobias. It is also the Welsh for Thomas.

TRISTRAM. (Lat.) From *Tristus*, sad, sorrowful.

UCHTRED. (Sax.) High counsel.

URBAN. (Lat.) Civil, courteous.

URIAH. (Heb.) The fire of the Lord.

VALENS. (Lat.) Puissant, brave, able.

VALENTINE. (Lat.) The same as Valens.

VICTOR. (Lat.) A conqueror.

VINCENT. (Lat.) Victorious, a conqueror.

WALTER. (Sax.) *Waldher*, from *Wald*, a wood, and *heer*, a master—the master or lord of the wood, like the Latin, *Sylvanus*, or *Sylvester*.

WIBERT. (Sax.) From *Wi*, holy, and *bert*, bright—holy, and bright or shining.

WILDRED. (Sax.) Much fear.

WILFRED. (Sax.) Much peace.

13

290 DICTIONARY OF CHRISTIAN NAMES.

WILLIAM. (Ger.) *Wilhelm.* Some derive it from the Belgic, *Guild-helm,* harnessed with a gilded helmet, and others, with more probability, from *Wil-helm,* the shield or defense of many, *wel,* and *wil,* being used by the Germans in the sense of *many* or *much,* as in *Wildred* and *Wilfred* above; Wilibert, and Wilwald.

WIMUND. (Sax.) Sacred peace, or holy peace, from *Wi,* holy or sacred, and *mund,* peace.

WISCHARD. (Nor.) Wily, crafty, a shifter. Sometimes written, *Guiscard.*

WOLFERT. A corruption of *Wulpher,* helper.

WOLSTAN. (Sax.) Comely, decent.

WULPHER. (Sax.) Helper.

ZACHARY and **ZACHARIAH.** (Heb.) The memory of the Lord.

ZADOC. (Heb.) Just, justified.

ZERAH. (Heb.) East or brightness.

ZOPHAR. (Heb.) Rising early.

NAMES OF WOMEN.

ABIGAIL. (Heb.) The father's joy.

ADA. (Sax.) A corruption of *Eade*, an old Saxon name, signifying happiness. *Eadith*, now *Edith*, and *Ida*, are from the same. (See *Edith*.)

ADELAIDE. (Sax.) Noble, from *Adeliz*, the same as Alice.

ADELINE. (Sax.) Noble, descending from nobles.

AGATHA. (Greek.) Good, from 'Αγάθη.

AGNES. (Greek.) Chaste, from Αγνή.

ALETHEIA. (Greek.) Truth, from 'Αλεθεια.

ALICE. (Sax.) Abridged from *Adeliz*, noble, the same as Adeline and Adelaide.
The French make it *defendress*, by turning it into *Alexia*, in their language.

AMY. (Fr.) *Amie*, beloved, from the Latin, *amata*.

ANASTASIA. (Greek.) Given in remembrance of Christ's glorious resurrection, and ours in Christ, from ἀνάσταῦις, the act of rising up—the resurrection.

ANNE and **ANNA.** (Heb.) Gracious or merciful.

ANNETTE. A diminutive of Ann; little and pretty Ann.

ANTOINETTE and **ANTONIA.** Feminine of Antony or Anthony, from the Greek, ἄνθος, a flower.

ARABELLA. (Lat.) A fair altar, from *ara*, and *bella*.

292   ETYMOLOGICAL DICTIONARY

AURELIA. (Lat.) Feminine of *Aurelius*, golden—little golden dame.

AURORA. The morning, the dawn; as if "*Aurea hora*," the golden hour.

BARBARA. (Greek.) Strange, of unknown language, a barbarian.

BEATRICE. (Latin.) From *beatrix*, blessed, happy.

BERTHA. (Sax.) Bright and famous.

BLANCHE. (Fr.) White or fair.

BRIDGET. (Gaelic.) *Brighid*, "fiery dart." The name of the muse who was believed to preside over poetry in pagan times, in Ireland. *Brighid*, in the Gaelic, also signifies a hostage, a pledge of security.

CAROLINE. (Ger.) The feminine of *Karl*, or Charles, the manlike, the strong, the daring.

CASSANDRA. (Greek.) Inflaming men with love.

CATHERINE. (Greek.) Pure, chaste, from Καθᾶρὸς.

CECILIA. (Latin.) Grey-eyed.

CHARLOTTE. The French feminine of Charles.

CHLOE. (Greek.) The verdant, springing, blooming; an epithet of Ceres, the goddess of husbandry, from *Chloe*, springing grass or corn.

CHRISTINE. Feminine of Christian.

CLARA. (Lat.) Clear, bright, renowned, illustrious—the feminine of Clarence.

CLAUDIA and CLAUDINE. (Latin.) Feminine of Claudius.

CLEMENTINE. (Lat.) Feminine of Clement, kind, gentle, merciful, from *Clemens*.

OF CHRISTIAN NAMES. 293

CONSTANCE. (Lat.) Constant, firm, unyielding.

CYNTHIA. (Gr.) An epithet of Diana. Apollo was called *Cynthius*, and Diana *Cynthia*, from *Cynthus*, a mountain in the island of Delos, in which they were born. She was called also *Delia*, from the name of the island.

DEBORAH. (Heb.) A bee.

DELIA. (Lat.) A name given to the goddess Diana from being born on the island of *Delos* (manifest, conspicuous), so called because having previously been hidden under water, it was brought to the surface and made manifest, in order that Apollo and Diana might be born upon it.

DIANA. (Greek.) Jove's daughter, from Διός, the genitive of Ζεὺς, Jove,—the ancient name of the moon or the moon-goddess. She was called also *Delia, Phœbe*, and *Cynthia*. Some have derived it from *Dianus, Janus*, fem., *Diana*, a Roman god with two faces, symbolizing the sun and moon.

DIDO. A Phœnician name signifying a manlike woman.

DORCAS. (Greek.) A doe, a roe-buck. Lucretius says that by that name amorous knights were wont to call freckled, warty, and wooden-faced wenches.

EDITH. (Sax.) From *Eadith* or *Eade*, an old Saxon name signifying happiness or blessed, from *Eadig*, happy, blessed, honorable. It has been corrupted to *Ada* and *Ida*.

ELEANOR. The same as Ellen or Helen, pitiful, compassionate.

ELIZA. A contraction of Elizabeth.

ELIZABETH. (Heb.) The oath of God, or God hath sworn.

ELSIE. A corruption of Alice.

294 ETYMOLOGICAL DICTIONARY

EMMA. (Ger.) From *Amme*, a nurse, one who nurses, cares for, and watches over another, tender, affectionate, the same as *Eutrophine*, among the Greeks. Emma, daughter of Richard, the first Duke of Normandy, was called in Saxon *Elgiva*, help-giver. It was sometimes written *Imma*, the name of the daughter of Charlemagne. Some have derived it from *imme*, a bee, busy, industrious.

EMMELINE. A diminutive of Emma, little Emma.

EMILY. The same as Emmeline.

ESTHER. (Heb.) Secret or hidden.

ETHEL. (Sax.) Noble.

EUGENIA. The feminine of Eugene, which is from the Greek εὐγενής, nobly born.

EVE and EVA. (Heb.) Life-giving.

FANNY. A corruption of Frances.

FELICIA. The feminine of Felix (Lat.), happy, fortunate.

FLORENCE. (Lat.) Flourishing, prosperous, from *Florens*.

FRANCES. The feminine of Francis, from *Frank*, free, not servile or bond.

GEORGINA and GEORGIANA. Feminine of George, which see.

GERTRUDE. (Ger.) All truth, amiable.

GILLIAN. A corruption of Julian, feminine of Julius, Greek, soft-haired.

GOODITH and GOODY. Contracted from Good-wife. King Henry the First was nicknamed *Goodith*, in contempt.

GRACE. The signification of this name is well known.

GRISHILD. Gray lady.

OF CHRISTIAN NAMES. 295

HAGAR. (Heb.) A stranger.

HANNAH. (Heb.) Gracious, merciful.

HARRIET. The feminine of Harry or Henry; the same as Henrietta. See Henry.

HELEN. (Greek.) Pitiful, compassionate. Ellen is a different form of the same name. It is often contracted to Nelly and Nell.

HENRIETTA. The feminine of Henry, which is derived from the German *Einrich*, ever rich.

HONORA. (Lat.) Honorable, graceful, handsome.

HULDAH. (Heb.) The world.

IDA. The same as Ada and Edith. From *Eade*, or *Eadith*, Saxon, happy, blessed.

IONE. (Greek.) From the island *Ionia*.

ISABEL. (Spanish.) The same as Elizabeth with the Spanish, as they always translate Elizabeth into Isabel. It is also said to signify olive-complexioned or brown.

JANE. Anciently Joane, the feminine of John, gracious.

JANET. A diminutive of Jane, little and pretty Jane.

JEMIMA. (Heb.) Handsome as the day.

JOSEPHINE. (Heb.) The feminine of Joseph, which signifies increase, addition.

JUDITH. (Heb.) Praising, confessing.

JULIA and JULIANA. (Lat.) The feminine of *Julius*, Greek, soft-haired.

KATHARINE. (Greek.) Pure, virtuous, from Καθάρος.

KATHLEEN. (Celtic.) Little darling.

LAURA. (Lat.) Bay or laurel, crowned with laurel, from *laurus;* corresponding to the Greek name *Daphne.* The feminine of Lawrence.

LETITIA. (Lat.) From *lœtitia*, joyfulness, mirth.

LETTICE. A corruption of Letitia.

LETTY. A corruption of Lettice and Letitia.

LOUISA. The feminine of Louis or Lewis. (See Lewis.)

LUCRETIA. (Lat.) The feminine of Lucretius, from *lucrum*, gain, a name proper for a good housewife.

LUCY. (Lat.) From *lux*, light, lightsome, bright, a name given first to children that were born when daylight first appeared.

LYDIA. (Greek.) From *Lydia*, in Asia, because born in that region.

MABEL. From the French *ma belle*, my fair maid. Camden thinks it a contraction of the Latin, *amabilis*, lovely, amiable, as it used to be written in old deeds, Amabilia, and Mabilia.

MADELINE. The same as Adeline (which see).

MAGDALEN. (Heb.) Majestical.

MARGARET and **MARGERY.** (Greek.) From Μαργαρῖτες, a pearl, precious.

MARIA and **MARIAN.** The same as Mary, exalted.

MARTHA. (Heb.) Bitter.

MARY. (Heb.) Exalted. It is a famous name in both sacred and profane history; in all ages it has literally been exalted.

Some derive the name from *maria*, bitter, a drop of salt water, a tear.

MATILDA. (Ger.) A noble or honorable lady. (See Maud.)

MAUD. A corruption of Matilde or Matilda. From the German *Matildis* or *Mathildis*, Latin, *Matilda*, noble or honorable lady.

MELICENT and MILICENT. (French.) Honey-sweet.

MIRIAM. (Heb.) Bitterness of affliction, exalted, bitterness of the sea.

NANCY. A corruption of Ann.

NANETTE and NINON. (Fr.) Nan, Nancy, same as Ann, little Ann.

NICIA. (Greek.) Victorious, from νική, a victory, a triumph.

OLIVIA and OLIVE. (Lat.) The feminine of Oliver. From the Latin *Oliva*, the olive tree, an emblem of peace.

OLYMPIA. (Greek.) Heavenly, from Ὄλυμπος, heaven.

PAULINE. The feminine of Paul, from the Latin, *Paulus*, little, small in stature.

PENELOPE. (Greek.) The name of a kind of bird, with a purple neck. The name of the most patient, true, constant, and chaste wife of Ulysses, given to her because she carefully loved and fed those birds.

PERNEL. (Fr.) From *Petronilla*, pretty stone.

PHŒBE. (Greek.) The feminine of *Phœbus*, from the Greek φοῖβος, light, splendid, radiant, a name of Diana. Phœbus, denoting Apollo, or the sun; Phœbe, Diana, or the moon.

13*

298 ETYMOLOGICAL DICTIONARY

PHILIPPA. (Greek.) Feminine of Philip (which see).

PHILLIS. (Greek.) Lovely, dear, cherished from φίλη.

POLYXENA. (Greek.) One that will entertain many guests and strangers, from πολλοὶ, many, and ξένοι, strangers, guests.

PRISCA. (Lat.) Ancient.

PRISCILLA. (Lat.) A diminutive from Prisca,—little, ancient dame.

PRUDENCE. (Lat.) *Prudentia,* wisdom, corresponding to the Greek name, *Sophia.*

RACHEL. (Heb.) A sheep.

REBECCA. (Heb.) Fat and full.

REGINA. (Lat.) The queen, queen-like.

RHODA. (Greek.) A rose, from ρόδον.

ROSALIA. (Lat.) From *Rosa,* fair as a rose.

ROSALIND. The same as Rosalia, from *Rosa,* a rose.

ROSAMUND. Rose of the world, from *rosa,* and *mundi;* or from *rosa,* Latin, and *mund,* Saxon, a mouth, from her rosy-colored lips; a name made famous by Fair Rosamund, mistress of Henry the Second. .

ROSE. (Lat.) From that fair flower, like a rose.

ROWENA. (Sax.) From *Rouw,* Dutch, peace, and *rinnan,* Saxon, to acquire. The name of the beautiful daughter of Hengist, a renowned leader of the Saxons, "who, having the Isle of Thanet given him by King Vortigern for assisting him against the Picts and Scots, obtained as much ground as he could encompass with an ox-hide, on which to build a castle, which being finished, he invited King Vortigern to a supper. After supper Hengist calls for his daughter Row-

OF CHRISTIAN NAMES. 299

ena, who, richly attired, enters the room with a graceful mien, with a golden bowl full of wine in her hand, and drinks to King Vortigern in the Saxon language, saying, 'Be of health, lord, king,' to which he replied, 'Drink health,' which, I think, is the first health we find in history, and claims the antiquity of about 1400 years. Vortigern, enamored with her beauty, married her, and gave her and her father all Kent."

RUTH. (Heb.) Satisfied.

SABINA. (Lat.) As chaste and religious as a Sabine, a people who had their name from their worshiping of God.

SARAH. (Heb.) Lady, mistress, or dame.

SOPHIA. (Greek.) Wisdom, from σοφία.

SOPHRONIA. (Greek.) Modest and temperate; prudent, from σωφροσύνη, modesty, chastity.

SYBIL. God's counsel; others derive it from the Hebrew, signifying *divine doctrine*.

SYLVIA. (Lat.) From *Sylva*, a forest—belonging to the forest.

TABITHA. (Heb.) Roe-buck.

THEODORA. The feminine of Theodore, Greek, the gift of God.

THEODOSIA. The same as Theodora, the gift of God.

URANIA. (Greek.) Heavenly, from Οὐρανὸς, heavenly.

URSULA. (Lat.) A little bear. The name of the virgin saint of Britain, martyred under God's scourge, Attila, king of the Huns.

DICTIONARY OF CHRISTIAN NAMES.

VENUS. (Lat.) Coming to all, as Cicero derives it, from *veniendo*. In Greek, Venus was called Aphrodite, some say from the foam of the sea whence she sprung, but Euripides says from *Aphrosune*, mad folly.

VIOLA. (Lat.) *Viola*, a violet, pretty and modest.

VIRGINIA. (Lat.) Virgin-like, chaste, maidenly.

WILHELMINA. (Ger.) The feminine of Wilhelm or William. (See William.)

WINIFRED. (Sax.) From *Win*, and *fred*, get peace.

THE END.

Printed in the United Kingdom
by Lightning Source UK Ltd.
127400UK00001B/104/A